# Under God's Good Hand

***A history of the traditions which have come together in the United Reformed Church in the United Kingdom***

David Cornick

ISBN 0 85356 175 9


Published by
The United Reformed Church
in the United Kingdom
86 Tavistock Place, London WC1H 9RT



Printed by Healeys Printers, Unit 10, the Sterling Complex,
Farthing Road, Ipswich Suffolk IP1 5AP
Cover design and photograph by Sara Foyle

# Contents



*Continue overleaf .....*

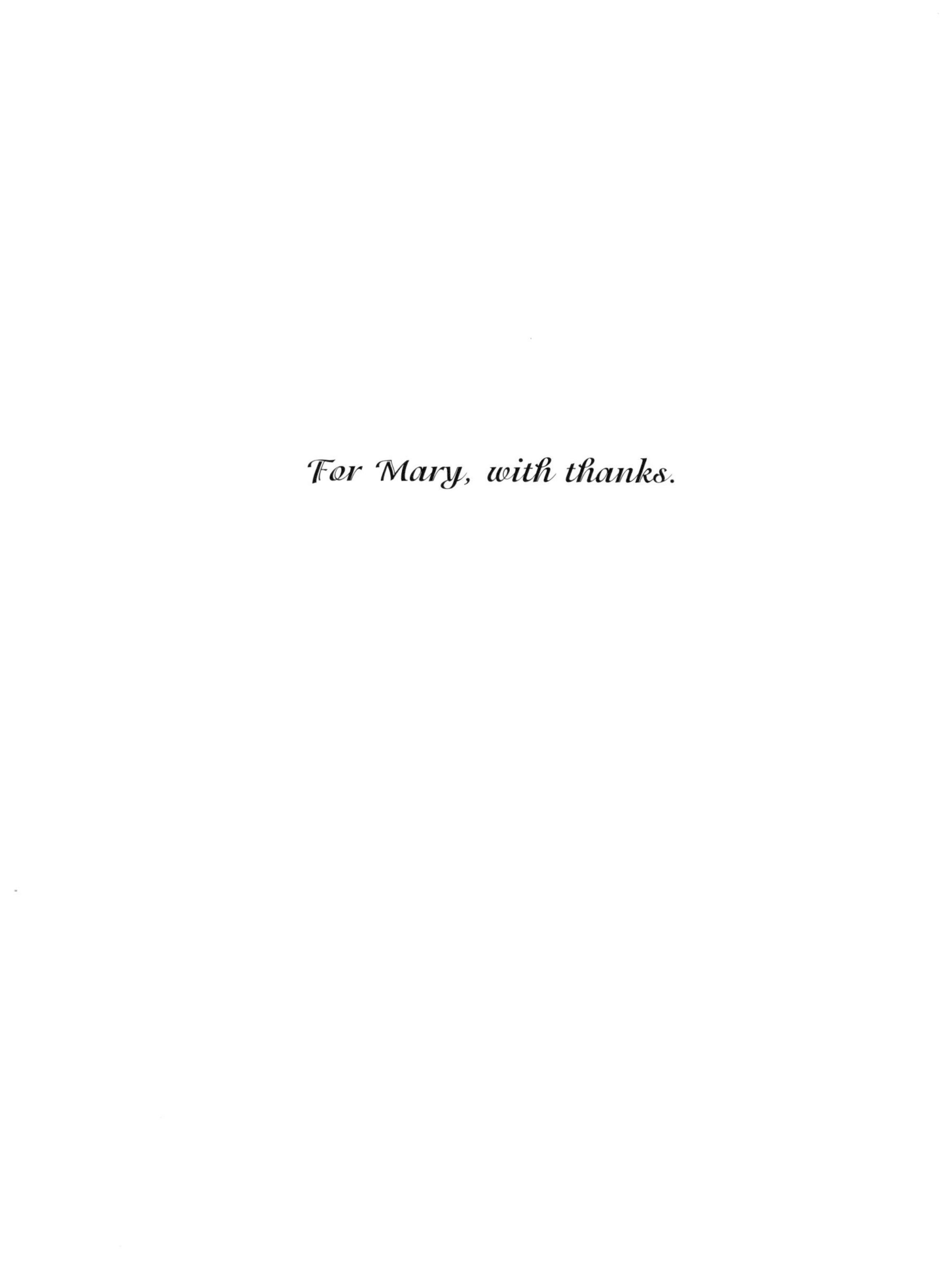

*For Mary, with thanks.*

*In the beginning God created the heavens and the earth . . .*

*Then*

JOHN CALVIN
led reformation thought from Geneva in 1536

Elizabeth made the church partly protestant.

Thomas Cartwright led puritan demands for more reforms -
simpler worship, Biblical beliefs and Presbyterian form of church government.

Independents formed breakaway local congregations; John Greenwood imprisoned for leading unauthorised worship; Henry Barrow arrested while visiting him; John Penry suspected of writing critical tracts; they were hanged in 1593

*Elizabeth*

tolerated Presbyterianism in the Channel Islands in 1576

Independents from Scrooby, Lincs fled to friends in Holland and later led the migration of the PILGRIM FATHERS in 1620.

Hoping for political help from Scotland, Parliament set up the Westminster Assembly of English Divines to give the English church more presbyterian shape. Charles I disagreed but it nearly succeeded.

Civil war led to the King's execution in 1649 and Olivers Cromwell's republic favoured Independency. Over 3,000 clergy were dismissed.

Cromwell died in 1658. Parlaiment supported the return of Charles II, thinking that he would include them in a comprehensive church. But he enforced Anglicanism & outlawed all non-conformity. 2,000 ministers were ejected & laymen lost civil rights.

Richard Baxter had briefly united all protestant ministers in Worcestershire & supported the return of Charles II.
But he was among those who refused to conform and was persecuted after 1662.

In a bloodless coup William became King in 1688. As a reformed protestant from Holland he restored freedom of worship but dissenters still lacked civil rights.

Presbyterian and Congregational ministers in London achieved a short-lived 'happy union' in 1690.

Denied access to the universities the nonconformists founded DISSENTING ACADEMIES which greatly influenced English education.

1700

London Congregational minister ISAAC WATTS began writing hymns about 1700.

***'When I survey the wondrous cross Where the young Prince of glory died'***

Protestant Dissenting Deputies gain direct access to the Sovereign on civil rights issues from 1732.

The Wesleys' revival (1740- ) boosted flagging Congregationalism but younger Presbyterian ministers were increasingly attracted to unitarian theology.

The London Missionary Society started in 1795, supported by Congregationalists; it sent abroad John Williams, Robert Moffat & David Livingstone. English Presbyterians sent missionaries to Bengal, Malaya & Taiwan.

Congregational churches founded a national union in 1832 and expanded in the new towns and rising middle classes.

Presbyterianism was boosted by Scots moving south due to business and industry; for a while they remained in a synod of the Scottish church but in 1876 a united Presbyterian Church of England was formed.

From 1870 the Free Churches found common ground supporting the Liberal party & opposing catholic renewal in the Church of England. Great preachers and industrialists were prominent in national & church affairs.

An international Alliance of Reformed (Presbyterian) Churches was formed in 1875 and Congregationalists started to hold international councils in 1891.

By the turn of the century there were as many Free churchmen as active Anglicans in England. But the tide was turned by biblical criticism, social mobility and disillusionment bred by the Great War.

John Cairns and John Oman were outstanding among Presbyterian theologians, & RW Dale & PT Forsyth among Congregationalists. Willian Paton & AE Garvie made leading contributions to early ecumenical conferences.

Presbyterians & Congregationalists joined in the United Ch. of Canada (1925), the Ch. of Christ in China (1927), the Ch. of South India (1947). A union of Congregationalists & some Presbyterians created the United Ch. of Christ in the USA in 1957

An English attempt to unite the two churches failed in 1947, but in 1951 a covenant 'to walk together' led to some local united churches.

Present discussions began in 1963. The parliamentary Bill received the Royal Assent on 29 June 1972. THE UNITED REFORMED CHURCH was constituted on 5 Oct 1972 with 2,000 congregations, 1,900 ministers & 200,000 members.

New readers will start here.

1981 The United Reformed Church united with the Reformed Association of Churches of Christ to become the United Reformed Church in the United Kingdom.

*An extract from the Service of Thanksgiving for the inauguration of the United Reformed Church, held at Westminster Abbey, 5 October 1972 at 3 pm*

## DEDICATION AND COMMITMENT

*The people rise and say together:*

God of our fathers, God of our own time, God of the hidden future: we accept anew the gift of life from thee; we pledge ourselves to one another in thy service; we commit ourselves to seek unity with all Christian people; and in all this we rely solely on thy grace. Confirm and strengthen us in this resolve, for the sake of Jesus Christ our Lord. Amen.

*All remain standing.*

*The Archbishop of Canterbury addressing the Moderator and the Congregation will say:*

On behalf of the Church of England, I give thanks with you for this union, and share your resolve to seek that wider unity which is Christ's will.

*The Moderator of the United Reformed Church will say:*

May God enable us all to find and do his will.

*The Cardinal Archbishop of Westminster will say:*

On behalf of the Roman Catholic Church in this country, I give thanks with you for this union, and share your resolve to seek that wider unity which is Christ's will.

*The Moderator of the United Reformed Church will say:*

May God enable us all to find and do his will.

*The Moderator of the Free Church Federal Council will say:*

On behalf of the Free Churches in this country, I give thanks with you for this union, and share your resolve to seek that wider unity which is Christ's will.

*The Moderator of the United Reformed Church will say:*

May God enable us all to find and do his will.

# Preface

This book has a simple aim. It seeks to introduce members of the United Reformed Church and others to the history of the traditions which joined together to form the United Reformed Church in the United Kingdom. I am grateful to Lesley Husselbee for seeing the need, and for encouraging me to meet it.

That aim has consequences. An introduction is intended to whet the appetite for more! This is no more than an entrée to some delicious main courses. Our traditions, and the history of dissent, have been well served by fine historians. The sadness is that so many of their works are out of print. The works of Geoffrey Nuttall and Tudor Jones, Clyde Binfield, David Thompson and Elaine Kaye are veritable feasts, but many of them can only be found in libraries and second hand shops. The honourable exception is Michael Watts's monumental *The Dissenters*, now in two volumes of a projected longer series. A section on further reading is intended to open the way for readers to make their own journeys, and the book will eventually be supplemented by a unit for the Open Learning Centre.

This work makes few claims to originality. The historian of the United Reformed Church has to consider not one denomination but three, as well as the united church itself, and cast an eye over four centuries. That is probably why there is a gap in the market! Like all academic disciplines, history relies on specialists in particular areas. The writing of a history like this is the most collaborative of all exercises. I am indebted to the expertise of countless others whose books and articles have helped me on my way. In order that the book might be more user-friendly I have deliberately not included footnotes. The danger of doing that is that I have risked not acknowledging the precise nature of my indebtedness to other scholars' work. This book has grown out of many talks, lectures and seminars, and inevitably the sources of some quotations have been lost. I have given a list of sources at the end of the book, and I crave the indulgence of those whom I have missed, and will gladly remedy any omissions in future editions.

Time-charts have been provided to help the readers orientate themselves to the period under discussion in the following chapter(s). Wherever possible I have tried to give the dates of those who play a significant part in the narrative. There are still gaps in our understanding of our past. One of my hopes (which is becoming more and more eschatological) is to close one gap by writing the history of modern English Presbyterianism; another is that colleagues might look again at its decline in the eighteenth century; yet another that the years since 1945, including the formation of the URC and its subsequent history, might excite the imagination of future students.

There are countless friends in the URC who have contributed to this book by their friendship and conversations. It would be invidious to name them all, but some deserve particular words of thanks - to Carol Rogers and Sara Foyle of Communications and Editorial, whose patience is unlimited; to John Taylor and David Thompson for reading the manuscript, saving me from more errors than are here, and generously sharing their ideas and research; to Robert Pope of the University of Bangor who put his knowledge of Welsh church history at my disposal; to Clyde Binfield, David Thompson, and Elaine Kaye for many years of conversations, friendship and the highest ideals of scholarship; to Arthur Macarthur for allowing me to use his words loosely echoing Oliver Cromwell in his article 'The background to the formation of the United Reformed Church (Presbyterian and Congregational) in England and Wales in 1972' *JURCHS* vol 4 no 5 (1987) which form my title; to my colleagues and students in the South Western Province and at Westminster and the Cambridge Theological Federation whose questions have forced me to reconsider my own understandings of the past; to Margaret Thompson who kindly offered her skills as proof-reader; but above all to my long-suffering family, Andrew, Peter and Mary who have borne my hours in the study with humour and grace. Mary has shared our marriage with ecclesiastical history. She knows more about it now than she ever wished or wanted to know. This book is for her.

*David Cornick*
*Westminster College, Cambridge*
*The Feast of St Bartholomew, 24 August 1997*

# The Reformation - a time chart

| Date | Continental Europe | England | Scotland |
| --- | --- | --- | --- |
| 1483 | Luther b. | | |
| 1509 | | Henry VIII | |
| 1516 | Erasmus's Greek New Testament published | | |
| 1517 | Luther's 95 theses posted | | |
| 1518 | Zwingli called to Zürich | | |
| 1519 | Luther's disputation with Johannes Eck | | |
| 1520 | Luther publishes *An address to the Christian nobility* *The Babylonian captivity of the church* *On the Freedom of a Christian* | | |
| 1521 | Karlstadt celebrates 'reformed' communion in Wittenberg | | |
| 1525 | | | Act prohibiting importation of Lutheran books |
| 1526 | | Tyndale's NT | |
| 1528 | | | Patrick Hamilton executed |
| 1529 | Colloquy of Marburg (Luther and Zwingli) | 'The Reformation Parliament' meets | |
| 1531 | Zwingli killed in battle | | |
| 1532 | | Act of Annates | |
| 1533 | | Act in restraint of Appeals Henry m. Anne Boleyn Cranmer archbishop of Canterbury | |
| 1534 | Radicals in control of Münster | Act of Supremacy | |
| 1536 | | Tyndale executed | |
| 1541 | Calvin begins second Genevan ministry | | |
| 1545 | Council of Trent (to 1563) | | |
| 1546 | Luther d. | | George Wishart executed |
| 1547 | | Henry d. Edward VI to throne | |

| Date | Continental Europe | England | Scotland |
|---|---|---|---|
| 1549 | | First Prayer Book | |
| 1550 | | Laski given licence | |
| 1552 | | Second Prayer Book | |
| 1553 | | Edward VI d.<br>Mary to throne<br>Re-introduction of Catholicism | |
| 1557 | | | Lords of the Congregation formed |
| 1558 | | Mary d.<br>Elizabeth to throne | |
| 1559 | Final edition of Calvin's *Institutes* | Elizabethan settlement | |
| 1560 | | | Scottish reformation<br>*Scots Confession*<br>*First Book of Discipline* (Knox) |
| 1564 | Calvin d. | Vestments controversy (1560s) | |
| 1567 | | | James VI to throne |
| 1570 | | Cartwright's lectures on Acts<br>Elizabeth excommunicated | |
| 1571 | | Thirty-Nine articles sanctioned | |
| 1572 | | John Field's *Admonition* | Concordat of Leith |
| 1578 | | | *Second Book of Discipline* (Melville) |
| 1582 | | Robert Browne<br>*A brief treatise..* | |
| 1588 | | Spanish Armada | |
| 1592 | | | Presbyterianism ratified |
| 1593 | | Greenwood, Barrow and Penry executed | |
| 1603 | | Elizabeth d.<br>James VI of Scotland and I of England to throne | |

## Chapter 1

# Where did it all begin?

There is a small, leather bound book in the archives of Cheshunt College. It is a copy of William Tyndale's translation of the New Testament which was first produced in 1525. This copy was probably produced in the 1530s or 40s, but it still includes Tyndale's translation of Luther's prologue to Romans. What is remarkable about this copy is that we know that two hundred years later it was a treasured possession of Selina, Countess of Huntingdon, the patroness of George Whitefield and one of the lay leaders of the Evangelical Revival of the eighteenth century. It then passed into the hands of the college she founded in Trevecca in Breconshire to train young men for ministry and was kept by it throughout the many changes of its history until in 1967 Cheshunt College, Cambridge (as it was then known) united with Westminster College. That small and precious book symbolises the relationship between the United Reformed Church and the events which turned Europe upside down in the 1520s and 1530s which historians label 'the Reformation.' There was, of course, no United Reformed Church in 1525, nor Congregationalists, Presbyterians or members of the Churches of Christ, but if we are to understand why our church is as it is we must pay due attention to the days of William Tyndale and try and appreciate why that book was so treasured.

The trouble with history is that we know the ending, and we therefore unconsciously let the ending determine our understanding of the course of events. That is the way powerful myths are born. One great overarching myth of Western history which dominated the nineteenth and early twentieth centuries was the myth of progress, that things were getting better all the time. That in turn affected the way in which the Reformation was understood. It was written as the account of the inevitable triumph of Protestantism. That caused distortion. The startling diversity of the reformation was lost to view. The life of the pre-reformation church was seen through the spectacles of

the reformers - abuse-ridden, unspiritual, ripe for change. Luther was pictured as the first modern man, the forerunner of the quest for freedom and liberty which occupied the European political agenda for the next two centuries.

The series of events which rocked Europe between 1500 and 1550 which are labelled 'the Reformation' were a heady mix of theological ideas, political realities, economic stresses and personal spiritual journeys. It sometimes seems that the more historians study them, the more complicated they become. One historian has suggested that it helps to think of the reformation having three 'phases'. The first was intimately tied up with the spiritual journey of a German monk, Martin Luther, and concluded with the condemnation of his views by the Diet of Worms in 1521 (a diet was a meeting of the electors, princes and representatives of the towns and cities of the Holy Roman Empire, a kind of 'parliament' which provided opportunities for important issues to be discussed). The Reformation was in large measure an urban phenomenon because cities contained the people, political structures and literary sophistication essential to the reception of reforming ideas. The second phase of the reformation, which lasted roughly from 1521-1548 saw reforming ideas triumph in many of the city states of what are now known as Germany and Switzerland. That in turn overlapped with the third phase, 'the reformation of the refugees' which was centred on Geneva when Calvin was senior minister there (1541-64). Those who were discontented with the reformation in their own towns and cities journeyed to Geneva to see how things should be done properly.

Local studies are illustrating the varied ways in which this process happened. The study of popular religion has recovered something of the vitality and effectiveness of the pre-Reformation church, and Luther himself has been placed firmly in a late medieval context as (in Geoffrey Elton's words) '*..the demon-ridden man who saw the Devil walking at noonday about God's creation and knew himself called to mortal combat in order to save immortal souls.*'

The term 'Reformation' used to describe the upheavals of the first part of the sixteenth century is a seventeenth century term. It became the accepted way to talk of those events after the 1830s, following the work of the great German historian, von Ranke. The Latin word *'reformatio'* from which it derives was used in three technical ways in the sixteenth century. It was used to describe new legal codes, changes in university curricula and internal church reforms. However, there was also a popular, non-technical, meaning. The early 1500s were tinged with apocalyptic dreams and hopes. God's intervention in history was eagerly awaited. A prophet, a *'reformator'*, was expected. Luther fitted the bill perfectly in the eyes of the peasantry.

Sixteenth century people understood their world to be charged with holiness, alive with the supernatural, encountered in holy places like shrines, touched in the relics of the saints, harnessed through the sacraments of the church and the work of healers and 'cunning folk'. Angels and demons were only just beyond the veil, taking a keen interest in lives and loves of ordinary people. The church sought to monopolise and control these potent forces. Hence the ferocity and violence of the campaign against witchcraft in the fifteenth century. The church provided a cycle of sacraments which embraced the life-cycle from the cradle to the grave, and extended the power of the sacraments through a plethora of sacramentals. These were as frequent as the life-cycle sacraments were rare. Objects and commodities like candles and salt and water were blessed, and that blessing was thought to lend them the power of Christ so that ordinary men and women could use them to fend off demons, disease and disaster. Prayers were also said over crops to try and ensure good weather, and exorcisms to repel demons were common.

At the heart of this spiritual economy was the eucharist, the miracle of God present with his people, really, tangibly in the wafer host. The entire architectural structure of the late medieval church and the whole movement of the liturgy was focused on this visual and visible miracle. However subtle the theologians might be in their discussions of transubstantiation, in the common mind God was made real in the act of consecration during the eucharist, and the chattering congregation dropped to their knees in adoration.

## Martin Luther (1483-1546)

Luther was a man of that universe. His parents, rising peasants made good, intended him for the legal profession, but he became a monk because he had been caught in a dreadful thunderstorm on his way home from Erfurt University, cried out to St Anne for protection and been saved by her. He joined the Augustinian order, a monastic community which originated in the eleventh century. At his first mass he was struck dumb in sheer terror at the awesomeness of God's presence and only gentle coaxing by the prior (or novice-master) stopped him running away. He heard the Devil rummaging around in the monastery food store whilst he was frantically writing the next day's lecture. He knew the Devil to be *'Lord and God of this world'* and he understood his life to be part of the cosmic battle between God and the Devil. On his later travels he used to keep his wife Kate informed of the state of the beer. In one town it was excellent, in the next dreadful because the devil got there first and poured tar into the kegs. Emotionally Luther belongs firmly in the sacramental universe of the sixteenth century.

Intellectually he was part of a movement which was de-constructing it. The Augustinians quickly realised that their new recruit was a bright lad. They pushed him through a doctoral programme and let his talents blossom as a university teacher in the new University of Wittenburg. From 1512 onwards Luther was a theology don, lecturing twice a week, and as Gordon Rupp once characteristically put it, '*In between lectures, so to speak, he attended the deathbed of a world and assisted the birth of a new age.*' Luther had been trained at the University of Erfurt, which was a noted centre of nominalism.

Medieval theology faculties were dominated by a method known as scholasticism. It sought to show that the Christian faith was rational, and it used Aristotelian philosophical methods of logic and deduction. From *c.*1350-1500 scholasticism was dominated by nominalism. Nominalism was inherently sceptical. It replaced a system known as realism. Realism and nominalism were profoundly different. An illustration will help us appreciate the difference. A realist looked at human beings and said, 'I exist because humanity exists.' In other words there is a universal concept, 'humanity', and without that universal concept I could not be. A nominalist said, 'I know I exist. I look at other human beings and I name them "Humanity". That name (nomen) is a product of my mind and intellect. "Humanity" doesn't have an independent existence as a concept. There are no such things as universals. They are simply models that describe the ways things are.' Nominalism was radical. It shunned the great authorities like Aquinas and Duns Scotus who were the great realists, but counted among its adherents some of the sharpest thinkers of the fifteenth century - the French theologian Pierre d'Ailly, Gabriel Biel who taught at Tübingen, and the Italian Augustinian Gregory of Rimini. In 1497, just 5 years before Luther matriculated at Erfurt, the Arts Faculty revised their programme on thoroughgoing nominalist principles. Nominalism had a high view of human rationality, a deep appreciation of the mystery of God and the necessary limits of theological knowledge, but above all it subordinated speculation to experience.

Luther's spiritual journey was precisely about the subordination of speculation to experience. He was, he tells us, a diligent monk who '*kept the rules of my order so strictly that I can say: if ever a monk got to heaven through monasticism I should have been that man...I would have become a martyr through fasting, prayer, reading and other good works had I remained a monk much longer.*' But it did not work. The peace that he longed for eluded him. He felt himself the object of the wrath of God. The medieval sacramental and penitential system which operated on the premise that good works, confession and absolution were the building blocks of the path to salvation just did not work for him. His life was a continual wrestling with the majesty and holiness of

God, and with the attempt to discover how he, a sinful man, could stand in the presence of the holy God. *'I felt myself in the presence of God to be a sinner with a most unquiet conscience, nor could I believe him to be appeased by the satisfaction I could offer....I hated this just God who punishes sinners.'*

The seriousness of that spiritual quest was also part of his professional work as a professor of Biblical theology. It was whilst he was about that work, struggling with the meaning of Scripture and preparing his lectures, that the breakthrough came. We don't know precisely when, because Luther left three slightly different accounts of it.

*At last as I meditated day and night, God showed mercy and I turned my attention to the connection of the words, namely - 'The righteousness of God is revealed, as it is written: the righteous shall live by faith' - and there I began to understand that the righteousness of God is the righteousness in which a just man lives by the gift of God, in other words, by faith...At this I felt myself straightway born afresh and to have entered through the open gates into paradise itself.*

The rest of Luther's career was devoted to working out the implications of that experience.

Theologically there was little that was new in his theology of salvation. Research has shown that much of it was prefigured in the writings of the Augustinian nominalist Gregory of Rimini and elsewhere. But there was a crucial difference. All the medieval commentators on Augustine wrote of Christ's righteousness as if they were talents distributed by the church which could be increased by good works and holy living. In other words, the righteousness of Christ put people in the position to become righteous, it did not make them righteous there and then. Luther brought salvation out of the future into the present. Through faith the believer shares in Christ's righteousness now. Salvation is now.

The implications were staggering. William Tyndale (*c.*1494-1536) admired Luther because he saw in his career the possibility of a new way of being the church, and of a closer, more satisfying walk with God. He included Luther's prologue to Romans in his translation of the New Testament because it was through his reading of Romans that Luther had 'discovered' the doctrine of justification by faith which had been the answer to his spiritual quest. If his reading was correct, if the relationship between humanity and God was determined by faith, then the entire system of penance was rendered redundant.

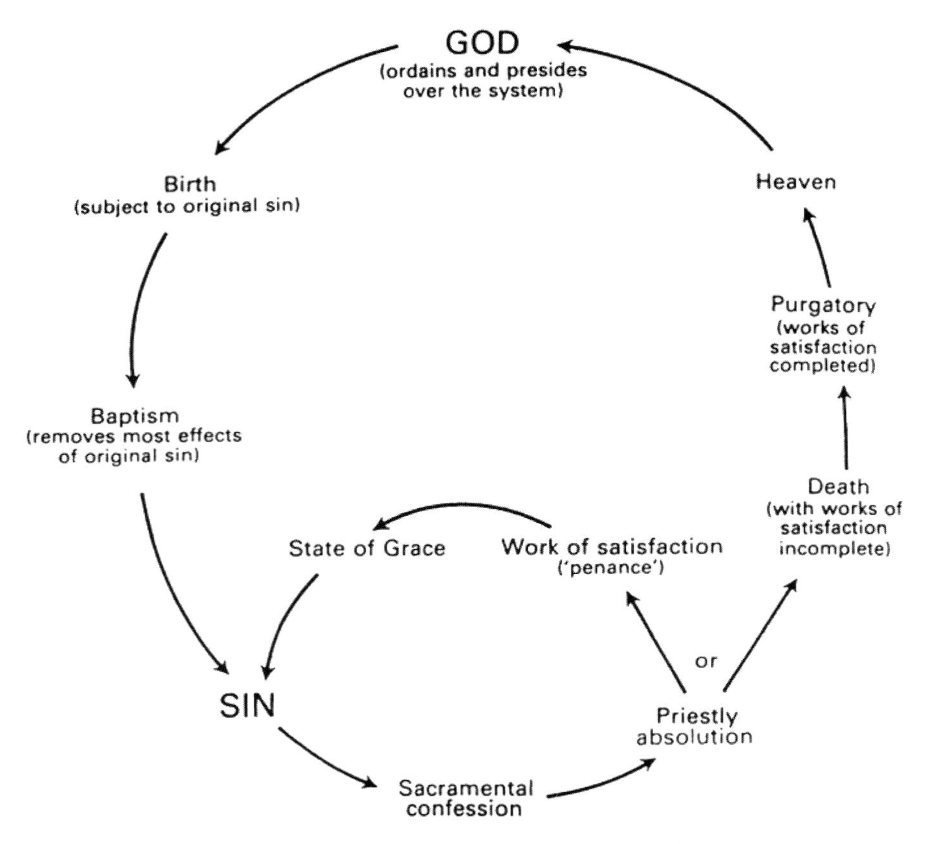


FIG. 1. The Penitential Cycle in Late Medieval Catholicism

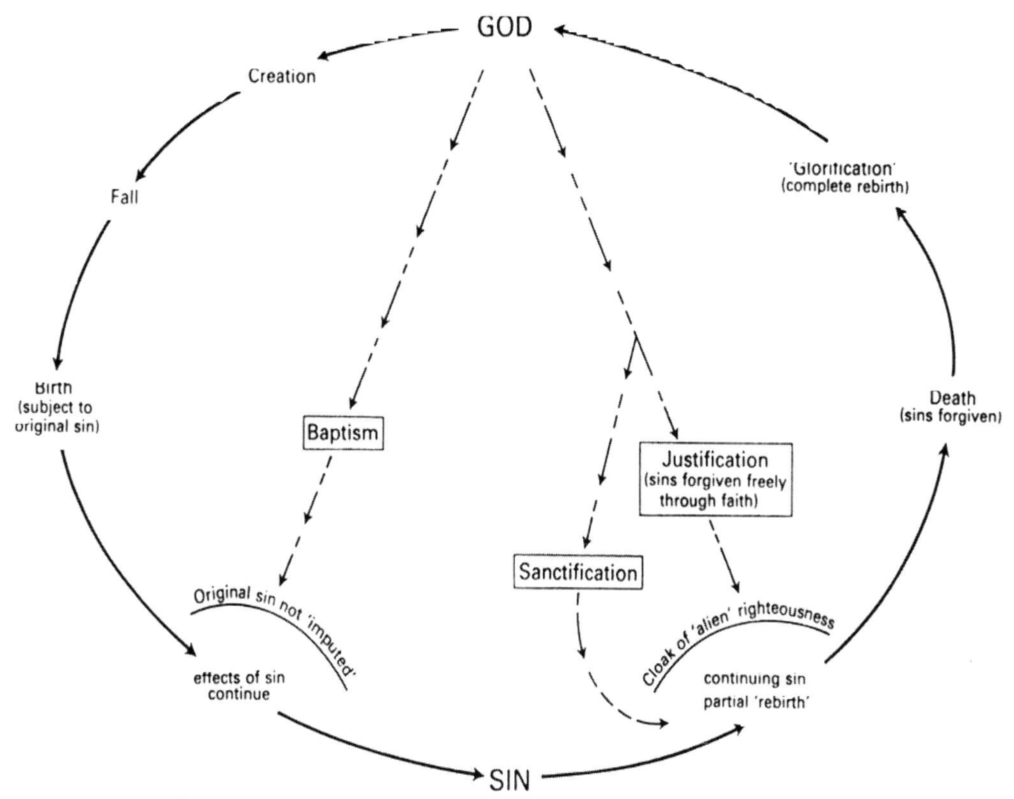

FIG. 2. The Scheme of Human Salvation in the Teaching of the Leading Reformers

*Fig.1 & 2 from*
*Euan Cameron's "The European Reformation"*
*(Oxford 1991) pp 80 and 124*
*OUP ©*

The diagram shows the difference made by Luther's 'discovery'. The believer is no longer subject to the penitential cycle of confessing sins, receiving absolution, doing penance and being restored to a state of grace. Baptism now deals with the effects of original sin, and the believer's faith in Christ means that he or she is righteous in God's sight because believers share in Christ's righteousness. God, as it were, 'sees' the righteous Christ rather than the sinner.

At this point the private spiritual struggle of an unknown academic in a fifth rate university in an obscure part of the empire became part of the politics of Europe.

In 1514 Prince Albert of Mainz, whose family, the Hohenzollerns, were trying to control the empire, was presented with the possibility of adding the Archbishopric of Mainz and the Primacy of all Germany to the sees of Halberstadt and Magdeburg, which he already held. A fee to the pope - 31,000 ducats - was needed. That was a great deal of money. It was to be raised partly by a bank loan, from the Fuggers banking house, and partly by the sale of indulgences. An indulgence was an act of piety or charity which enabled the faithful to gain remission from the pains of purgatory for themselves or a loved one. Pope Leo X was in the midst of putting up that grandiloquent pile, St Peter's Rome, and he was strapped for cash. A deal made good sense, and the Dominican Johannes Tetzel was dispatched at a salary of some twenty times that of a university professor plus expenses to preach the indulgence. The elector of Saxony, Frederick the Wise, was livid, not least because the sale of indulgences just over the border threatened lucrative income from his collection of relics, which included 17,433 fragments of bones and the entire body of one of the Holy Innocents. Luther became involved when some of the citizens of Wittenburg who had travelled to Mainz to secure their salvation came back with their indulgence papers and asked his opinion. Newly and emotionally aware of the nature of salvation from his Biblical studies, he considered the indulgence campaign blatant exploitation, and composed his ninety five theses, conventional notice of an academic debate. There it might have remained, had they not been translated into German, printed, and circulated throughout southern Germany within a fortnight. It is impossible to overstate the importance of the printing press in the history of the German reformation.

The authorities were alarmed. Luther was summoned to debate, firstly with his own order, then with Cardinal Cajetan, the General of the Dominicans, at Augsburg in 1518. The ground of debate was shifting. What began as a discussion of the salvific function of indulgences was quickly transformed into an analysis of the authority of the pope and the church. Did the church have the right to issue indulgences? Luther refused to bow to Cajetan's demand that he recant in 1518, and in June 1519, in a public debate with Johannes Eck, the professor of theology at Leipzig, Luther declared that a simple layman armed with the Scriptures was superior to the pope and the councils of the church. The authority of Scripture, he had come to believe, could not be circumscribed by either the Pope or the General Councils of the church. When the bull of excommunication eventually arrived in mid 1520, Luther threw it on the bonfire.

That summer he produced three extraordinary essays that spelt out the practical consequences of his theology - *The address to the Christian nobility*, *The Babylonian captivity of the church*, and *On the Freedom of a Christian*. The first proclaimed the God-given responsibility of the rulers to bring about reformation of the church and presented a twenty-eight point plan for them to implement; the second reduced the seven sacraments to three - baptism, penance and communion, re-instituted the chalice for the laity, and emphasised that the mass was neither a good work, nor a sacrifice; the third was a small treatise on the inner life, exploring the paradoxical nature of the Christian life, free from all law, yet subject to all in love. Summoned before the Imperial Diet at Worms in 1521 Luther again refused to recant. He was declared an outlaw, was kidnapped by friends for his own safety, and lodged in the castle at Wartburg. There he remained, cut off from the world for a year, coping with the isolation by writing and translating the Scriptures into German.

Back in Wittenberg reformation continued without him. The Most Reverend Lord Professor Andreas Rudolff-Bodenstein von Karlstadt (*c.*1480-1541), Doctor of Theology, Doctor of Canon and Secular Law, Archdeacon and Canon of All Saints Wittenberg, a senior colleague of Luther's in the Faculty of Theology, took over. He dressed as a peasant and demanded to be known as 'Brother Andy'. In many ways he is a tragic figure, unfairly mocked by history. He was formidable scholar in his own right. Ten years before Luther joined the Faculty he had taught himself Hebrew using Reuchlin's *Grammar* so that he might study the Old Testament in its original language. With Luther off the scene, he and another Augustinian colleague, Gabriel Zwilling, pursued liturgical reform vigorously. On Christmas Day 1521 Karlstadt celebrated a drastically revised mass with no sacrificial language, no vestments, and offering communion in both kinds, in express defiance of the Elector of Saxony. The next day he announced his engagement to a sixteen year old peasant girl, and on 19 January he secured his place in history by becoming the first reformer to marry. Meanwhile reform was degenerating into riot and altar wrecking. The atmosphere was not helped by the arrival of three apocalyptic prophets from Zwickau, one student and two weavers who announced the coming millennium. On 25 January the Town Council adopted a new church order written by Karlstadt, but drawing on Luther's ideas in his *Letter to the Nobility*. At this point

Frederick the Wise became seriously concerned. He refused to accept the reforms, which caused confusion, and summoned Luther back from the Wartburg to sort out the mess.

Luther was in essence a conservative. He slowed the pace of reform dramatically, re-introduced the elevation of the host (which continued in Wittenberg until 1542), allowed a variety of liturgical forms until he published his German Mass in 1526, and in 1529 introduced his own Catechism. He and Karlstadt parted company on bad terms - reconciliation was never Luther's strongpoint. However badly Luther treated him, they had profoundly different understandings of the implications of reform. Karlstadt wanted to create a Christian commonwealth, 'the Christian city of Wittenberg', subject to the rule of God as revealed in Scripture. Initially at least he wanted rid of lay and clerical distinctions, and the introduction of democratic structures. It was, as it were, the city as monastery under Christ the abbot. It was a vision which appealed immensely in the city states of Switzerland, and Karlstadt finished his days as a professor at Basle. Luther, however, never thought it the job of Christians to create the Kingdom of God. For him the preaching of the cross was for the strengthening of the saints in the Last Days. Change was undoubtedly needed, but it was to be carried out under the banner of Christian freedom, not imposed on the unwilling as a new legalism.

Theology never operates in a socio-economic vacuum. As the events of the 1520s unfolded, Luther's protest blended with the politics of empire in all their bewildering complexity. He found himself the unwitting and unwilling focus of nationalism and anticlericalism, and his longing for a cleansed and renewed church ended in division and institutionalism. As early as 1520 the papal legate had written home, *'All Germany is in revolution. Nine tenths shout "Luther!" as their war-cry; the other tenth cares nothing about Luther, and cries "Death to the court at Rome!"'* In 1529, at the Diet of Speyer, six Lutheran princes and fourteen imperial cities signed a protestation, affirming their right to be answerable to God alone in matters of religion. The second phase of the reformation, the reformation of the cities, had begun. Those who signed the protestation became known as Protestants, and the history of the church had taken a decisive turn.

Luther was one of the giants of the Christian story, a theologian of originality and vision, but it would be quite wrong to think that he was the first or only Christian thinker of the fifteenth and sixteenth centuries to criticise the church or study the Scriptures. His work belongs in the context of the intellectual and spiritual debates which had characterised the church from at least the mid fourteenth century. The fourteenth century had seen the high ideals of the theorists that the papacy might become a universal monarchy reduced to cruel absurdity. In 1309 Pope Clement V tried to escape the political infighting of Rome by moving to Avignon. That upset the Italians, and although Gregory XI tried to solve the problem by moving back in 1377, the result was disastrous. From 1378 there were two popes, both correctly elected by the College of Cardinals, and a third was added by the council of Pisa in 1409. The papacy was behaving as just another European political power.

Many were scandalised by this. Some theorists re-examined the nature of the church and considered anew the way it should be governed and relate to the state. These theories, known as conciliarism - the belief that authority in the church should rest with a General Council rather than the pope - seemed to offer genuine hope. It was a General Council (of Constance) which ended the Great Schism in 1415. However, the lesson was not learnt, and in 1460 appeals to a General Council were forbidden under canon law. That was one of the tragic mistakes of church history. Luther was part of a long tradition of those who sought the reformation of the church. He was also the heir to a long tradition of theological debate about the nature of salvation which ran through the mainstream of scholastic theology as well as the work of radicals like John Wiclif (*c.*1330-84), a turbulent Yorkshireman and Oxford philosophy don who gave Scripture a distinctive prominence in his theological method, and Jan Huss (*c.*1372-1415) who developed similar ideas in Bohemia. Luther's originality grew out of his participation in scholarly debates about the freedom of the will and the gift of grace. If one part of Luther's mind was formed by that theological agenda, another was determined by humanism.

## Humanism

'Humanism' in the fifteenth and sixteenth centuries was a name given to the new resurgence of interest in human history, in particular the history and literature of the classical civilisations of Greece and Rome, which was the mainspring of the Renaissance, that glorious flowering of art and architecture which gave the world Michaelangelo and Leonardo da Vinci. It was an intellectual movement which swept all before it in European universities. It has nothing to do with the way the word is now used to refer to a 'secular' philosophy.

The outstanding humanist of Luther's day was Erasmus of Rotterdam (*c.*1469-1536). He recovered the Greek text of the New Testament, published a critical edition of it, and stimulated the renewed study of the Greek and Latin fathers by producing new editions of their work. Erasmus is a paradox, a gentle scholar with a savage wit, a bitter critic of the hierarchy, yet when the crunch came, a faithful member of the church, finding stability and security in the traditions that his scholarship and ironic pen had done so much to undermine. However, the scholarly tools he provided, in particular the Greek text of the New Testament, played a vital role in the history of the reformation.

Almost all the early reformers were trained humanists. The humanist agenda of the study of languages and texts opened doors into the study of Scripture and the early fathers. The precise balance of humanism and Lutheranism in the blend of reforming zeal that led to the reformation of the cities during the 1530s and 40s is debated by historians. It is clear, for example, that Huldrych Zwingli (1484-1531), who led the reformation in Zürich, owed far more to his study of Scripture than to his reading of Luther, and the Genevan reformer John Calvin trained initially as a lawyer. His first publication was an edition of Seneca's *De Clementia* (On mercy), and he took the skills which he developed as a commentator on humanist texts into his life's work of Biblical scholarship. However, whether inspired by humanism or Luther, or both, reforming ideas swept through the city states of Germany and Switzerland between 1520 and 1550. The spread of reforming ideas was part of the battle for autonomy in the city states. The rulers or 'magistrates' be they princes, electors, or city councils became the arbiters of religious allegiance.

The German reformation was immensely complex because Germany was immensely complex. It was not a unified state like England but an amalgam of city-states of some two thousand towns and sixty-five imperial cities. The political structure of Germany was fragmented. The Holy Roman Emperors had little power and they were mostly broke. Real authority lay in territorial structures - in a great number of nobles and prince bishops. There were no central structures or institutions, no uniform coinage, and no effective legal system. Power was localised, and provincial culture was vibrant and autonomous. This hectic pluralism explains why the reformation took on so many different shapes in Germany. Part of Luther's legacy was a Protestant pluralism as each of the city states adopted its own religious stance. The spiritual energy and dynamism which Luther unwittingly unlocked in 1517 could not be contained by the official structures authorised by princes and councils.

## The radical reformation

Beyond the 'magisterial reformation' in the cities was the so-called radical reformation. These radicals rejected the idea of a state church which would serve the whole community. They looked rather for the separation of the 'godly', and for many that was symbolised by believer's baptism. They have been seen as the ancestors of those who later argued for 'free' churches and religious liberty. There were literally hundreds of different groupings, many of them very small. Their contemporaries regarded them at best as eccentric individualists, at worst as the very incarnation of anarchy and they were cruelly persecuted. In an age tormented by fear of civil unrest, such an attitude was understandable because radicalism occasionally had dreadful consequences, as in the city of Münster in 1534 when a brutal and bizarre régime under Jan Beukelsz of Leiden instituted compulsory polygamy. Münster was a notorious and isolated case, but it grew to symbolise the fears of the Protestant majority.

The challenges facing the second generation of reformers, then, were very different from those which had confronted Luther. They faced splintering pluralism as each state dealt with reform in its own way, the seeming anarchy of the radical left and from 1545 onwards a reforming Catholic church. Luther's fight had been a pastor's fight - for truth, against the oppression of the masses, for a symmetry between the teaching of Scripture and the system of salvation practised by the church. That meant that preaching and reading Scripture gained new prominence. Luther himself is remembered as a great Scriptural translator. The belief that people should be allowed the Word in their own language was an essential part of his programme. Allowing people access to Scripture was dangerous, because it meant they could make up their own minds about weighty issues like the nature of church government. During the 1530s and 40s they did, and they didn't agree.

Major headaches for the second generation reformers were therefore, 'what shape should the church be?' and, 'where are the limits of the church?' In the previous 1,200 years unity had been provided by episcopal structure. That was now no more, and the reformers had to work out different formulae. It is in their work that the first glimpses can be caught of the ideas which were later to become congregationalism and presbyterianism.

## John Calvin (1509-64)

The greatest of the second generation reformers was John Calvin (1509-1564). He was eight when Luther published his theses in 1517. Luther died in 1546, five years after Calvin had begun his second, momentous Genevan ministry in 1541. If Luther was a fiery prophet, thinking on his feet and producing something like a book or pamphlet a fortnight throughout his life, then Calvin was a systematiser, a man of logic and order, who spent his twenty-three year ministry as the senior minister in Geneva working out appropriate ecclesiastical and social shapes for a world which Luther had turned upside down.

Calvin's significance is immense. His theological work provided the basis for Reformed theology. The system of church government he developed in Geneva became the blueprint for presbyterianism, and Geneva became a centre to which protestant refugees fled from all over Europe when persecution threatened in their own lands. Frequently they returned home to use the Genevan system as models for civil and ecclesiastical reform in their own lands. Calvin's influence was also disseminated by a vast international correspondence. He gave advice freely to all the major reformers of Europe.

Throughout history church and national state have battled for supremacy. Sometimes the fight has been on the grand scale, as in the Investiture Controversy which raged in Europe during the eleventh and twelfth centuries when successive popes and Holy Roman Emperors battled over the right to appoint abbots and bishops. At other times the skirmishes have been domestic, as in 1928 when Parliament refused to accept the Church of England's proposed revision of the Book of Common Prayer. The same struggle marked the reformation of the cities in the 1530s and 40s. In 1538 the Genevan City Council flexed its muscles and Calvin's first ministry there ended in expulsion. He was called back in 1541, and the same struggle marked the first decade of his new ministry. From the first he was determined that the church was not going to be a department of state. The church of Jesus Christ was not to be subject to any town council. Its independence was to be jealously guarded. The city council, on the other hand, had no intention of being pushed around by a group of upstart, arriviste ministers. Calvin prepared a new constitution for the church - the *Ecclesiastical Ordinances* - the City Council radically revised them. Calvin wanted weekly communion. The city fathers refused. Calvin wanted ministers to be chosen by their colleagues. Only if they swear an oath of loyalty to Geneva said the Council. There was a border between church and state, but its precise location was unclear because everyone was a Christian, every citizen a member of the church - '*As the magistrate ought by punishment and physical restraint to cleanse the church of offences, so the ministers of the word should help the magistrate in order that fewer may sin. Their responsibilities should be so joined that each helps rather than impedes the other.*' (*Institutes* IV.i.5)

Geneva was a small town of a few thousands, parochially intense and petty, yet alive with the tensions and difficulties which were sweeping Europe. Calvin had a vision for Geneva. It was cultural revolution, turning an easy-going Swiss city into the epitome of psalm-singing godliness. It is scarcely surprising that there was resistance. All societies control the behaviour of their citizens. Across Europe there were laws against swearing and blasphemy, regulations controlling public amusements and private vices. Almost a century before Calvin's ministry the Cathedral chapter in Geneva had issued regulations controlling prostitution, abhorring gambling and blasphemy, and punishing adultery with banishment. During the ministry of the first Genevan reformer Guillaume Farel, before Calvin's foot fell on Genevan soil, the sale of drink was forbidden after 9pm or during sermons, and women who had dressed a bride over luxuriously for her wedding were put in prison.

Calvin inherited a tradition of discipline administered by various city councils with long traditions of independence. They did not take over kindly to clerical interference. Indeed there is some evidence that Calvin failed to stop the councils being manipulated by those whose views were narrower than his. The case-book of the Genevan consistory from 1542 onwards shows the negative side of Calvin's vision - it deals with such terrible sins as laughing during sermons, singing obscene songs (not during sermons !), possessing dubious books, playing cards and dice. It shows the consistory trying to control the names given to children (forbidding those with pagan associations) and intervening in family quarrels. This was a régime that regulated the style of women's hats, investigated the insides of tankards and saucepans, disciplined a barber for shaving a priest in Catholic style, and punished three young men for eating thirty-six pâtés, and (most ill judged and short-lived of all) shut all the taverns and replaced them with cafés equipped with Bibles for light reading. But such a reading is too negative. It misses the nurturing of a decent system of public education, the liberalism that insisted that parents had no right to force their children to marry, the attempt to alleviate the misery of poverty and reduce the amount of domestic violence and cruelty to children.

Creating a godly society is dangerous affair. Hypocrisy is just beyond the sermon on the mount, and few Christian social reformers avoid its shadow. Calvin was no exception. Whether Calvin's Geneva was *'the maist perfect school of Christ since the Apostles'* as John Knox called it, or an exercise in Christian Stalinism will remain a matter of debate. By the mid 1550s Calvin's position in Geneva was secure, and the 'moderator of the Genevan company of pastors', as he styled himself, became in 1555 the defender of republican independence against an attempted putsch by Ami Perrin. In 1559 Calvin became a Genevan citizen. The sixteenth century was a harsh age when good people caused dreadful suffering for the best of motives. In 1553, the year Mary came to the English throne, Calvin lodged a complaint of heresy against a wandering Spanish theologian, Michael Servetus, a notable Unitarian heretic. He was found guilty, and sentenced to be burnt. Calvin pleaded with the council for a more humane death, but as so often, he lost. Servetus was burnt, by an inexpert executioner, and he took half an hour to die in the extremes of agony. By the standards of our day it is a grievous blot on Calvin's career, but it must be seen in the context of the times. Heretics were the sixteenth century equivalent of terrorists, those who threatened the very fabric, cogency and coherence of society. They had to be put down. After Servetus' execution the Christian world expressed its warm approbation of Calvin's decisiveness.

Calvin believed magistrate and minister had complementary functions, and in theory, if not in practice, he kept them distinct. It was not his job to rule. It was his job to preach. The Bible was at the heart of Calvin's life devotionally and professionally. He was, in effect, a local minister for twenty-eight years, and the pulpit was the focus of his work. It was his job to expound Scripture week in, week out. Every week he preached on the Old Testament on weekdays at 6 in the morning (7 in the winter). He dealt with the New Testament on Sunday mornings, and the Psalms on Sunday afternoons. It has been estimated that he preached 170 sermons a year - almost 4,000 sermons after his return to Geneva. If, in between sermons, he changed the shape of the church, that was an incidental spin off. If, in between sermons, he wrote a primer of Christian doctrine which grew to become the definitive work of Reformed dogmatics, that was a bonus. Calvin's influence and greatness lies in his work as a Biblical scholar. That is amply demonstrated by comparing his simple, elegant concentration on the text with the cumbersome works of his predecessors. Calvin seems refreshingly modern.

Unlike his predecessors, Calvin separated out theology and commentary, and from 1536 until 1559 he developed the *Institutes of the Christian Religion* from a catechetical primer into the definitive work of Reformed dogmatics.

It is a work of towering significance, a rich, subtle wrestling with God's self-revelation in creation and Christ, as systematic as Luther was incisive, the Protestant equivalent of Thomas Aquinas's *Summa Theologica.* It is a fugue on the theme of God's gracious fatherly goodness and sovereignty. Sadly, many associate it only with the doctrine of predestination. Calvin did not invent predestination. It is there in Scripture, in Augustine, and in a veritable host of medieval theologians. It was the Calvinists, the embroiderers of his tradition, who gave it disproportionate status within their theological system. Calvin was far too astute a theologian to fall into that trap.

Calvin regarded theology as an ordering of the witness of Scripture. However, although he considered Scripture to be the focus of God's revelation, he opens the *Institutes* by exploring the revelation of God in creation. Nonetheless, the primary source of our knowledge of God and of ourselves is Scripture, for we cannot truly appreciate what it is to be human apart from our relationship with God. Later Reformed thinkers insisted that Scripture was the sole source of theology. A careful reading of Calvin suggests that although he subordinated reason and tradition (the two other sources of Catholic theology) to Scripture, he did not eliminate them. Indeed, he was the sixteenth century's greatest patristic scholar, with a particular love for Augustine and St John Chrysostom. He uses their writings as a critique of contemporary Roman theology, and in that sense he may be said to reverence tradition. Few theologians have ever addressed their subject with more intellectual rigour than Calvin. What he refuses to do is use reason and tradition to dissolve Scripture's paradoxes.

His thinking is deeply trinitarian. He lets God be God, in all God's majesty and glory and otherness. A recent study has shown us that Calvin was an anxious, driven man caught between order and chaos, longing for cogency and coherence, yet celebrating the paradoxes and mysteries of existence. Maybe living with that tension is part of everyone's Christian pilgrimage. The *Institutes* strive to make religion rational, logic, coherent, but in the end God cannot be tamed, cannot be reduced to the parameters of human language and concepts. God is other, holy, transcendent, and the proper response is to worship. God's *'wonderful method of governing the universe is rightly called an abyss, because when it is hidden from us, we ought reverently to adore it.'* (*Institutes* I.xvii.2)

If Luther was the theologian of the cross, Calvin was the theologian of the incarnation. Salvation for Calvin flows from Christ's life-long, death-long obedience to the Father,

*This is the wondrous exchange, which out of his boundless goodness, he has made with us. Having become Son of Man with us, he had made us with himself Sons of God. By his own descent to earth, he has prepared our ascent to heaven. Having received our mortality, he has conferred his immortality upon us. Having taken our weakness, he has strengthened us by his power. Having submitted to our poverty, he has transferred his wealth to us. Having taken up himself the burden of impurity with which we were oppressed, he has clothed us with his righteousness.* (*Institutes* IV.xvii.2)

He had a profound understanding of the work of the Holy Spirit. Two examples must suffice, both of contemporary importance. There is much discussion in the church and amongst professional theologians about the authority of Scripture. This was a problem Calvin pondered thoughtfully. The authority of Scripture, he considered, rested not on the opinions of the church, but in the testimony of the Holy Spirit who worked in human hearts to bring the Word of God to life. The second example is of ecumenical importance. Calvin is being recovered as a eucharistic theologian of the first importance. Here mystery and rationality meet, and rationality kneels and adores. Huldrych Zwingli, the leader of the reformation in Zürich spoke of holy communion as a memorial. Believers broke bread because Christ commanded them to, but Christ was not really present in the elements because his body was in heaven. Calvin had a different understanding. He addresses the paradox that here we feed on a Christ whose body is in heaven. The bread and Christ are spatially separate, but it is the Spirit's work to unite things which are separate. At communion we are taken up into heaven and we feed on the reality of Christ. It was mystery, paradox, not to be reduced from its strangeness and wonder to crass comprehensibility. (*Institutes* IV xviii, see particularly 26) That his followers made it so should not blind us to Calvin's perception.

## The origin of presbyterianism

Calvin is rightly regarded as the father of Reformed theology. He is also the originator of the Reformed ordering of the church. All the reformers tried to use the New Testament as a source book for the shape of the church. The trouble is, the New Testament writers didn't have a list of their questions in front of them, any more than they have a list of ours. Modern New Testament scholarship has shown that it is impossible to extract a blueprint for being the church from the New Testament - because it reflects the early Christian experience that there were many ways of being the church.

Calvin didn't know that, and in book IV of the *Institutes* he presents what he thought was the New Testament way of being the church. It is what became know as presbyterianism, the rule of the church by presbyters -

ministers. Calvin identified four offices in the church - ministers who preached the Word and administered the sacraments, deacons who looked after the poor, elders who maintained spiritual discipline and order in the community, and doctors who were theological teachers. It was definitely not democracy - no-one in Geneva doubted that Calvin was in charge, although the City Council continually tried to limit his authority. Nonetheless, it is interesting to note in his correspondence with English reformers that he was fairly flexible. He would have been quite happy with a modified form of episcopacy, and regarded such concerns as the wearing of surplices (which was to take on symbolic power in England) as a matter of indifference.

## The origins of Congregationalism

Presbyterianism then, traces its origins to Calvin. Excavating the origins of Congregationalism has long been a temptation to historians. In one of the committee rooms in the United Reformed Church's London offices hangs a painting which shows King Edward VI handing a licence to John Laski, the Polish minister of the Strangers' congregation in London, in 1550. This was the first officially recognised independent congregation in England. Eighteen months later a similar congregation was established in Glastonbury under the ministry of Valérand Poullain. It went into exile during Mary's reign, never to return. However, Laski's congregation became a permanent part of the religious life of London, always conscious of its links with the Reformed churches of the Netherlands. It is significant that it received official blessing, for that shows the government was not hostile to reform. But it is all the more significant that it was a 'Stranger's' congregation, for the roots of Congregationalism reach down to the radical left-wing of the reformation, to reformers like Konrad Grebel of Zürich (1497-1526) who felt that they could not wait for the 'godly prince' to carry on the work of reform and tried to force the pace.

These radical ideas which emphasised the discontinuity between church and state, the voluntary nature of religious commitment, and the right of God's people to order their own life under the gospel were later to flow into Congregationalism. Both radical and mainstream Reformed ideas of how to be the church spread across Europe. The Christian scholarly community had always been international, and the invention of printing meant that ideas circulated more widely and rapidly than ever before. Every city state and nation in northern Europe was affected by the reformation. They all responded in characteristically individual ways, blending politics and religion in varying reactions.

## The reformation in England

### Henry VIII (1491-1547)

The upheaval in England stretched across the reign of Henry VIII and his three children, from the 1520s to the end of the sixteenth century. It began in about 1527 when Henry became increasingly anxious that his marriage to Katherine of Aragon (1485-1536) was failing to produce an heir. He seems genuinely to have believed that this was a sign of divine displeasure because their union was contrary to God's will. Katherine had been married to his elder brother Arthur (1486-1502), and that was forbidden by Leviticus 18.16 and 20.2. The pope had granted the necessary dispensation when he had married in 1509, and Henry also seems to have thought that the pope had had no right to grant that original dispensation. At the same time he was falling in love with Anne Boleyn (*c.*1501-36), and so set in train a process to gain a divorce. He gave no encouragement either to native dissenting groups (the Lollards), or to continental reforming ideas. The break he initiated with Rome in the 1530s was a political rupture, intended to make the English church independent, and the King master in his own house. It was not theologically motivated.

However, in spite of Henry, reforming Lutheran ideas spread from the continent, along trade routes and into the universities where small groups gathered, like the one at the White Horse Inn in Cambridge, to consider these new ideas. There may have been willing ears to hear them amongst the Lollards, dissenters who had originally been followers of John Wiclif (*c.*1330-84), but whose reforming platform had widened. However, their influence is hotly debated by historians of the English reformation.

Reforming ideas also had powerful, aristocratic sympathisers. Notable amongst them was a group at court centred on the Boleyns and Thomas Cromwell (*c.*1485-1540), the king's new chief minister. They patronised the evangelical and humanist critics of the church. Anne certainly fed Henry with reforming concepts during the divorce crisis, and we know that she kept a copy of Tyndale's New Testament open on a lectern in her private quarters when it was still a proscribed book. Tyndale was martyred in 1536, but the following year a translation gained royal approval, and in 1538 it was placed in every church by royal command. Amongst the bishops, Thomas Cranmer (1489-1556) and Hugh Latimer (*c.*1485-1555) emerged as important forces within the church, challenging such traditional practices as masses for the dead and redefining doctrine in the Ten Articles of 1536. There was a conservative backlash in the late 1530s, and in 1539 the Act of Six Articles restored the doctrinal *status quo*, and that was how matters remained until Henry died in 1547. The English church was still in spirit a catholic church. The Henrician reformation had simply switched authority and control from Rome to Canterbury, or more precisely to the monarch himself. Some think Henry may have been modelling himself on the Roman Emperor Constantine!

## Edward VI (1537-53) and Mary (1516-58)

He was succeeded by his ten year old son by his third wife Jane Seymour (*c.*1509-37). During Edward's reign Thomas Cranmer, Henry's archbishop, moved the church gently towards Protestantism, publishing two Books of Common Prayer in 1549 and 1552, and used his influence to bring leading reforming scholars to the English universities - Peter Martyr (1500-1562) to Oxford in 1548 and Martin Bucer (1491-1551) to Cambridge in 1549. Bucer in particular pushed the English reformers in a firmly Swiss direction, notably by his influence on Cranmer's 1552 Prayer Book which did away with traditional vestments, put the altar in the nave and removed any reference to the divine presence in the eucharist. The effect, however, was short lived, because the book was only published in the last year of Edward's reign. However, the true power of university professors lies in the way they form the thinking of the next generation.

Church leaders may change their minds, intellectual fashions may fluctuate in universities, but life in the average parish church changes at a more sedate pace. There is lively debate amongst students of the English reformation about how pervasive it actually was. In some places Cranmer's Prayer Book was fiercely resisted. In others a prudent caution greeted the changes and the vestments, statues and works of art outlawed by the new liturgies were quietly hidden away, to be brought out of store with alacrity in 1553 when Edward's half-sister Mary, the troubled, sad and holy daughter of Katherine of Aragon, came to the throne. There is no doubt that the old catholic faith was rapidly restored, perhaps because 800 of the leading Protestant clergy had read the writing on the wall and disappeared into exile in such reformed havens as Frankfurt and Geneva where the reformation of the refugees was in full swing. Edward's Protestant reforms were repealed, and the fires of Smithfield were stoked with the bodies of Protestant martyrs - including the five famous bishops - Cranmer, Ferrar, Hooper, Ridley, and Latimer. It was neither vindictiveness nor political necessity but conscience that lit the fires. Mary was not a bad woman. It was, as martyrdom has frequently been, the best way to ensure survival. Protestantism did not go away. After five years on the throne Mary died of cancer, and her twenty-five year old half-sister Elizabeth, the daughter of Anne Boleyn came to the throne. Mary was scarcely in her grave before the Marian exiles returned, full of ideas picked up in those living academies of reform, the city states of Germany and Switzerland. The debate about the shape of the English church now began in earnest. Although Calvin's ideas were to gain primacy, the refugees returned having been influenced by many different patterns of reform. It was the reforming movement which captivated them rather than the work of one individual.

## Elizabeth (1533-1603), presbyterian ideas, and the emergence of separatism

Elizabeth I was Anne Boleyn's daughter. It is tempting to see the roots of Elizabeth's temperate protestantism in the faith of the mother who promoted reform in the dangerous days of the late 1520s and 1530s. Elizabeth was decisive and forceful. She acted with extreme speed in ecclesiastical affairs on her succession.

Within three days, on 20 November 1558 she had appointed William Cecil (1520-1598) as her principal secretary, a clear signal that she wished to return to the policies of Henry VIII and Edward VI, for he had been secretary to the privy council in her half-brother's reign and had been deeply involved in the production of the 1552 Prayer Book. Whilst Mary had been on the throne he had been quietly employed as the surveyor of Elizabeth's estates. Cecil arranged for a protestant sermon at Paul's Cross on the day the Privy Council met for the first time, and when the bishop of Winchester attempted to have the preacher arraigned for heresy, the Privy Council imprisoned the bishop instead. Just a month later, at Christmas, Elizabeth walked out of mass when the priest attempted to elevate the host. The signals were clear for all to read.

In the first weeks of the reign Elizabeth's attention turned to the bench of bishops, which had suffered a marked number of vacancies during Mary's last months, including the see of Canterbury, for Cardinal Pole (1500-1558) (Mary's archbishop) had died on the same day as his queen. In the early days of December 1558 Elizabeth's advisors were already sounding out Matthew Parker (1504-75), who was soon to be Pole's successor.

By Easter 1559, in spite of spirited opposition from the Lords and the remaining Marian bishops, Elizabeth's first parliament passed the Act of Supremacy and the Act of Uniformity. The former established her as

'Supreme Governor' of the church (her father had been Supreme Head). As John Parkhurst, a Marian exile, pointed out to the Zürich reformer Heinrich Bullinger (1504-1575), *'the queen is not willing to be called the head of the church of England, although this title has been offered her; but she willingly accepts the title of governor, which amounts to the same thing.'*

It was however, the latter, one of the most cannily drafted of all the statutes of the reformation, which gave Genevan noses the first whiff of Elizabeth's distinctive and unwelcome policy of moderation. It imposed the 1552 Prayer Book as the pattern of worship in the English church, but with significant conservative alterations. The words of administration which had been clearly memorialist in 1552, were changed in an attempt to balance memorialism with a theology of the real presence. Equally conservative were the omission of the so-called 'black rubric' of 1552 which stated that kneeling to receive the sacrament need not imply the *'real and substantial'* presence of Christ in the elements and the inclusion of the 'ornaments rubric' which stated that eucharistic vestments should be worn *'as in the second year of Edward VI'*. This splendidly vague phrase was to cause untold havoc in the later history of the Church of England. However, the Act itself seemed to hold out the hope of future change in a reforming direction, for it stated that the ornaments should be used *'until other order be taken therein'*, but when the Queen issued the Royal Injunctions which set out how the book was to be used, they stipulated the use of wafers rather than the 'common bread' spoken of in the Prayer Book.

To many contemporaries the settlement looked like the triumph of protestantism, and they assumed that there would be room for manoeuvre. They were wrong on both counts. It was actually a triumph for the Queen, and once it was enshrined in statute, she refused to budge from it. The reformers had wanted reformation at the hands of a godly prince. And that was what they got, like it or not - thorough-going Erastianism, a neat political middle way between catholic and protestant extremism. From the very beginning Elizabeth was as clear as her father had been about who was running the English church - she was. As bishops who crossed her found to their cost, in her eyes they were first and foremost royal servants.

It was a settlement which rapidly ran into difficulties. During the 1560s there were clashes between the bishops and more advanced Protestants over the wearing of surplices. The white surplice was a red rag to Genevan bulls! It conjured up images of the Roman priesthood, and behind that the Jewish priesthood, clean contrary, some Protestants believed, to the gospel. That view was not confined to radical fanatics - it was shared by

Laurence Humphrey, the Regius Professor of Divinity at Oxford, and his colleague Thomas Sampson, the Dean of Christ Church, by bishops like Grindal and Horne, by the dean of St Paul's and the three archdeacons of the diocese of London. But the surplice was a symbol of much more. Was the church to be governed the Queen or Christ? What were the limits of conscience? Could the authority of Scripture be so lightly cast aside? It was a debate that had raged amongst the Marian exiles in Frankfurt, and Elizabeth's letter telling Parker to establish uniformity and the wearing of surplices, which Parker translated into policy in 1566, re-lit that smouldering fire.

The vestments controversy showed the depths of the division within the Elizabethan church. Forty clergy in London alone were suspended just before Easter 1566. It provoked the first of many furious Puritan pamphlet campaigns, caused furore in the universities, triggered the first manifestations of separatism, and (more significantly) contributed to the development of presbyterianism. Some trace the 'fault-line' between the establishment and dissent to this point. Those bishops who had had sympathy with the 'precisionists' who refused to wear surplices quickly lost it when they were faced with the horror of separatism.

In 1567 about a hundred Londoners were caught in Plumbers' Hall, using Genevan forms of worship rather than the Prayer Book. It is probably misguided to see this as a manifestation of proto-Congregationalism. In 1570, Thomas Cartwright (1535-1603), one time Marian exile, Fellow of Trinity College, Cambridge and Lady Margaret's Reader in Divinity, electrified the university with a lecture series on the Acts of the Apostles. This was the first systematic exposition of presbyterian theory in England.

The Elizabethan 'presbyterians' were moderates. They strove for reform of the Church of England from within. They wanted changes in worship, modifications in episcopal government, the introduction of *classes* (best understood as a mix between Bible study and in-service training for the clergy). It was a significant and dangerous movement. In Cartwright's view the only possible Biblical pattern of church government was a conciliar system in which congregations were ruled by ministers and elders, with representative councils above them. Such radicalism would have swept away the entire Elizabethan hierarchy. Unfortunately, Cartwright was an academic theorist. He had no stomach for the Russian roulette of Elizabethan church politics.

However, his theories were translated into political threat by John Field (1545-1588), an Oxford trained priest who launched a furious *Admonition to Parliament* in 1572. There are good times and bad times to launch revolutions. This was a bad time. The Pope had excommunicated Elizabeth in 1570. The country was in fear of Spanish invasion, and remained so until the Armada was defeated in 1588, and parliament responded to the uncertainty of the political climate by tightening the uniformity screw. Religious conformity was a badge of political rectitude. Presbyterianism was perceived as a threat to national unity, and archbishop Whitgift and bishop Richard Bancroft of London used the Court of High Commission to silence it.

Presbyterianism, though, was never inherently dissenting. It was an alternative ideology of establishment, not a revolutionary manifesto. Congregationalism, on the other hand, was. If presbyterianism is a system, congregationalism is a walk, a way of being Christian. If presbyterianism was formulated by Calvin, congregationalism is historically eclectic. If presbyterianism is about good order and reformation at the hand of the divinely inspired godly prince, congregationalism is about the expectancy of the Spirit, the freedom of God's people and the autonomy under Christ of the local community of Christians.

There are three pairs of windows in the apse of Emmanuel URC in Cambridge. To the left are two men who were rough contemporaries with Cartwright at Cambridge, John Greenwood (d.1593) and Henry Barrow (*c.*1550-1593). In the centre are two of the great figures of English history, Oliver Cromwell (1599-1658) and John Milton (1608-1674), both of whom came to prominence during the Commonwealth and Protectorate, and to the right two men of the later seventeenth century, Francis Holcroft (*c.*1629-1693) and John Hussey (1660-1726). These windows epitomise the difficulty the historian faces in discussing the origins of Congregationalism. Students of church history have made cogent cases that Congregationalism could begin with all three.

John Greenwood and Henry Barrow were amongst the tiny minority of Elizabethan Christians who wished to separate from the national church because they felt that the Queen and the established structure would never reform the church as Christ wished it to be reformed. They therefore formed their own 'separatist' congregations, separating from the godless multitudes in their parish churches to live lives of true holiness. A thousand years earlier the same impulse had led to Benedictine monasticism. It had been seen before in England, perhaps in Laski's 'Strangers' congregation, in the shadowy underground world of Protestantism in Mary's reign and in Richard Fitz's so-called 'Privy church' of the 1560s.

The separatists believed the Church of England to be so hopelessly corrupt that nothing save a new beginning would suffice. Following Christ demanded a distinctive life-style, as Barrow put it *'..reducing all things and actions to the true and primitive pattern of God's Word.'* The English church was far from that. It was as apostate as ancient Israel. Parish churches thronged with the godless multitude, ministered to by those ordained by bishops and maintained by tithes rather than presbyters chosen, appointed and paid by the people. Its worship was un-Scriptural, based on a Prayer Book all too Romish in tendency; its government an unhappy mingling of courts sacred and secular. All that had to be rejected for the narrow way, the faithful walk.

It was only in the 1580s that separatism began to develop a coherent ideology through the writings of Robert Browne (*c.*1550-1633), Henry Barrow, Robert Harrison (d.1585), John Penry (1559-1603) and John Greenwood. They were all Cambridge men. Greenwood, Barrow and Browne all emerged from the radical tradition fostered around the urban centres of East Anglia - Norwich, Thetford and Bury St Edmunds. Browne was a man of some substance, a kinsman of Elizabeth's chief minister, William Cecil, Lord Burghley. He and Harrison had been undergraduates at Cambridge when Cartwright was electrifying the university with his lectures on Acts. It was Browne who first inveighed against the condition of the bishop-ridden state church, judging that *'..the kingdom of God was not to be begun by whole parishes, but rather of the worthiest, be they never so few.'* and getting on with reformation, in his famous phrase, *'without tarrying for anie.'* Bishop Freke did not welcome such views from the pulpits of his diocese of Norwich. Browne was harried and imprisoned until he and Harrison and some of the other members of their congregation decided life would be easier in the Netherlands. They settled at Middelberg in Zeeland. During 1582 Browne set out his views in a series of books, *A brief treatise of the reformation without tarrying for anie*, *A treatise upon the 23 of Matthew*, and *A book which sheweth the life and manner of all true Christians.* There he set out his understanding of the church as a gathered company of Christians, in covenant together under God, with minister, officers and people held together in mutual contract. Life proved less than easy in exile. Harrison and Browne disagreed. The relationship between Browne and his congregation broke down and he left for Scotland. The Kirk wanted no truck with such independent radicalism, and a chastened Browne returned to England in 1584, which was either foolhardy or brave because his books were proscribed. He was arrested, but recanted and returned to the Church of England, eventually becoming rector of Achurch in Northamptonshire in 1591 thanks to the influence of Lord Burghley. However, something of his separatist principles seems to have survived, because he was suspended from his duties and excommunicated in 1631, finally dying in prison in 1633, having been arrested for striking the village constable! Harrison died in Middelberg around 1585.

In 1583 John Whitgift (*c.*1530-1604) was translated from the bishopric of Worcester to Canterbury. Ambitious and able, he had been Master of Trinity and Vice-Chancellor of Cambridge University during the vestiarian controversy and was the main opponent of Cartwright's presbyterian theories. Whitgift was a man of order, and it was no surprise that he began his episcopate by insisting that all clergy should subscribe to the Prayer Book as *'containing nothing contrary to the Word of God.'* One of few whose conscience baulked at this was John Greenwood who joined up with a separatist congregation in London. In 1587 Greenwood and twenty others were arrested while they were meeting near St Paul's. One of his visitors in the Clink was Henry Barrow, Cambridge graduate, member of Gray's Inn, and former courtier. It was a fatal visit. Whitgift had him arrested. During the six years of their imprisonment they produced a steady stream of apologetic writings which were fiercely critical of the Elizabethan establishment.

Their works were printed in Holland. The English ambassador tried to have them suppressed in 1591. He used as his agent Francis Johnson (1562-1618), another Cambridge Puritan, minister to the English Merchant Adventurers at Middleberg, a presbyterian who had no time for separatism. Johnson managed to get the stock of books burnt, but he saved two from the fires so that he could read them. So impressed was he, that he travelled to London, met Barrow and Greenwood in prison, joined the London separatists and became their minister in 1592. Not long afterwards Johnson welcomed a distinguished new member, John Penry. Penry was Welsh, and an ardent advocate of reform for the Welsh church. In 1587 he had published *Aequity of an Humble Supplication*, arguing for the provision of Welsh speaking clergy in Wales, the establishment of proper pastoral care, and the use of lay preachers to cope with the shortfall of clergy. Whitgift imprisoned him for his pains. On his release he went to Scotland, and what he saw of presbyterianism there persuaded him of the value of separatism. Penry had played a part in the printing of the scurrilous and wickedly satirical Marprelate tracts which incensed Whitgift. His days were numbered. He was arrested in 1593 and hanged, six weeks after Barrow and Greenwood. Only Francis Johnson escaped with his life after four years' imprisonment, eventually returning to his church in Amsterdam in 1597.

Separatism had been effectively obliterated in England by Whitgift's use of the Court of High Commission. It is impossible to establish any continuity of personnel between those brave dissenting congregations and the radical sects which were to explode into activity following the Civil War some sixty years later. Even those radical groups did not constitute a denomination. That was not to happen until after the restoration of Charles II in 1660 and the Restoration settlement of 1662 which forced presbyterians and congregationalists outside the national church into a life of their own. However, it was as men like Cartwright and Field and Barrow and Greenwood wrestled with Scripture and tried to be the church they felt Christ was calling them to be, that the upheavals orchestrated by Calvin and Luther took on specifically English forms and provided the impetus which would later be harnessed into the traditions which were to create the United Reformed Church.

# The Seventeenth Century - a time chart

| Date | Politics | Church Affairs |
|---|---|---|
| 1603 | Elizabeth d.<br>James VI of Scotland to throne of England | |
| 1604 | | Hampton Court Conference |
| 1605 | The Gunpowder Plot | |
| 1606 | | Separatist church at Scrooby |
| 1608 | | Robinson's congregation to Amsterdam |
| 1610 | | *Remonstrance* of Dutch church |
| 1611 | | The Authorised Version |
| 1618 | Outbreak of Thirty Years' War (to *c.*1648) | Synod of Dort |
| 1620 | | Mayflower takes first Puritan settlers to America |
| 1623 | | Jesuits establish an English Province |
| 1625 | James VI & I d.<br>Charles I to throne | Rise of 'Arminianism' |
| 1628 | Assassination of Buckingham | |
| 1629 | Beginning of eleven years 'personal rule' | |
| 1633 | | William Laud archbishop of Canterbury |
| 1637 | Trial of Bastwick, Prynne and Burton<br>Rebellion in Scotland | Attempt to impose Prayer Book in Scotland |
| 1638 | National Covenant in Scotland | |
| 1640 | Long Parliament<br>King leaves London | |
| 1641 | Grand Remonstrance | |
| 1642 | First Civil War | |
| 1643 | | Westminster Assembly<br>Execution of Laud |
| 1646 | End of first Civil War | Abolition of episcopacy |
| 1648 | Second Civil War | |
| 1649 | Execution of Charles I<br>Commonwealth | Dean and chapter lands sold |
| 1651 | | John Owen Dean of Christ Church, Oxford |

| Date | Politics | Church Affairs |
|---|---|---|
| 1653 | Barebones Parliament<br>The Protectorate<br>(Oliver Cromwell) | Baxter's *Reformed Pastor* |
| 1656 | | |
| 1660 | The Restoration<br>Charles II to throne | |
| 1661 | Cavalier Paraliament<br>Venner's Fifth Monarchist 'rebellion' | Savoy Conference |
| 1662 | | The Act of Uniformity<br>The Great Ejection |
| 1664 | Conventicle Act | |
| 1665 | The Five Mile Act | |
| 1666 | The Great Fire of London | |
| 1673 | The Test Act | |
| 1675 | | The re-building of St Paul's |
| 1678 | | John Bunyan's *Pilgrim's Progress* |
| 1679 | Exclusion crisis (to 1681) | |
| 1683 | | John Owen d. |
| 1685 | Charles II d.<br>James II to throne | Catholics organised under vicars-general |
| 1688 | James II flees<br>The Glorious Revolution<br>William and Mary to thrones | John Bunyan d. |
| 1689 | The Act of Toleration | The 'non-jurors' refuse oath to William and Mary |
| 1690 | | Presbyterianism established in Scotland |
| 1691 | | Richard Baxter d. |
| 1701 | James II d. | |

# Chapter 2

# *Britain's religious wars - the early Stuart church.*

Presbyterianism and Congregationalism were international phenomena. Their origin can be traced to the theories and practice of being the church which emerged during the continental reformation, and they became an important part of the struggle to establish the shape of the English church during Elizabeth's reign. However, the United Reformed Church in the United Kingdom is a British church, and the histories of Wales and Scotland contribute much to its shape and flavour.

## The reformation and its aftermath in Wales

The roots of the Welsh church were Celtic, part of the remarkable process of evangelisation and mission which developed along the western seaboard, linking the Celtic cultures of Ireland, western Scotland, north-western England, Cornwall and Brittany during the fifth and sixth centuries. The British Isles and Ireland were effectively cut off from mainland Europe from the fall of Rome to the Goths in 421 until the late seventh century, and during this time it fell back on its own resources and traditions. The churches of these islands thus developed their own emphases - a monastic, ascetic spirituality, a flowing, exquisite curvilinear art, deep devotion to Scripture, and an intimate veneration of the saints. In the late seventh century the British churches were re-united with the continental church in the wake of Anglo-Saxon invasions. The English church assimilated quickly. The Welsh did not. It was not until the Norman conquest in the eleventh century that the nature of Welsh Christianity began to change as territorial bishoprics replaced monasteries as the powerhouses of Christian living. However, they maintained their distinctiveness. The Welsh never accepted clerical celibacy, never readily accepted the overlordship of Canterbury, and took more easily to such ascetic forms of monasticism as practised by Cistercians and Franciscans, and they continued to reverence their own saints like David and Illtud.

The problems of the Welsh church really began when Edward I conquered Wales in 1282-3 and subordinated it to the English state, using Welsh bishoprics as part of a system of rewarding the English, turning them into administrators and drawing them away from their dioceses. Resentment against colonial oppression boiled over in Owen Glydwr's rebellion (1400-1415). For a while it looked as if he could build an independent state and ecclesiastical province, but the comet soon burnt itself out and the main legacy of his campaign for the church was a great deal of physical damage, the disruption of worship and the shattering of church discipline. By 1500 the church had recovered from most of these problems, but at a price. Most bishops were royal servants, most were not Welsh, and the structure of pastoral care was haphazard. Monasteries had declined into ease. None of the great reforming movements of the late middle ages had a significant impact on Wales.

Nor did Henry's break with Rome. For Wales the Henrician reformation meant the dissolution of the monasteries and a consequent reduction in the number of pilgrimage centres. The Edwardine reformation, however, was deeply resented because it swept away much that was deeply loved and imposed an English-language prayer book on Welsh speakers. The Welsh thought they were being forced to become heretics, to forsake their ancient faith rooted in the work of the Celtic saints for the hated religion of the Saxons.

It was only during Elizabeth's reign that the reformation made any appreciable impact, for the 1567 parliament ordered the production of a Welsh Bible and Prayer Book, which didn't appear until 1588. The Bible was prefaced by a superb 'Letter to the Welsh people' by bishop Richard Davies (*c.*1501-1581). He provided a brilliant re-interpretation of Welsh church history. The gospel, he argued, had been introduced into Britain by Joseph of Arimathea. The Welsh had preserved that pristine faith until they had been dragged down into error by the English who had introduced wicked Roman error. The reformation was a restoration of the 'second flowering' of the gospel - the great purpose for which God had chosen the Welsh. Wales had its Puritans - John Penry for example - but he had more impact in England than his native Wales. Puritanism didn't make the same inroads in Wales - possibly because of its extreme poverty and the lack of a middle-class. Even during the reigns of the early Stuarts its influence was mainly in the borders and the south which was within easy reach of Bristol.

## The Scottish reformation

The reformation also came late to Scotland. Whereas in England Henry and his ministers engineered a break with Rome in the 1530s and Edward sanctioned reformed liturgies in the 1549 and 1552 Prayer Books, reformation did not become an official part of Scottish national life until 1560.

In the previous forty years, from the publication of Luther's theses in 1517 to the death of Mary Tudor in 1559, reforming ideas touched Scotland in two main ways. There was a brief but unimportant flirtation with Lutheranism in the mid 1520s. Laws are rarely passed unless behaviour needs regulating. In 1525 an act was passed prohibiting the importation of Lutheran books. It is therefore a reasonable assumption that some of his works had entered Scotland by the east coast ports. Three years later Patrick Hamilton, who had studied at Marburg and defended Lutheran theses there, was executed at St Andrews. His execution was followed by a spate of others. Over three hundred years later the English Presbyterians joined with their Scottish cousins in honouring his martyrdom as the first shoots of the Scottish reformation, and the then Principal of the English Presbyterian College, Peter Lorimer, wrote a biography of him which is still in use.

Second, more radical, probably Calvinist, ideas were in the air in the 1540s, centred on Dundee and Angus in the east, Ayr in the south-west and in certain parts of Lothian. George Wishart (*c.*1513-46) was executed in 1546 as the Scottish government pursued a pro-French policy. The Scottish church read the reforming straws in the wind and began to put their house in order. Even as late as the 1550s it looked as if conservative, catholic reform could save the Scottish catholic church. John Hamilton, the archbishop of St Andrews was deeply influenced by the patterns of reform in continental catholicism which were given legislative shape by the Council of Trent (1545-63). He instituted catechetical and educational reforms in the 1550s. However, Protestant pressure was increasing simultaneously. In 1557 leading Protestant nobles banded together as the 'Lords of the Congregation', drawing up a covenant, pledging themselves *'to labour at our possibility to have faithful Ministers purely and truly to minister Christ's Evangel and Sacraments to his people.'*

South of the border Mary Tudor was dying. The international scene was dangerous. Mary, Queen of Scots (1542-1587), was married to Francis, the French dauphin (heir to the throne). There was at least a serious theoretical possibility that Scotland could become a French province. When Elizabeth came to the throne in 1559, she saw essential allies in the Lords of the Congregation and lent them her aid.

In 1559 the pressure for reform became a revolution in Scotland. In 1560 the Scottish parliament broke all ties with Rome, abolished the mass, and a reformed church was created. Prior to the calling of parliament, the Great Council of Scotland had appointed a commission of six religious leaders to draw up a Confession of Faith and a Book of Discipline. They were a fascinating group - all called John, but with contrasting backgrounds and hopes. Two were St Andrews' men, John Wynram (*c.*1492-1582), sub-prior of the Augustinian monastery and John Douglas (*c.*1494-1574), the Rector of the University. Both had been leading players in the conservative reform programme in the previous quarter of a century. Three had been south of the border, had tasted the Church of England and hoped that Scotland would move in a similar direction. John Spottiswoode (1565-1639) eventually became archbishop of St Andrews, and was throughout his career a convinced royalist, fleeing to Newcastle after the signing of the National Covenant in 1638. John Willock (d.1588) had been chaplain to the Duke of Suffolk, and was to end his days as rector of Loughborough. John Row (*c.*1525-1580) had returned from Rome, where he had been much taken by the reforming process within Catholicism. And then there was John Knox (*c.*1513-1572), in effect the leader of the group. A difficult, outspoken and courageous man, he had been chaplain to Edward VI, and a formative influence on the revised Prayer Book of 1552 before fleeing to Geneva on Mary's accession. He had spells as pastor to the exiled English congregations at Frankfurt and Geneva, before returning to Scotland in 1559. Knox was a Genevan Calvinist through and through, and his hand lies behind the Scots Confession (1560), *The First Book of Discipline* and *The Book of Common Order* (1560-64).

The group worked fast and harmoniously. Parliament accepted their Confession of Faith (which became known as The Scots Confession of 1560) without demur. However, their radical proposals for re-structuring the church, *The First Book of Discipline*, were too much to stomach. Parliament could not envisage the old order disappearing so smartly, although they eventually acquiesced in the following year. *The First Book of Discipline* proposed a fairly 'Genevan' polity, dividing Scotland into ten areas, each under a superintendent, who was a bishop in all but name. Worship was re-organised according to the *Book of Common Order*, based on the material Knox had used with his English congregation in Geneva. Parish discipline was administered by Kirk sessions and elders, and great efforts were made to improve parish education.

For 130 years, from the establishment of the reformation in 1560 until the accession of William and Mary to the Scottish as well as the English throne in 1689, Scottish church history was a see-saw battle between church and state. The path of reform was rough and difficult, unlike the English experience. Part of the problem was the sharing of monarchs between the Scottish and English thrones throughout the period, and the fact that most English monarchs had little idea what made Edinburgh tick, let alone St Andrew's or Aberdeen.

## The Jacobean period (1604-1625 in England; 1567-1625 in Scotland)

However, that could not be said of the first of those kings, James VI of Scotland (1567-1625) who had thirty years of Scottish kingship behind him before he came to the English throne in 1603. James was canny and clever, and one of the sharpest intellectuals ever to occupy the throne, with volumes of poetry and Biblical exegesis to his credit. He was also lazy and a dreamer, but one person's dreams are another's visions - the toleration of Catholics, the union of the kingdoms and the plantation of Ulster have seemed statesmanlike to posterity. He was also extravagantly, recklessly generous (in his first five years on the English throne he added a quarter to the national debt), married to a giddily spendthrift queen, Anne of Denmark, who managed to accumulate debts of £40,500 in two years, mainly on clothes, and he was cheerfully bisexual. He played the Scottish ecclesiastical scene from the inside, and under the terms of the Concordat of Leith (1572), nearly managed to introduce episcopacy as part of the presbyterian system. It might have worked, but for some unfortunate appointments, and some clear signals that the government intended to use the episcopate as a way of diverting ecclesiastical revenues into the crown's coffers.

The reformers reacted by preparing *The Second Book of Discipline* in 1578. This was largely the work of Andrew Melville (1543-1622), recently returned from Geneva as Principal of Glasgow University. It pressed a far harder line than *The First Book*, laying down the Calvinist four orders of ministry (minister, doctor, elder and deacon), stating clearly that the authority of the church was derived from Christ, not the king, and declaring that there was not a trace of episcopacy in the New Testament.

Relationships between the reformers and the king were not easy. James tried to limit the power of the presbyterian party. Melville promptly told him that there were two kings in Scotland, and king though he might be in his own realm, he was *'but a member of the Kirk'* in Christ's kingdom.

For just over half a century, during the reign of James and his son Charles, English and Scottish church life influenced each other more than ever before, or ever since. James VI and I used his instinctive awareness of the subtleties of Scottish church affairs to try and bring the two national churches into a closer relationship with each other. Ruling the two kingdoms of England and Scotland was rather like riding two horses simultaneously - never easy, but possible if both beasts moved in roughly the same direction. James's ecclesiastical policy attempted to do just that. Politically adept and theologically acute as he was, he understood Edinburgh from the inside and was sharp enough to develop a rapid appreciation of the English church and its liturgies. Writing of the differences between moderate Puritans who wanted the English church pushed in a more Scottish direction and those who were content with the English church as it was, he protested - *'I am so far from being contentious in these things (which for my own part I ever esteemed as indifferent) as I do equally love and honour the learned and grave men of either of these opinions.'*

In 1610 he managed to persuade the Scottish General Assembly to accept the royal supremacy *'in the conservation and purgation of religion'*, acknowledge that the king had the right to call the Assembly, and accept a particularly reformed style of episcopacy - they were more permanent moderators of presbyteries than English-style prelates. James never attempted a clumsy union or takeover between the two national churches. Rather he sought reform and true catholicity for both. His attempt to introduce a reformed episcopate to Scotland was balanced by his consistent campaign to encourage both a higher standard of preaching in the English church and a higher standard of education amongst its clergy. It has been suggested that James's ecclesiastical policy is best described as a search for 'congruity' between the two national churches. He sought to bring the Scottish and English churches as close together as possible. In 1618 he persuaded the Scottish parliament to enact the Five Articles of Perth which prescribed kneeling to receive the communion elements (administration had previously been carried out with the congregation seated around a table), introduced private communion for the sick, private baptism in cases of necessity, confirmation by bishops and the observation of the five main festivals - Christmas, Good Friday, Easter, Ascension and Pentecost. Some Scottish Christians accepted this happily. Others thought it a step too far.

Yet others objected not to the substance of the Articles, but to the method of their introduction, for it seemed to place the authority of the king above that of the church, and therefore of Christ.

South of the border James's ecclesiastical inheritance was far from easy. First, the English church was marked by vigorous divergence of theological opinion. The Elizabethan church was a church in tension about the relationship between scripture and the church, the status of Rome, the shape of the liturgy and the nature of church government. Part of the achievement of Elizabeth's reign was the fashioning of a cherished institution out of those tensions. The Elizabethan church was a middle way, Calvinist in doctrine yet Catholic (or pseudo-Catholic) in organisation. It was marked by enthusiastic and frequently bitter disagreements.

The most vocal opponents of the *status quo* were the Puritans, those who sought further reform of the church from within. The Puritan storms of the 1570s and 80s had abated, largely through the heavy handed use of church courts, but Puritanism had not gone away, it had simply been driven underground. One recent estimate suggests that roughly 10% of the Jacobean clergy were 'Puritan'. During James's reign Calvinism remained the theological orthodoxy of the English church - as the formal adhesion of the Church of England to the Synod of Dort in 1618 showed.

The advent of a new, presbyterian, King seemed like a new dawn to the Puritans, and they promptly made their requests known. On his journey south from Scotland to London, they presented him with a petition, which has become known as the Millenary Petition because it was supposedly signed by a thousand ministers. It was a moderate document, proposing *'not a disorderly innovation, but a due and godly reformation.'* Many of their demands were old favourites. For example, they wanted the making of the sign of the cross at baptism to be discontinued, and the wedding ring and the surplice to the outlawed. However, it was not simply a negative document. They also sought better education for the clergy, a higher standard of preaching, and a proper exercise of church discipline, most particularly in excommunication.

James was initially impressed. He too longed for the church to be more properly equipped to do her work, and he called a conference at Hampton Court in 1604 to consider their demands. Unfortunately some of the Puritans tried to increase the pressure during the run-up to the Conference. That gave the establishment the opportunity to fight back. The conference was a good-tempered affair, but both bishops and Puritans soon realised that James was his own man. Under his chairmanship it became a whip-cracking exercise, and it took the sting out of the church questions. In essence, the bishops were told to put their house in order and the Puritans to behave themselves. Fresh from the headaches of Scottish presbyterianism, he overestimated the democratic thrust of English Puritanism, and told their principal spokesman, John Rainolds, in a famous explosion at the end of a tiring day of theological argument,

*Then Jack and Tom and Will and Dick shall meet, and at their pleasure censure me and my council and all our proceedings...Dr Rainolds, till you find that I grow lazy, let that alone...No bishop, no King...I will make them conform themselves or I will harry them out of this land or else do worse.*

After a night's sleep he was in a better temper, if not half so perceptive, and agreed to collaboration on minor changes in the Prayer Book and the production of what was to become the Authorised Version of the Scriptures, which pleased the Puritans.

The second problem James inherited was closely allied to the strength of Puritanism. The power of the laity which had been unleashed by the reformation was potent. It found expression in pressure for godly preaching and the willingness to go outside the structures of the parochial system to obtain it by the creation of extra-parochial lectureships.

Thirdly, finance was the great unsolved problem of the English reformation. Such money as there was was all tied up in the wrong places. The clergy were paid by tithes, a tax of 10%. Most tithes had been commuted into money payments by the end of the middle ages. Unfortunately, inflation was rampant between 1540 and 1640, and it eroded the real value of tithes. Henry VIII's dissolution of the monasteries had not helped because it had transferred a huge amount of church land into lay hands, along with the right to the income of many benefices. It has been estimated that of *c.*9,250 livings in 1603, 3,850 rector's shares had been impropriated. All attempts to alter this (and there were several) seemed doomed to failure. The vested interests of nearly 4,000 landowners who were the backbone of parliament could not be gainsaid.

James attempted to grasp the ecclesiastical nettles of Elizabeth's reign. He achieved little more than the preservation of the unity of a pluriform, potentially fissiparous institution, but that in itself should be recognised as a considerable achievement. Historians heatedly debate the anatomy of the parties within the Jacobean church, but none doubt that being its Supreme Governor was like sitting on a powder keg.

## Jacobean separatism

There were of course a few, statistically insignificant, but historically important for the history of our tradition, who stepped beyond the boundaries of the national church into separatism. Two years after James's coronation, in 1606 in Scrooby in Lincolnshire and along the lower Trent valley, a group of Puritan radicals which included William Brewster (*c.*1560-1644), the Scrooby postmaster, Thomas Helwys (*c.*1550-*c.*1616), a landed gentleman of Broxtowe Hall near Nottingham, and William Bradford, a farmer's son of seventeen, along with several clergy and two Cambridge dons, John Robinson (*c.*1575-1625) and John Smyth (*c.*1554-1612), formed a separatist church. Within two years this church had split into two, one under Smyth, the other under Robinson, and both congregations migrated to the Netherlands. In Amsterdam Smyth's congregation was soon in controversy with Francis Johnson's separatist church which had settled there after Whitgift's assault on the separatists in 1597.

Johnson's church had had a miserable decade. Francis and his brother George (who was a member of the church) fell out over Francis's marriage to Tomasine Boys, the widow of a fellow separatist who had been a prosperous haberdasher. She continued to dress fashionably and flamboyantly, in a way George thought ill became the wife of a pastor. To make matters worse, there were rumours of financial mismanagement in the congregation, coupled with an acrimonious dispute over the election of two deacons, and relations with the Dutch reformed authorities were strained. Tittle-tattle and gossip laid the foundations for published assaults on the congregation's life and accusations of sexual misconduct which led to legal action.

Smyth was a true radical. He and Johnson (who had been his tutor at Christ's College, Cambridge in the 1580s) parted company on two issues. The Puritans had always placed the highest value on the reading of Scripture in worship. Smyth took that position one stage further by arguing that the Scriptures should only be read in the original Biblical languages of Hebrew and Greek, for in that form alone were they truly inspired of God. At this point he and his followers split from Johnson's church and formed 'the brethren of the Separation of the second English church at Amsterdam.'

Smyth also objected to the way Johnson's church was organised. Johnson had attempted to produce order in his chaotic and divided church by exercising proper church discipline through the use of elders. It was clear that he and his elders ruled the church. Smyth thought that this was the tail wagging the dog. He understood proper church government to mean that the elders should be governed by the whole body of the local church, not the other way round. Smyth's most significant and far-reaching innovation was the rejection of infant baptism. In 1609 his congregation adopted a believer's baptism policy. Smyth re-baptised himself, then Thomas Helwys and the remainder of the congregation. They thus became the precursors of the Baptists.

Robinson's congregation arrived in Amsterdam in 1608. They quickly took stock, and decided that would be better off in Leyden, with some miles between them and Smyth's fiery radicalism and Johnson's divided congregation. The church grew rapidly under Robinson's sensitive and intelligent pastoral care. Of all the exiled separatist congregations, his alone remained intact and unriven by dissension. However, Holland was not an ideal home for English Puritans. Language was a barrier, and the English and Dutch had differing theological emphases, not least on Sabbath observance. It was not surprising that some eyes began to look to a far horizon. As early as 1560 Admiral Coligny (1519-1572), the French Protestant leader, had sent a party to settle in Florida. Unfortunately, they had been wiped out by the Spanish. However, the early seventeenth century was the 'golden age' of exploration and expansion. Virginia fever was in the air. The Virginia Company of London was trying to raise funds through advertising. Captain John Smith (1575-1631), the Company's Virginian adventurer and frontiersman, launched a literary campaign which began with a map of 'New England' and was followed in 1616 with his *Description of New England*, full of promises of nature's bounty and the fortunes which awaited the resourceful. At the same time the Dutch were building on the work of Sir Henry Hudson, an independent seaman in their pay, who had discovered the Hudson river in 1609. In 1613 they had established a trading post 150 miles upstream - Fort Nassau - now Albany, the capital of New York State. It is therefore not surprising that in 1620 a section of the church, including the young William Brewster, left Leyden to sail first for Southampton and then for New England. They are better known to posterity as the Pilgrim Fathers, and Brewster as the first Governor of Plymouth colony. It was a daunting venture. The voyage itself was full of danger and difficulty; the first five years of life in the colony were beset with problems as they sought to build, farm, fish and trade. Their history, and that of those who followed their pioneering path, is beyond the scope of this book, but we can note in passing the significant contribution made by the separatists to the development of American political and religious institutions, perhaps indeed to the American character.

Separatism was far from dead in England. Congregations began to sprout elsewhere in Jacobean England, particularly in Kent, Essex and East Anglia. There was no uniform practise. Some shunned their local parish churches as tainted fleshpots. Others maintained a dual allegiance to their separatist meeting and their parish church. Many who adopted this position were influenced by an Oxford trained Puritan, Henry Jacob (1563-1624). He had been one of the organisers of the Millenary Petition, and was to be one of the most influential Puritans in Stuart England. Historians have been unable to categorise Jacob. He is a man who eludes labelling. He had deep sympathies with separatist thought, believing that the true visible church consisted of individuals who had freely covenanted together under God to live a holy life. Unlike the separatists though, he did not believe that necessarily meant breaking communion with the Church of England, protesting that all congregations of faithful people were in communion with each other under Christ. He also disagreed with the separatists over the role of the godly magistrate or prince in the government of the church. He had no difficulty in accepting that the civil authorities had a place in the government of the church. His views may have developed in response to James's refusal to take the English church in a presbyterian direction at the Hampton Court conference. His thought was to prove influential amongst those who sought exile in Holland. The separatists were a small undercurrent, but they were a sign of the stresses and strains to come.

The problems of the Jacobean church were intimately related to events across the channel. Calvinism was a pan-European ideology. The Thirty Years' War (*c.*1618-48) forms the diplomatic backdrop to the latter years of James's reign and the high drama of Caroline England. As Catholic was set against Protestant across Europe, it seemed necessary to many that England should take sides. The English parliament, bred on a stringently anti-Catholic diet of Foxe's *Book of Martyrs*, the Spanish Armada, the Spanish Inquisition, the St Bartholomew's Day Massacre and the Gunpowder Plot, were vociferous in their support of the Protestants. James was a man of peace, a seeker of middle-grounds. He refused to accept that the strife in Europe was confessionally based and sought a diplomatic solution which involved weighing the possibilities of marrying his son Charles to the Catholic Spanish Infanta.

When Parliament demanded that the matter be discussed, James promptly dissolved it. Three years later, the scene had changed. Britain was now at war with Spain. The Duke of Buckingham decided that that demanded an alliance with France, and he promptly had Charles married off to Henrietta Maria, a devout Catholic. Thus, by a series of thoroughly virtuous political misjudgments, James appeared to favour the Catholics.

That, plus some notable and politically significant conversions to Catholicism in court circles, heightened the antagonism between king and parliament. The court seemed a hot-bed of Catholic sedition. Relations between king and parliament were sour in James's final years. However, a new king offered new possibilities, and in 1625 Charles came to the throne on a spring tide of goodwill which he made ebb at astonishing speed.

## Charles I and the Civil Wars

Charles lacked his father's political deftness and his innate sense of knowing just how far he could go. He was everything James was not - sober, clean, virtuous, dignified, courteous, chaste, an aesthete rather than an intellectual. His court was magnificent without vulgarity. He had exquisite taste. Whether Charles was an Anglican saint, one of the most inept monarchs in history, the hapless victim of revolutionary fanatics, or a mixture of all three is still debated.

His accession actually did nothing to sweeten relations with Parliament. In 1626 it attacked the hated Buckingham. Charles dissolved parliament. Parliament had not voted him any income, but he continued to collect it. Five knights refused to pay their taxes to him. He imprisoned them. Parliament responded with a Petition of Right in 1628/9 which declared arbitrary imprisonment and the collection of taxes without parliamentary permission to be illegal. The quarrel led eventually to the dissolution of parliament and eleven years of personal government by the king.

During the period of personal rule the court became more and more isolated from ordinary life. Charles was a quiet aesthete who sought solace in ritual and proportion. Stately acts of worship, masques and banquets became the routine of court life - the mood of the period can be caught in the architecture and art - the Banqueting House in Whitehall, the Queen's House in Greenwich, the van Dyke portraits. Unfortunately, his sophisticated taste merely emphasised his distance from those around him.

Part of the problem was Charles's religion. His wife, the vivacious Henrietta Maria, to whom he was devoted, was a Catholic. He allowed her freedom to practise her own faith. It was widely perceived that the court favoured Catholicism. This is difficult to quantify. There were certainly notable Catholics in the Queen's household. Beyond the rarified world of the court Catholic influence increased in Caroline England - the number of English Catholic priests almost tripled between 1603-30 (250 - 700). To the very Protestant eyes of parliament, Charles seemed a Catholic. His delicate aesthetic sense, his appreciation of beauty and ceremonial sat ill with Calvinism and Prayer Book liturgy. But Charles was not a Roman Catholic. He was a child of the Church of England, and the Church of England was not what it used to be. The Calvinist orthodoxy of the Elizabethan church had been waning for a generation.

In the early years of the seventeenth century theological fashions began to change across Reformed Europe. Calvin's magisterial theological system was subject to probing re-evaluation amongst Reformed theologians. The revisionists concentrated their attention on the question of predestination. Chief among them was Jacob Arminius (1560-1609), star pupil of Calvin's successor at Geneva, Theodore Beza (1519-1605) , who was to become Professor of Theology at Leyden 1606-9. The nature of the dispute, although it seems complex when clothed in the technical language of Calvinist scholasticism, was in fact very simple. It boiled down to the question of who was responsible for salvation. Was salvation the work of God, or humanity, or God and humans together? The orthodox position was that it was the work of God, for the image of God in human beings had been all but obliterated by the Fall, and salvation was therefore entirely the work of God's saving grace. Calvin regarded predestination as a great mystery, and he devoted little space to it. Later followers of Calvin, including Arminius's teacher, Beza, elaborated the system. They argued that God's decree of election (ie. God's knowledge of who would eventually be saved by responding to Jesus) pre-dated the Fall. That is to say, God's plan for the world included the Fall. All people therefore deserved damnation. Those who responded to God's saving grace in Christ were known to God before the Fall, and could therefore be regarded as chosen by God before the world began. That position became known as supralapsarianism. It was this position that Arminius found impossible. He protested that he could find this doctrine neither in Scripture nor the creeds of the early church, nor in the confessional statements of the Reformed churches. It undermined the doctrine of creation because it suggested God created that which was not good. It abused the doctrine of humanity, for it suggested that human beings were not free, and it completely subverted the work of the church, because if salvation is pre-determined, what is the point of preaching and calling the world to repentance?

The matter came to a head after Arminius's death. Pupils of his turned his thought into a credal statement - the *Remonstrance* of 1610. It caused chaos in the Dutch church, and in 1618 the Synod of Dort, a synod of the Dutch Reformed Church, was called to evaluate Remonstrant teaching. The Remonstrants lost, with grievous consequences for the Dutch church, and for the immediate theological future of the Reformed churches.

The spin-off in England was a polarising of attitudes. English anti-Calvinists sought each other out for mutual support and encouragement, and that loose grouping was dubbed the 'Arminian' party - initially a term of abuse. How much any of the so-called English Arminians owed to Arminius is debatable, but just as Arminius presented a liberal version of Calvinism, so the English Arminians were theological liberals, but their liberalism was tied to a recovery of sacramental theology, given added spice by the Prayer Book. The 'group' emerged in the early years of the seventeenth century. It included Lancelot Andrewes (1553-1626), bishop of Ely 1609-19, then of Winchester, whose sermons and prayers in the finest and most beautiful English prose are one of the high points of English spirituality. However, the most significant and powerful man amongst them was William Laud (1574-1641), archbishop of Canterbury 1633-41. The king found their theological stance and liturgical practice much to his taste. By 1626, when Laud emerged as the government's chief religious spokesman, the English church had undergone a complete theological turn around. All Calvinist teaching was forbidden - the university presses succumbed in two years.

Laud attempted to create uniformity and order in worship. Services were to be conducted according to the Book of Common Prayer. The clergy were to wear surplices. Communion tables were to be raised and railed at the east end of the church. People were to kneel to receive the elements. To the Protestant House of Commons this looked like the introduction of Catholicism through the back door, and they weren't in favour. Laud was a complex, innately ambitious man whose ambition was married to a deep love of the Church of England. He was an energetic and efficient archbishop, but he had an unfortunate tendency to interfere - in the affairs of the province of York, in Scottish and Irish ecclesiastical business, even trying to curb the 'religious deviations' of English settlers in the Netherlands and America. Laud's vigorous enforcement of the rubrics of the Prayer Book, his recovery of the beauty of catholic holiness, had the significant effect of narrowing the band of what was acceptable within the Church of England. Poor old bishop Davenant of Salisbury was not the only leader of the previous generation who felt like a stranded theological dinosaur

*Why that should now be esteemed Puritan doctrine, which those held who have done our church the greatest service in beating down Puritanism, or why men should be restrained from teaching that doctrine hereafter, which hitherto has been generally and publicly maintained (wiser men perhaps may) but I cannot understand.*

The 1630s subsequently saw an increase in prosecutions for nonconformity. Just as in Mary's reign, a Protestant diaspora developed, this time centred on the Netherlands and New England rather than Geneva. Puritan ministers who found the Laudian church impossibly restrictive found ready employment amongst congregations of English merchants and soldiers in the Netherlands, and in the theological faculties of the Dutch churches. William Ames (1576-1633), a thinker influenced by Henry Jacob, and one of the most distinguished Calvinist theologians of his day spent the last decade of his life as Professor of Theology at the University of Franeker in Friesland, using his influence to find pastoral work for a number of Puritan ministers silenced by Laud.

The harder Laud tried to extinguish Puritanism, the more resilient it seemed. In the late 1630s Laud's campaign of harsh repression backfired. In 1637, at his instigation, three men were tried for sedition by Star Chamber - William Prynne (*c.*1602-1669), John Bastwick (1593-1654) and Henry Burton (1578-1648). Each was fined more money than they possessed and sentenced to exile. Before that sentence was carried out they were to stand in the pillory, have their ears cut off, and Prynne was to have his face branded 'SL' (Seditious Libeller). Prynne was a pedantic Calvinistically inclined lawyer who had written a learned and intemperate attack on the behaviour of Charles's court. Bastwick was a physician who had penned a delicious satire on the bench of bishops. He was a parishioner of Henry Burton's. Burton was the popular Puritan minister of St Matthew's, Friday Street, London. A Cambridge man, he had been dismissed from his position of Clerk to the Closet for warning Charles against Laud's 'popish' ways. He was a staunch champion of both Charles and the Church of England, and he sought to defend both against what he considered to be the subversive tendencies of Laud and his fellow bishops. Laud's persecution of the three men, and the subsequent outcry in their favour, turned Burton from a Puritan into a separatist, and he became a scourge of the established church. Writings poured from his prison cell in Castle Cornet on the Channel Island of Guernsey, all proclaiming the anti-Christian nature of the Church of England.

If Laudianism pushed men like Burton from Puritanism to separatism, it also lay behind the increase in Puritan militancy of the 1640s. It was unfortunate for the government that the years of Laud's supremacy co-incided with the eleven years of the king's personal rule, for the common mind identified absolutism (rule by the king alone) with Arminianism.

England was heading towards political crisis. Ironically it was Scotland that brought matters to a head. Whereas James understood Edinburgh from the inside, Charles barely knew where it was. Scotland had been slipping through Charles's fingers throughout his reign. In 1637 he tried to do what his father would never have done - force a modified version of the Prayer Book on the Kirk. What Charles actually wanted was order, both in worship and in the organisation of the church under the crown, not an anglicised version of the Scottish Kirk. Unfortunately the way he and Laud tried to achieve that end was high-handed and authoritarian, and the end result was rebellion.

In 1638 representatives of the Scottish people gathered in Greyfriars Kirk in Edinburgh to sign a protest - the National Covenant, the nobles signing it one day, the burgesses and ministers the next. It declared their resistance to any change in worship not previously approved by free assemblies and parliaments. They pledged to defend their religion against all threats, whilst carefully maintaining their loyalty to the Crown. Charles, never a skilled politician, played into their hands by declaring all the signatories to be rebels. He raised an army, but then changed his mind and called the General Assembly instead, and was then horrified when it abolished bishops. He responded by declaring the Assembly illegal and gathered an army. The Scots replied by raising their own army of the covenant.

For the leaders of Scottish presbyterianism this was a day of the Lord, a chance to purge the church and bring about a second reformation. It was evidence that Scotland was a nation elect of the Lord, the new Israel, the bride of Christ. They had been given the opportunity to liberate the oppressed Church of England. They marched, and occupied Newcastle.

Charles was now in desperate need of funds and fighting men, and the only way he could raise either of those was to call Parliament. He did. The Long Parliament met on November 3rd 1640. It was not to be dissolved until 1660. It was a momentous occasion in English history. The Triennial Act was passed which required Parliament to meet on a regular basis, and a further act prevented Parliament being dissolved against its will. It thus became a permanent part of the English constitution. The Long Parliament also impeached Laud.

The following year, 1641, Parliament passed the Grand Remonstrance, a comprehensive indictment of royal policy. Charles tried to arrest five opposition leaders, failed, left London, the conflict spread and the result was Civil War.

To rebel against a king threatened the whole order of the nation. It undermined the very nature of being and society. It was a terrifying step for Parliament to take in 1642. It did so because it believed that the country was on the brink of chaos, that the forces of Anti-Christ were about to be unleashed. However unfounded, sincere belief in the existence of a Papal plot and hatred of Laudian innovation which seemed to be attacking the very core of the nation's Protestant being, led to the conviction that the king was morally and politically incapable, that he must be stopped. Unless we appreciate the depth of parliament's Protestant passion, we shall misunderstand the civil wars.

In the following year, 1643, the Scots and the English parliamentarians entered into a Solemn League and Covenant, designed to impose presbyterianism on England *'according to the Word of God and the example of the best reformed churches.'*

The work of reforming the Church of England was given to an Assembly which met at Westminster Abbey in 1643 - hence the name, the Westminster Assembly - 121 divines, ten peers, twenty members of the Commons and some Scots commissioners. The first Civil War only lasted four years. Charles threw in the towel in 1645, and the attention of parliament now centred once more on religion. The dismantling of the church took place between 1641 and 1646. It was a piecemeal and unsatisfactory affair from all points of view. Laudian innovations were reversed, most particularly the railing of altars at the east end; the Commons assumed wide-ranging powers to suspend so-called 'scandalous ministers', and the Westminster Assembly slowly led the attack on episcopacy, church courts, the Prayer Book and the Anglican calendar. It sounds drastic, but in an odd way it was nibbling at the edges. At no time was there any thought of re-defining the Elizabethan acts of supremacy and uniformity. Similarly, the bill to abolish episcopacy was never turned into an ordinance, and although fourteen of the twenty-six bishops had their temporal possessions sequestered in 1643, twelve were left to enjoy their property and powers to the full and six of them became members of the Westminster Assembly. Similarly, up until the mid 1650s bishops alone had the right to ordain, and some of them did so with gusto. The attempted replacement of the Prayer Book with the Westminster Directory was a dismal failure. The new book, a guide to the construction of free liturgies, did not catch on. One estimate suggests that only 10% of parishes had obtained a copy six months after it was introduced, and there is no extant evidence of the penalties for using the old Prayer Book ever being used.

In 1645 the Westminster fathers presented a scheme for a presbyterian Church of England, albeit with a minority separatist dissenting report. It was accepted in 1646 with the crucial modification that parliament should be the supreme authority in religious matters rather than a General Assembly. As far as there was a national church during the Civil War and the Protectorate it was presbyterian, but once again the structures were never put in place to turn plan into reality. Only eight out of forty English counties introduced presbyterian structures and there was no proper national system of councils. Doctrine suffered a similar fate. The old doctrinal formularies were revoked in 1645, but they were never officially replaced. The Assembly fathers drew up a Confession of Faith, the Westminster Confession, stringently Calvinist, written largely by the vicar of Boston, Anthony Tuckney. It is one of the rich ironies of church history that it was never adopted in England, but became the defining doctrinal standard of the Church of Scotland. Various attempts were made to get rid of the calendar - to lose Christmas, Easter, Whit Sunday, Holy Days and Saints Days and replace them with a monthly day of thanksgiving every second Tuesday. They were generally ignored.

The whole re-organisation was fumbled. This was not the way to implement revolution. What was achieved by 1649 was toleration, and toleration meant that most parishes stayed with the comfort and security of the old patterns. What is fascinating is that when the crunch came, people turned out to be really rather fond of the national church and its funny ways.

The second Civil War lasted from 1646-9 and ended with regicide and the establishment of Oliver Cromwell as Lord Protector. If deposing a king was a terrifying work, executing one was the most serious and theological act a nation could take. Charles, as ever, was his own worst enemy. Militarily defeated in 1646, he refused to negotiate. For some, most particularly the New Model Army, their victory was a sign of God's favour, of his judgement writ large in political providence. Charles's decision to start a new war was an act not of treason, but sacrilege. God, for Cromwell, was presiding over the national destiny of England, working out his purposes in the texture of English politics, and bringing about *'such things among us as have not been known in the world these thousand years.'* Cromwell's is one of the most extraordinary stories in British history - in twelve years he rose from being a yeoman farmer in the backwaters of Huntingdon and St Ives to be the Lord Protector, and to refuse the crown, although in the judgement of a contemporary he was *'one that is worth more than all the others put together, and in effect a king.'*

It is hard to 'place' Cromwell religiously. The most formative influence on his faith was the religious radicalism of the New Model Army, meeting in small covenanted gatherings. Beyond that he cannot be categorised. He was deeply convinced he was the servant of God's providence, seeking God's will for the country, longing to be part of the godly commonwealth. In power from 1653-8, his innate conservatism and tolerance furthered the pluralism that had emerged in the 1640s.

The Commonwealth and Protectorate (1649-1660) was a decade unlike any other in English church history. It was as if the lid had suddenly been lifted from the ecclesiastical pot, and the stew of Puritan and radical ideas which had bubbling away since Elizabeth's day suddenly, dramatically, boiled over. For twenty years all controls were lifted. Censorship was abolished. Thought was free. Cromwell himself had considerable sympathy for liberty of conscience and religion. He looked for an all-inclusive national state church. The *Instrument of Government* insisted that although *'the Christian religion as contained in the Scriptures should be held forth and recommended as the public profession of these nations'*, yet *'none shall be compelled by penalties or otherwise'* provided they did no harm by the practice of their liberty. It was a wide provision, and held out a real prospect that all but hard-core Laudians could be reconciled to a state church. The figures speak for themselves - only two Catholic priests were executed under the Protectorate - compared with twenty-one under the Commonwealth. At the other end of the scale, Independents (who theoretically believed in the separation of church and state) felt able to remain within the state church. Some, like Ralph Josselin (1616-1683), the vicar of Earls Colne in Essex from 1641-1683, ministered both to their own gathered church *and* to their parish church and saw no friction between them.

The question contemporaries asked was whether this was a state church at all, or just anarchy. It was so comprehensive that there was no structure, no discipline. Where was the power of excommunication? That worried episcopalians, presbyterians and independents alike because they were all social conservatives, all worried by the radicalism of the sectarians.

The sectarians emerged in the 1640s when censorship was lifted. Quite where these fecund and fascinating ideas sprang from is one of the unsolved problems of history, as is where they disappeared to when the clamp of censorship was re-introduced in 1660. The 1640s were years when the world turned upside down, when the old order was laid waste and anything seemed possible, politically and religiously. The flood gates opened and radical groups and movements rose and fell with astonishing rapidity in the 1640s and 50s. In 1646 one commentator counted 199 heresies. Most were tiny. However, some major groups can be identified. The Levellers dominated the 1640s. They were on the left wing of the parliamentary party. They believed in political and religious freedom. They had no need for the clergy because they believed that God's message was for the simple, the poor and the uneducated. Faith flowed into politics - subscribing to the principles 'Do unto others as you would have them do unto you' meant resisting oppression and poverty, looking for the re-distribution of wealth, living a communal life, and loving foreigners. The 'true Levellers' set up a commune near Kingston-on-Thames which collapsed as quickly as it rose.

They were replaced by the fifth monarchists in the 1650s. The interpretation of Daniel and Revelation was a serious business in the mid seventeenth century. Isaac Newton (1642-1717) was as much interested in that as the laws of gravity. By the 1640s there was a scholarly consensus, based on mathematical principles, that the four monarchies of Babylon, Persia, Greece and Rome had ended and that the fifth monarchy of Christ was imminent. The fall of anti-Christ, the conversion of the Jews, maybe even the Second Coming, were scheduled for the 1650s. By 1653 it seemed that God had suffered a time-tabling lapse, and the fifth monarchists decided to force the pace and help the birth of the kingdom by a few well chosen acts of violence.

They in turn were eclipsed by the Quakers. They were not the quiet campaigners for peace that we know so well. Their founder George Fox (1624-91) did not find the spiritual sustenance he sought in the parish churches of England, or amongst the Separatists, so he abandoned both and went on his own spiritual quest. Peace came to him, he said, only by a personal revelation of Jesus Christ - *'Christ it was who had enlightened me, that gave his light to believe in, and gave me his hope, which is himself, revealed himself in me, and gave me his Spirit and gave me his grace, which I found sufficient in the deeps and in weakness.'* For Fox this was the dawning of a new age, and he stumped the country proclaiming that the true light was to be found within everyone. Following the light was the path to perfection. He claimed that the Spirit was superior to the witness of Scripture, saw visions, foretold the future and claimed healing powers. His followers swept the land in a magnificent outburst of missionary zeal - by 1660 there were between 50-60,000 Quakers in the land. Ecstatic, charismatic, wild - they were widely considered a dangerous threat, and of all nonconformist groups they were to be the most viciously persecuted in the 1660s.

The dramatic experience of political and religious freedom died with Cromwell. His son Richard was not in his father's mould. Parliament, essentially 'presbyterian-royalist' in composition, met on 25 April 1660 and recalled the king. Christ's kingdom had not come; Charles II's had.

Chapter 3

# From the Restoration to the Act of Toleration, 1660-1689

*Charles, by the grace of God, King of England, Scotland, France and Ireland, defender of the faith...To all our loving subjects of what degree or quality soever, greeting. If the general distraction and confusion which is spread over the whole kingdom doth not awaken all men to a desire and longing that those wounds which have so many years together been kept bleeding may be bound up, all we can say will be to no purpose....nor do we desire more to enjoy what is ours than that all our subjects may enjoy what by law is theirs, by a full and entire administration of justice throughout the land, and by extending our mercy where it is wanted and deserved.....And because the passion and uncharitableness of the times have produced several opinions in religion, by which men are engaged in parties and animosities against each other; which, when they shall hereafter unite in a freedom of conversation, will be composed, or better understood; we do declare a liberty to tender consciences; and that no man shall be disquieted, or called in question, for differences of opinion in matters of religion which do not disturb the peace of the kingdom; and we shall be ready to consent to such an act of parliament, as, upon mature deliberation, shall be offered to us, for the full granting of that indulgence.*

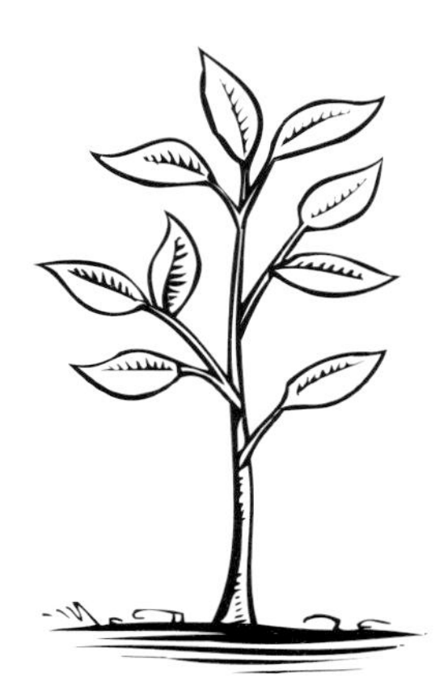

That is part of the offer Charles II (1630-1685) made to the English parliament and people on 4 April 1660 from the small Dutch town of Breda. It was an offer of reconciliation, of healing. It held up the possibility of order in place of chaos, and the hope of religious liberty if such rights did not harm the peace of the kingdom. Those who recalled the religious history of the preceding century might have been excused if they had considered that a pious hope. Pious or not, it was sincere. A mood of rejoicing swept the country. Church bells rang to welcome the king home. In Cambridge soldiers fired volleys of shots from the roof of King's

College chapel, and in Ripon girls dressed in white were crowned with garlands 'in honour of their Virgin-King', which was a nice irony because Charles distributed his sexual favours generously. Many things he might have been, virgin he most emphatically was not. There were official days of thanksgiving throughout May and June. An analysis of over twenty surviving sermons preached on those days reveals a telling reticence - there is little mention of such matters as the restoration of the episcopate or the re-introduction of the Prayer Book. In the Chapel Royal Gilbert Sheldon (1598-1677), the newly appointed dean, Oxford don, convinced Royalist and later archbishop of Canterbury was positively eirenic, speaking of the need to put passions away and not *'be at enmity among ourselves for trifles.'* Across the country preachers echoed the tone of the king's declaration. Pamphlets began to appear suggesting ways forward. Archbishop Ussher's *Reduction of Episcopacie unto the Form of Synodical Government Received in the Antient Church* of the early 1640s was reprinted in June 1660, and its suggestion of episcopacy exercised with the assistance of senior parochial clergy proved a meeting point for presbyterians and moderate episcopalians.

However, reconciliation was not to prove an easy option. There were difficult obstacles to be overcome. During the Commonwealth and Protectorate a considerable number of Royalist clergy had had their livings sequestered in favour of men mainly of presbyterian and independent views. Should they be restored, or should the present incumbents be allowed to continue? Should those who had not been episcopally ordained be re-ordained? What liturgy should the restored church have? Should it be the *Directory of Public Worship*, which had been the legally prescribed form since 1645, or should the Prayer Book be re-introduced? The king's business managers put pressure on both camps in the late summer and autumn of 1660. The presbyterians gave way on sequestered livings, and the question of liturgical reform was deferred.

Presbyterians and Independents/Congregationalists reacted differently to the restoration. The return of the king meant the return of an established church, doubtless with a form of episcopacy, although its precise shape was yet to be determined. The Presbyterians had dreamt of an inclusive, more fully reformed, national church for a century. They hoped and prayed that their dream would now be realised. Few Congregationalists entertained such dreams. Indeed, their ecclesiology raised significant theoretical questions about such a future. It is therefore scarcely surprising that most obeyed their consciences and quietly had withdrawn from the structures of the new national church in the months immediately following the restoration. 194 Congregationalists can be identified amongst the ejected of 1660-62.

108 of them (55%) left in 1660. They were therefore observers of, rather than participants in the struggles and debates of the following two years, devoting their considerable energies and abilities to the creation of a Congregationalist witness beyond the confines of the national church.

## John Owen (1616-1683)

Amongst their number were distinguished theologians and church leaders, the greatest of whom was John Owen. The son of the incumbent of Stadham, he was educated at Queen's College, Oxford. A convinced presbyterian, his acute theological mind soon manifested itself, and in 1643 he published a thorough Calvinist critique of Arminianism. In the same year Parliament offered him the living of Fordham near Colchester. He replaced the sequestered rector, John Alsop, who had been chaplain to archbishop Laud. He remained there for 3 years before moving to become 'the minister of the gospel' at Coggeshall, which had long been a centre of Puritanism. During the late 1640s his views were changing, and he slowly became a convinced Congregationalist. He put his ideas into practice by ministering both to the parish church and a 'gathered congregation'. As the tumultuous and terrible events of the late 1640s unfolded Owen's Independent views drew him into the purview of the Parliamentary army. General Fairfax and Henry Ireton laid siege to Colchester in 1647 and Owen was invited to minister to the encamped soldiers. He rapidly became a popular preacher, both locally and before parliament. It was Owen who preached before the Commons on the fast day following Charles I's execution, interpreting it as God's righteous judgement on the House of Stuart for its support of false religion and tyranny. Later in 1649 Cromwell invited him (perhaps ordered him would be more precise) to become his chaplain on his Irish expedition, and whilst there to conduct a survey of the future of Trinity College, Dublin. He was one of two chaplains to Cromwell's Scottish campaign of 1650, and it was Cromwell's support which led to his installation as Dean of Christ Church, Oxford in 1651 and as Vice-Chancellor the following year. During the 1650s he was at the centre of power, both within the university world and in the political life of the country, travelling up and down to London to preach before Parliament and sit on national committees, creating a network of relationships amongst Independent churches, and advising his friend the Lord Protector on policy. Owen briefly re-established Oxford as a centre of Puritan theology, and made a mark as a reforming Vice-Chancellor in a university which has ever resisted too much reform. Quiet, dignified, witty, an inherently conservative academic yet a radical ecclesiastic, Owen played a central role in Independency during the Protectorate, and it was his power and ability which did much to weld Congregationalism into a coherent entity after the Restoration. Offers of professorships in Holland and pastorates in New England were gently rejected in favour of the vocation of remaining in England and guiding the churches through the storms of political change. Unlike many of his fellows he was a man of substance and wealth both in his own right, and through his second marriage to a wealthy young widow. He was able to retire from public life, to write, to think, to become the finest English Protestant theologian of the seventeenth century and to plead the cause of toleration in the highest of circles where he was still trusted and admired.

## The Restoration settlement

Whilst the Congregationalists were withdrawing from the national church in the late summer and autumn of 1660, the Presbyterians were working for the re-establishment of an inclusive national church. The fruits of attempted compromise were reaped in October 1660 in the Worcester House declaration in which Charles re-iterated the promises of Breda, appointed a clerical commission to review the Prayer Book and asked a national synod to consider the nature of ceremonial. At the heart of the declaration was an Ussher-like modified episcopate in which bishops were to act in collegiality with senior diocesan and cathedral clergy. Although some have questioned the sincerity of Charles and his chief minister Edward Hyde, the first Earl of Clarendon (1609-1674), they do seem to have been genuine seekers after reconciliation. Certainly during this period they tried to fill senior appointments with men of all opinions. However, within a very few months, it was clear that compromise was a dead letter.

The threats to compromise came from three quarters. First, the Royalist gentry were gaining ground in vociferous support for the old order. Second, the Army, which had not yet been disbanded, was staunchly presbyterian and independent. Their support for the restoration had more to do with Charles's promise to pay their arrears than with an ideological approval of monarchy. The radicals were still a danger. In January 1661 Thomas Venner and his fifth monarchists launched a lunatic campaign to replace King Charles with King Jesus with the slogan 'King Jesus and the heads upon the gates'. In retrospect the thirty-five rebels who intended to capture London, then England and then the world, are a laughing stock. However, to a country haunted by the horror of regicide, their occupation of St Paul's cathedral was all too real a threat and swingeing repression fell on sectaries across the country. Within six weeks 4,688 Quakers were imprisoned, and hundreds of gathered churches were suppressed. The Congregationalists were so alarmed that they quickly dissociated themselves from Venner in a public pamphlet *'against the late Horrid Insurrection and Rebellion'*. Thirdly, and most significantly, a body of presbyterians in England, Scotland and Ireland believed that the king should be held to the terms of the Solemn League and Covenant which he had signed in 1650 in a desperate bid to gain Scottish support. Granted, the English presbyterians were less enthusiastic than their Celtic cousins, but it was clear that any settlement would have repercussions in three kingdoms. Charles also knew well that the attempt to impose a uniform settlement across the kingdoms in the 1630s had led to his father's downfall.

The commission to revise the prayer book met at the Savoy in the early months of 1661 against the background of Venner's uprising and the suppression of gathered churches. It was not an auspicious gathering. It was seen as an opportunity to include Presbyterians within the new established church, but as such it was a dismal failure. Theological differences about the nature of priesthood, the role of the liturgy and ceremonial practice which had been masked by a veneer of goodwill in the heady, optimistic days of the previous April were now laid bare. The coronation took place on St George's day. Historic precedent had been carefully studied, and as archbishop Juxon (1582-1663) placed the crown on the king's head, the powerful symbolic assertion of the union of church and state was plain. Politically Charles tried to be even-handed, distributing coronation honours equally between former royalists and parliamentarians. It was a touching gesture, but by now the writing was on the wall. Charles II's England was a different kingdom from his father's. Times had changed. If the fate of his father had proved anything to the thirty-year old king, it was that parliament could be neither avoided nor voided. Much as he longed to maintain the upper hand in ecclesiastical matters, much as he might dream of a unified country, it was parliament that was to decide the shape of the country's religious future.

The so-called Cavalier Parliament met for the first time in May 1661, less than three weeks after the coronation, and a Convocation of the clergy gathered simultaneously in St Paul's. Nearly half the members of parliament were true cavaliers - either those fined for their royalist convictions during the previous régime or sons of such men. It marked the re-assertion of the power of the country gentry. The moderate men were on the wane - only between forty and sixty were pro-presbyterian. Within ten days bishops were restored to the House of Lords and the house had voted that the Solemn League and Covenant should be burnt by the public hangman. All members were to receive the sacrament according to the rites of the Book of

Common Prayer. As the Savoy Conference was deadlocked, it was the Convocation and the bishops who decided what shape that book would have. Reconciliation was a thing of the past.

The Cavalier Parliament had two aims - the obliteration of the constitutional reforms of the Commonwealth and Protectorate, and the creation of a religious settlement. Charles continued to promote toleration throughout 1661, particularly for Catholics and Quakers. In general terms though he found himself outmanoeuvred by a parliament which held his purse strings. In July a bill of uniformity was passed, heralding a return to the laws which had prevailed before the Civil Wars. Throughout the winter and spring the King and the Earl of Clarendon tried to keep the door open for presbyterians, proposing a new clause which would enable the king to relieve certain clergy from the observation of specific clauses, but the Commons refused point blank to grant him such latitude. In the October Charles effectively abandoned the policy of comprehension by allowing Convocation to take up the task of revising the Prayer Book from the deadlocked Savoy commissioners. In December the Corporation Act was passed, the first piece of legislation aimed at outlawing nonconformity. It required all mayors, aldermen, councillors and borough officials to swear loyalty to the king and take the sacrament according to the rites of the Church of England. It effectively barred conscientious nonconformists from taking office and allowed unscrupulous corporations to make money by electing nonconformists and then fining them when they refused to serve. Although alleviated in the eighteenth century it was not revoked until 1828.

On 19 May 1662, parliament passed the Act of Uniformity. It demanded that all clergy should accept the Prayer Book, denounce the Covenant and submit to royal authority. Convocation simultaneously instructed congregations to observe greater ceremonial, standing for hymns, kneeling for prayers, bowing at the name of Christ and removing hats in church. All who refused to accept were to be ejected from their livings on 24 August, the feast day of St Bartholomew. The date in itself was a turning of the knife in the wound. The Commons had suggested St Michael's Day, 29 September. The Lords introduced the modification, thus ensuring that those who would not or could not conform would be deprived of the great tithes which would be a substantial part of their year's stipend. The legislation extended to extra-parochial lecturers as well as incumbents, and schoolmasters had to make the same declaration and receive a licence from a bishop to maintain a school. It was intended to eliminate nonconformity from church, university and education generally. Still Charles and Clarendon sought modification. Within a fortnight the king let it be known that he would extend protection to nonconformists. He called a conference of his advisors at Hampton Court. Sheldon, on behalf of the bishops, refused to co-operate. Some historians identify this as a turning point in the history of the Church of England, and in Sheldon's own career. He identified the Church of England with the wishes of the ruling classes, the provincial gentry, against both the monarch and wider populace.

About a tenth of the English clergy (961 to be precise) refused to conform. That was more dramatic than it sounds because there was considerable regional variation. A third of the London clergy were ejected, a quarter of those in Sussex, a fifth of those in Devon, Leicestershire and Essex. If that is added to the expulsions of 1660-1 and the 129 who were ejected at some point in the Restoration before St Bartholomew's Day, a picture emerges of widespread disruption. 2,029 clergy, lecturers and fellows gave up their jobs, many with the utmost reluctance. 194 have been identified as Independents. 19 were Baptists. The remaining 1,816 were either presbyterians, or 'mere' Puritans who had shunned all labels but in all conscience could not accept a church designed to exclude. The restoration brought turmoil to parochial life. Two well researched examples suggest that three quarters of the parishes in Cheshire and Leicestershire changed hands in the three years following Charles's return.

The ejected included some of the sharpest, ablest minds in the church. They went in deep sadness, yet sure of the leading of God. One, Dr William Bates (1625-1699), preaching on his last Sunday in St Dunstan's London, said,

*It is neither fancy, faction nor humour that makes me not conform, but merely for offending God: and if after the best means used for my illumination, as prayer to God, discourse and study, I am not able to be satisfied concerning the lawfulness of what is required; if it be my unhappiness to be in error, surely men will have no reason to be angry with me in this world, and I hope God will pardon me in the next.*

The moderate Congregationalist Joseph Caryl (1602-1673), rector of St Magnus, London took as the theme of his farewell sermon 'Walking in white with Christ'. Why, he asked, do

*...the servants of Christ stand so strictly upon their terms with the Word, even while some call it peevishness, others ignorance, others wilful stubbornness. What is the reason? The reason is, because they understand in some measure, and have had experience in some measure, what it is to walk in some measure with Christ in white, and it hath left such a relish upon their souls that they would not lose it for all the dainty morsels of this world; they had rather walk with Christ in white, than walk with the world in scarlet..*

And so they went, some to uphold principles of independency and separatism deeply rooted in the doctrines of the reformation, others because they believed the ordering of the Restoration church was an affront to God and a denial of Scripture, yet others, like the great Puritan man of letters Richard Baxter, because they wished to keep doors open rather than closed.

## Richard Baxter (1615-1691)

Baxter was a remarkable man whose life spanned the discontinuities and divisions of the seventeenth century. He was a boy of ten when Charles I came to the throne, and he died two years after the passing of the Act of Toleration in 1691. In between he became a renowned, revered minister, a leader of moderate Puritan or 'presbyterian' opinion. He was appointed Lecturer at Kidderminster in 1641. Like Owen, he sided with the parliamentarians during the war and became an army chaplain. Unlike Owen, he was scandalised by the radicalism he discovered in the army, and when ill-health overtook him in 1646 he retired to Rous-Lench in Worcestershire, the home of Sir Thomas and Lady Lench where he wrote his devotional classic *The Saints Everlasting Rest*. When he was well enough he returned to his pastorate in Kidderminster and ministered there until Charles II returned to the throne. His was regarded as the very model of a Reformed pastorate, and he crafted one of the greatest books of pastoral theology, *The Reformed Pastor*, out of his experience. He was one of the most prolific writers in one of the greatest ages of English literature - it has been calculated that he wrote more words in English than any other seventeenth century writer! Baxter was singular - a prophet of ecumenism in bitterly divided times. Throughout his life he sought for reconciliation amongst Protestants - *'greater light and stronger judgement'*, he wrote, *'usually is with the reconcilers than with either of the contending parties'*. In 1653, during his ministry at Kidderminster he sought to bring together clergy of differing views - three Independents, one veering towards a Baptist understanding, *'three or four moderate conformists that were of the old Episcopacy; and all the rest were mere Catholicks; Men of no Faction, nor siding with any Party, but owning that which was good in all...'* into the Worcestershire Association; in his maturity it was his opinion that divisions between *'the Greek church and the Roman, the Papists and the Protestants, the Lutherans and the Calvinists, have woefully hindered the kingdom of Christ'*, and almost uniquely in the seventeenth century, he expressed a theoretical willingness to worship together with them.

During the 1650s and 60s Baxter was one of the leaders of moderate opinion, and it was therefore natural to find him amongst those invited to take up episcopates in 1660. He was offered the bishopric of Hereford, but he refused because *'..it will very much disable me from an effectual promoting of the Churches Peace.'* At the end of his account of the Savoy Conference he wryly noted that he *'should as willingly be a Martyr for Charity as for Faith.'* Baxter the 'mere Catholick' became a 'mere nonconformist' because he felt he could not minister in a church designed to exclude. For the rest of his long life he was legally barred from the preaching and pastoral work which he loved. Instead, he wrote - hymns, devotional books, and works of theology - played cat and mouse with the authorities as he kept up a limited preaching ministry and continued to strive for reconciliation between the Church of England and nonconformists.

## The 'heroic' age (1662-1689)

Nonconformity was a broad movement from its birth. After 24 August 1662 the Church of England was no longer the Church of England but a church in England. Comprehension had died. Pluralism had been born. The king and his ministers tried to find ways of alleviating the Act, but to no avail. In 1663 there was a pitifully abortive rising in Yorkshire - some former Army officers, a few sectaries, some artisans, small holders and tenant farmers who were convinced they were part of a national network. There was no bloodshed, and the government acted with predictable severity. There were twenty-four executions. The results of the rebellion were tragic, for it frightened parliament into trying to crush all centres of possible dissent, including all nonconformists. It is ironic that the repressive legislation of 1664-5 is known as the Clarendon Code, for Clarendon and Charles strove tirelessly to mitigate the effects of the Act of Uniformity. The principal architect of the repression was Gilbert Sheldon, now archbishop of Canterbury and an implacable opponent of nonconformity.

Times were grim. In 1664 England entered a disastrous war against the Dutch. Plague swept through the country in 1664/5, and everywhere there were rumours of rebellion. That explains but does not excuse the legislation.

The Conventicle Act of 1664 forbade religious gatherings of more than five people *'in other ways than is allowed by the liturgy.'* It was aimed at the laity. Heavy fines and imprisonment were enforced for the first two offences, transportation for a third. It was nicknamed 'the Banishment Act'.

In the first year of its operation 230 nonconformists were transported. When it became clear that nonconformity had not been eliminated, the government turned its attention to the relationship between ministers and churches. The Act for Restraining Nonconformists from Inhabiting in Corporations of 1665, otherwise known as the Five Mile Act, was aimed at ministers. It forbade all ministers who had not accepted the Act of Uniformity from going within five miles of any corporate town or place where they had previously ministered, except as travellers. It also prohibited them from teaching in schools unless they took an oath that it was unlawful to take up arms against the king. Failure to comply resulted in a £40 fine, of which a third was to go to the informer.

London was devastated by plague in 1665. That delayed the onset of this act. Many nonconformist ministers remained in the city at a time when some Anglicans fled their posts, and this made a great impact on the popular mind. Some nonconformists interpreted the Great Fire of London which followed in 1666 as the judgement of God.

A lot of romantic nonsense surrounds persecution. The blood of the martyrs may sometimes be seed of the church, but persecution can also obliterate the faith. The suffering and courage of the earliest nonconformists should neither be exaggerated nor underestimated. The persecution was a piecemeal affair, varying in severity both geographically and temporally. A few, ministers and people, were of independent means. Most were not. Some of the ejected ministers were desperately poor, with little means of replacing home and income. Some of the laity had their goods and working tools distrained to such an extent that they were unable to support themselves. In some places the penal code was enforced with grievous severity and not a little malice - one Congregationalist in Nottinghamshire had his goods distrained so violently that he lost £500 worth of goods and cattle and one of his children died of fright; Quakers were harried and force marched to prison for over twenty miles in Wales in 1662; the ejected curate of Halwell in Devon was fined £30 for *'praying with three gentlewomen who came to visit his wife, and comfort her on the death of her son and only child who was drowned at sea'*. Many died in the filthy stench of Restoration prisons where fever, plague and smallpox ruled. Francis Holcroft, the founder of the congregation which eventually became Emmanuel Congregational Church in Cambridge, was imprisoned for nine years, John Bunyan (1628-88) for eleven years in Bedford, although both were allowed out periodically to preach.

However, the policy did not work, and nonconformity showed no more signs of dying out than Puritanism had done under Elizabeth or in Jacobean England.

## The exclusion crisis and the Glorious Revolution

In 1672 Charles astonished and outraged parliament by issuing a Declaration of Indulgence which reversed all penal legislation against nonconformists and Catholics. It was revoked by parliament the following year, but it gave a much needed fillip to nonconformity. The times were changing. The heat was lessening on one wing of English dissent. It did so only to increase on the other, for 1673 saw a violent outburst of anti-Catholicism, and it is Catholicism which was to dominate the ecclesiastical history of England for the next decade. Charles's brother James (1633-1701), the Duke of York, was veering from Anglicanism towards Catholicism - he was eventually received into the Roman Catholic church in 1676.

In 1673 parliament passed the Test Act which stated that all civil or military office holders should accept the royal supremacy, receive communion according to Anglican rites and forswear the Catholic doctrine of the mass. The Duke of York resigned as Lord High Admiral rather than take the test. Under pressure from parliament, Charles enforced penal laws against Catholics in 1674 and 1675. Rumours of popish plots swept the land, the most famous of which is connected with the name of Titus Oates (1649-1705), a notorious fraud who fabricated a dossier about a Jesuit plot to kill the king.

It had dreadful consequences, for it unleashed a virulent anti-Catholic hysteria which led to state trials and roughly thirty-five executions. The violence of the reaction was out of all proportion to the threat. Catholics accounted for roughly 2% of the population, but the English nation had been fed on fear of the Pope since the days of John Foxe. The fires of Smithfield had seared into the national consciousness, and the ingenuity of the Jesuits knew no bounds in the minds of the credulous. Some even blamed them for the Great Fire of London in 1666, and in the minds of Protestant Parliament there seemed less distance than was proper between the king and the nobility and Catholicism. After all, Charles I had been married to a Catholic, and the Laudianism which precipitated the Civil War seemed like Catholicism by the back door to the undiscerning. Charles II too had continually striven to secure toleration for Catholics, and the Duke of York's position was becoming only too plain, particularly with his refusal to sign the test.

The anti-Catholicism which Oates so skilfully fanned into flame was to give rise to the Exclusion Crisis of the 1679-81. The Duke of York finally converted to Catholicism in 1676. For him and his wife it had been a long and often painful spiritual journey. He was a complex man, as sexually promiscuous as his brother, as convinced of the divine right of kings as his father, and genuinely religious. He claimed to have been convinced of the claims of Catholicism through his reading of the great Anglican apologist Richard Hooker, and to the end of his life couldn't understand why he was so hated and feared by the English. He saw in the Roman church the authority which was natural to a soldier-prince, and a power of forgiveness which could cope with his powerful sexuality.

In the wake of Oates's Popish plots James's position as heir became increasingly untenable. In 1678 Parliament passed the second Test Act which excluded all Catholics bar James from the Houses of Parliament. At first he weathered the storm. Memories of regicide were still tender, and the mood of the country changed. A Catholic king might be better than no king. The church rallied behind the principle of the divine right of the hereditary monarch and James II was crowned in 1685. He made it clear that he had no wish to turn the country Catholic, although he wished for the toleration of his co-religionists and the Protestant dissenters and to this end he moved the repeal of the Corporation Act of 1661 and the Test Acts of 1673 and 1678. He introduced his own Declaration of Indulgence, offering Protestant dissenters the freedom they longed for if they would only side with him rather than the Church of England. He tried to establish Roman Catholics as the Dean of Christ Church and the President of Magdalene College Oxford. He was pushing too hard, and naïvely underestimated the depth of the country's fear of Rome. In his naïvety he thought the Church of England would do what the king commanded. If his brother could have spoken from the grave he would have pointed to Gilbert Sheldon's stance against toleration in the early 1660s as evidence that the church had its own mind.

When seven bishops, including that most moderate royalist archbishop Sancroft (1617-1693), begged him on bended knee to withdraw his Declaration of Indulgence, he threw them into the Tower, and then subjected them to trial by jury. They were acquitted. Parliament responded by trying to get James's son-in-law, William of Orange (1650-1702), to mediate between king and people. William, who was neither naïve nor daft, played his hand carefully. He studiously avoided sullying his hands with the Duke of Monmouth's pathetically sad rebellion in 1687, and indeed gave naval aid to James.

What altered the situation irrevocably was the birth of a son to James and Mary of Modena in 1688. Now it was clear that Catholicism would not be an interlude in the life of the nation, but its future. William of Orange foresaw that future - at least in a possible short-term alliance with France against him, and he set sail. For whatever reason James's nerve went, and he fled for France. There at least he was happy. As his sexual energies waned, his devotional enthusiasm waxed. His wife Mary, no longer tolerating a succession of Anglican mistresses, took the upper hand in the marriage. He died in 1701. *'Consider Madam'*, he said to his tearful wife, *'I am going to be happy forever.'* In England Parliament offered the vacant throne to his daughter Mary and her Dutch Protestant husband, William. The bloodless Glorious Revolution was complete.

Two consequences need to be noted. First, of the seven bishops who had pleaded with James to renounce his Declaration of Indulgence, five remained loyal to him, including Sancroft, the archbishop of Canterbury, and Thomas Ken (1637-1711) of Bath and Wells, of 'Glory to Thee my God this night' fame. In a cynical age their loyalty and that of their four hundred 'non-juror' colleagues who refused to sign the Abjuration Act of 1702 lent credit and honour to their church. Like Baxter and Calamy in the previous generation, they too had learnt that not every act of Parliament deserves the accord of ministers of Christ.

## The Toleration Act

The second consequence was the Act of Toleration of 1689. It was a reward for those Dissenters who had refused to side with the king against the Church of England in 1687. Dissenters they may have been, but they made common cause with Protestants. In the closing decades of the seventeenth century no English Protestant could have dreamt of a day when dissenters would be observers at a council of the Catholic church, nor of a day when a pope and an archbishop would kneel together in prayer. It is a touching irony that a Catholic monarch's concern for his co-religionists led to the liberation of Protestant dissenters.

The Toleration Act was only part of the bargain struck between nonconformists and the new régime. As William of Orange set out for England he issued a Declaration which promised *'to endeavour a good Agreement between the Church of England, and all Protestant Dissenters'*. A nonconformist deputation met the King on 2 January 1689 to express their gratitude at his accession. He made it clear in his reply that he was committed to the union of Protestants, in other words to the creation of a more comprehensive national church. Presbyterian dreams of an inclusive national church were re-kindled. The Congregationalists advocated a broader toleration. They were naturally wary of a scheme which seemed to weaken the necessity of toleration by drastically reducing the size of the dissenting community.

The Comprehension Bill was introduced in line with the king's wishes. It was severely amended in the Lords, and provoked acrimonious debate in the Commons. The opposing parties, the Whigs and the Tories, came to an agreement that if the Comprehension Bill was dropped, the Toleration Act would be passed. That was what happened. The Toleration Act received royal assent on 24 May 1689. Freedom of organisation was to be granted to orthodox dissenters provided they were able to accept all but articles 34-36 of the Thirty-Nine Articles, the doctrinal standard of the Church of England. The exempted articles dealt with tradition, preaching and the ministry of bishops. Baptists were also exempted from Article 27 on baptism.

Long before in the reign of Elizabeth, the separatist theorist Robert Browne had argued for the right of congregations to choose their pastors and moved from that to suggest that citizens had the right to elect their rulers. Now, in 1689 that theory was given classic expression by John Locke (1632-1704), a philosopher who had listened to the greatest of all Congregationalist theologians John Owen when he was teaching at Oxford. He transposed the classic congregationalist idea of the church as a covenantal community into the theory that society was a covenant between men and women to protect life and liberty and property. Owen died in 1683, Bunyan in 1688, George Fox and Richard Baxter in 1691. The world belonged to their heirs. Locke wrote to the Dutch Remonstrant theologian Phillipus von Limbach:

*No doubt you will have heard before this that Toleration has now at last been established by law in our country. Not perhaps so wide in scope as might be wished for by you and those like you who are true Christians and free from ambition or envy. Still it is something to have progressed so far. I hope that with these beginnings the foundations have been laid of that liberty and peace in which the church of Christ is one day to be established.*

It was indeed something. But for more than a century social apartheid prevailed in English life for the Toleration Act allowed dissenters to worship and organise their own lives at the price of their political and civil rights. And that other stream of English dissent, the English Roman Catholic community enjoyed not even the limited freedom of their dissenting brothers and sisters. It could not remain that way. It was not to remain that way, for the truth the Toleration Act thinly veiled was that England was now, officially and legally, a pluralist country.

It was scarcely a generous piece of legislation. All dissenters had to swear oaths of allegiance and abjure the Catholic doctrine of transubstantiation. Each dissenting place of worship had to be registered with the diocesan bishop. All parliamentary attempts to rescind the provisions of the Corporation Act or to include all Protestant sacraments within its bounds failed. It was gloomily prophetic, for it destined nonconformists either to exclusion from public office or to a life of compromise through occasional conformity. In such an atmosphere it was unsurprising that the Comprehension Bill died. Such exclusion was to be fate of nonconformists throughout the long eighteenth century.

# The Long Eighteenth Century - a time chart

| Date | Politics | Church affairs |
| --- | --- | --- |
| 1689 | Act of Toleration | |
| 1690 | | Richard Davis called to Rothwell<br>Republication of Tobias Crisp's *Works* |
| 1691 | | 'Happy Union' |
| 1695 | | Congregation Fund f. |
| 1701 | William d.<br>Anne to thrones | Isaac Watts called to Mark Lane<br>Philip Doddridge b. |
| 1702 | War of Spanish Succession (to 1713) | |
| 1707 | Union with Scotland | Watts *Hymns and Spiritual Songs* |
| 1711 | Occasional Conformity Act | |
| 1713 | Treaty of Utrecht | |
| 1714 | Schism Act<br>Queen Anne d.<br>George I to throne | |
| 1715 | First Jacobite uprising | |
| 1717 | | Convocation prorogued |
| 1718 | | Subscription crisis (Salters' Hall) |
| 1720 | South Sea Bubble | |
| 1723 | | Regium Donum |
| 1727 | George I d.<br>George II to throne | |
| 1729 | | 'Holy Club' f. at Oxford |
| 1730 | | Strickland Gough *An enquiry into the decline..* |
| 1735 | | Conversion of Howell Harris |
| 1736 | | Whitefield begins field preaching |
| 1738 | | Whitefield to Georgia<br>Wesley's 'conversion' |
| 1739 | | Wesley preaches in open air for first time |
| 1740 | | 'Great Awakening' in USA |
| 1744 | | Methodist Conference meets for first time |
| 1745 | Second Jacobite Uprising | Doddridge *On the rise and progress of religion in the soul* |
| 1746 | Battle of Culloden | |
| 1751 | | Doddridge d. |
| 1753 | Lord Hardwicke's Marriage Act | |
| 1754 | | Lord Mansfield's judgement in Mansion House case |

| Date | Politics | Church affairs |
|---|---|---|
| 1756 | Seven Years' War (to 1763) | |
| 1760 | George II d.<br>George III to throne | |
| 1770 | | Whitefield d. |
| 1776 | American Declaration of Independence (war to 1783) | |
| 1778 | | Lady Huntingdon's chapels declared illegal<br>Charles Wesley d. |
| 1791 | | John Wesley d. |
| 1792 | | Baptist Missionary Society f. |
| 1795 | | London Missionary Society f.<br>George Roby called to Cannon Street, Manchester |
| 1797 | | Methodist New Connexion f. |
| 1806 | | Independent Methodists f. |
| 1811 | George, Prince Regent | Primitive Methodists f. |
| 1820 | George III d.<br>George IV to throne | |
| 1828 | Repeal of Test and Corporation Acts | |
| 1829 | Catholic Emancipation Act | |
| 1830 | George IV d.<br>Victoria to throne | |
| 1832 | Great Reform Act | |
| 1833 | | Congregational Union f. |

Chapter 4

# The long eighteenth century, 1689-1832

Historians sometimes talk about 'the "long" eighteenth century'. They mean the period which started with the Glorious Revolution of 1688 and ended with the great legislative changes of 1828-32 - the repeal of the Test and Corporation Acts and the Reform Act - which brought Roman Catholics and Protestant nonconformists into the mainstream of political life, and greatly extended the franchise. It was marked by the legislative union of the Church of England and the State defined by the Toleration Act which recognised a Christian pluralism by allowing dissenters to compete with the Anglican establishment for the souls of the English, but within a carefully constructed system of social and political apartheid which ensured that the only 'true' citizens were Anglicans. It ended with the so-called 'constitutional revolution' of 1828-32 which broke up the 'ancien régime' by extending equal political rights to Catholics and Dissenters. The Test Act had, of course, only applied to Catholics; Protestant Dissenters had been able to sit in Parliament during the eighteenth century, although few did because they lacked the necessary wealth and connections. However, to many Anglican commentators in the 1830s the reforming legislation seemed to signal the destruction of all they held dear. Parliament was no longer a 'lay synod' of the Church of England. Viewed from a different perspective, the legislation was a recognition that society had changed, and changed dramatically.

Those changes were part of the history of the 'long eighteenth century'. Eighteenth century life teemed with variety. The juxtaposition of beauty and brutality, prosperity and poverty has rarely been as sharp and revealing. The period began and ended in the shadows of revolution - English and French respectively. Between the shadows lay relative peace and growing prosperity. The treaty of Utrecht (1713) which marked the end of the War of Spanish Succession (1702-13) recognised Britain as a major player in the theatre of European politics, a position re-inforced by a series of victories against the French in mid-century. The union with Scotland in 1707 brought domestic peace and ensured the eventual failure of the 1715 and 1745 Jacobite uprisings. The seeds of commercial empire were being sown through the operations of the East India Company and military success in the West Indies and what was to become Canada.

Intellectually, it was the age of the Enlightenment, with its sure confidence in the range and power of human reason. Artistically it was an elegant, tasteful age, epitomised by the measured proportions of such churches as St Paul's, Deptford and St George's Hanover Square, and the Gibbs building at King's College, Cambridge which we now think contrasts so beautifully with the chapel. It was a world where all was in order and everyone and everything had its place:

> All are but parts of one stupendous whole,
> Whose body Nature is and God the soul;...
> All Nature is but Art, unknown to thee;
> All Chance, Direction, which thou canst not see;
> All Discord, Harmony not understood;
> All partial Evil, universal Good:
> And, spite of Pride, in erring Reason's spite,
> One truth is clear, 'Whatever is, is RIGHT.' *(Alexander Pope)*

However, the shadows of revolution gave birth to a politics of fear and conformity which continually denied civil rights to dissenters, and (far more seriously) resulted in the brutal slaughter of the Young Pretender's army at Cullodon in 1746. The beginnings of empire were counterbalanced by the deeply felt loss of the American colonies in the War of Independence 1775-1783. Its seeds were sown in the soil of slavery - even Selina, Countess of Huntingdon (1707-1791), the great lay patroness of the Evangelical Revival wanted a slave named after her. The measured elegance of Georgian architecture hid countless hovels and back alleys and gin palaces which have long since vanished, but which were pitilessly chronicled by William Hogarth (1697-1764). The intellectual self-confidence of the Enlightenment issued in sharp and persuasive questions about the nature of human knowledge and the limits of reason which were eventually to call into question the very concept of God, and which determine the way in which theology is done even now. The politics of peace rested on a culture of jobbery and corruption ruthlessly exposed by political cartoonists. Cruelty and poverty threatened civility. Beyond the Capability Brown landscapes England was slowly beginning to change. Towns were developing, employment patterns altering. The population rose gently from 5.1 to 5.8 million in the first half of the century, then took off dramatically to rise to 8.7 million by 1801. Although the country was predominantly agrarian throughout the century, 25% of the population lived in towns of 5,000+ in 1800, compared with 15% in 1750. Pre-industrial England was becoming industrial England.

The Anglican church of the eighteenth century has long been a by-word for indolence and inefficiency, indicted for almost every ecclesiastical negligence from pluralism to simony. Recent research is beginning to redress the balance. It will be a long time before a complete picture is available, but it is already clear that the church was neither moribund nor incompetent. Pastoral duties were performed, worship offered, spiritualities nurtured (albeit not ones our age finds congenial).

The Toleration Act changed the legal status of the Church of England dramatically and irrevocably. The switch from a policy of uniformity to plurality was a severe shock to many Anglicans who considered their church to be under threat well into the 1720s. The cry 'the church in danger' echoes through those early decades. As one popular song of the day put it:

> Bold Whigs and fanatics now strive to pull down
> The true Church of England, both mitre and crown,
> To introduce anarchy into the nation
> As they did in Oliver's late usurpation...
>
> We know the pretence, you for liberty bawl;
> But had you your fill, you'd destroy Church and all.

Although historians gifted with the benefit of hindsight may doubt the reality of such threats, the twin dangers of republicanism (considered a close cousin of dissent) and Rome were only too obvious to contemporaries. That goes some way to explain the anti-dissenting policies of Queen Anne's reign (1701-14) and the elaborate circumvention of dissent in Hanoverian England.

## Congregationalism and Presbyterianism in the long eighteenth century

### The Happy Union

1689 created a new world for dissenters. The phrases historians have used to describe this new world - 'a garden walled around' and 'a plain called ease' - are telling. Here at last was security and an end to the harrying and hounding of persecution. Here was the promise of better things. Congregationalists and Presbyterians now looked through their respective windows on to the same landscape.

The Congregationalists were genuine radicals, tracing their roots to the left-wing of the Reformation, to Grebel and the Swiss brethren and all who viewed state churches with anxiety. In England they were the deliberate outsiders, the heirs of Cromwell. Presbyterians, on the other hand, were natural conservatives, an establishment in waiting who would have liked nothing more than the widening of the Church of England to encompass their consciences by reforming the episcopate and the liturgy. Congregationalists and Presbyterians were odd bedfellows. They came together not because of conviction but by the force of circumstance.

The laws of 1662 and 1689 had made them both outsiders, fellow-citizens of the dissenting shadowlands. This common experience united them. There was little at first to differentiate them. Presbyterian church government cannot exist without a series of inter-related church courts. They never came into being in England, and presbyterian churches were therefore autonomous in practice, just as Congregationalist churches were theoretically intended to be. A theoretical scheme of union had been floated during Charles II's reign by Richard Baxter, but he had received short shrift from John Owen and other leading Congregationalists. However, there had been many local examples of co-operation after 1662. In the aftermath of 1689 money rather than theology provided a stimulus for further negotiations. Both churches were faced with the problems of clerical poverty and the need to educate new ministers. In the summer of 1690 representatives of both communions joined together to create a Common Fund to support poor ministers and provide for ministerial education. That laid the foundations for a more ambitious structure, and in 1691 a group of Congregational and Presbyterian ministers produced a document entitled *Heads of Agreement*. Almost all the ministers in London signed it and the 'Happy Union' was inaugurated in the Meeting House at Stepney on 6 April. The document was rapidly endorsed by associations of ministers in Devon,

Hampshire, Cheshire, Lancashire and the West Riding. Ecumenical documents risk blandness and sometimes evade divisive issues in the pursuit of the perceived greater good of unity. That was true of this hurried production. It was relatively easy for Congregationalists and Presbyterians to agree on such matters as the role of Scripture, the nature of the ministry and the importance of church discipline. The power of congregations, the nature of synods, the place of lay preaching and admission to communion (all of which had been matters of disagreement in the recent past) were more controversial, and the *Heads* skated over them with ominous ease.

The 'Happy Union' was doomed from the start. Congregationalists had not yet freed themselves from the anxiety that union with Presbyterians might be the first step on the path to an inclusive national church. The ministers who drew up the document had not consulted as fully as they should have done with their congregations. The two communions were profoundly different, and the true nature of those differences of conviction had been papered over.

The new context in which they found themselves had not severed their roots. Presbyterians were essentially parochial in organisation; Congregationalists believed that the gathered community of the saints was the true church. Presbyterians inclined to admit to communion all who lived respectable lives and professed some Christian conviction; Congregationalists restricted communion to church members. Presbyterians placed great store by an educated ministry; Congregationalists looked rather for evidence of the work of the Holy Spirit regardless of educational attainment. The differences between them were subtle and the historian's task is not made any easier by the fact that contemporaries used the terms 'Congregational' and 'Presbyterian' to mean what we mean by 'conservative' and 'liberal'. Within months of the inauguration of the Union arguments about these issues bubbled to the surface, and the happy union was looking more like an unhappy stand-off.

Matters came to a head in the Northamptonshire town of Rothwell. In 1690 the Congregational church issued a call to a dynamic, independently minded Welshman, Richard Davis. It was clear from the start that he had strong opinions. It was common practice, although by no means mandatory, for visiting ministers to take part in Congregational ordinations. Davis, however, was ordained by the elders of the Rothwell congregation (at this period some Congregational churches had a ministry of elders). It was a clear signal of a certain kind of austere Congregationalism, and the neighbouring ministers returned home grumbling. Davis's ministry was remarkably successful. He showed himself to be a capable evangelist, and during the next few years he and Rothwell congregation entered the business of what we would call church planting. A network of village churches was woven from the central congregation. Like Francis Holcroft in Cambridgeshire and John Bunyan in nearby Bedford, Davis created an itinerant ministry, drawing on the skills of lay preachers. Old dissent (the 'denominations' formed by the ejection of 1662) had its own tradition of itinerancy and lay ministry which pre-dated Wesley. Within three years Davis and his preaching team were operating over an eighty mile radius in at least twenty-nine centres. It was said that his influence spread through eleven counties and that thirteen Independent churches with between two and three thousand members owed their origin to his work. His ministry was accompanied by some of the hysterical manifestations of revival which were later to mark the work of the Wesleys.

At the end of 1690 events in Northamptonshire collided with the re-publication of the *Works* of Tobias Crisp (1600-1643), edited by his son Samuel. Tobias Crisp was a celebrated Antinomian of the early seventeenth century - the fathers of the Westminster Assembly had recommended that one of his works be burnt in 1643. Antinomianism was the belief that obedience to the moral law of Scripture played no part in human salvation, and it was employed in the seventeenth century as a useful tag for the more extreme Calvinists who believed that salvation was entirely the work of divine grace. In other words, a person might be saved and still continue to live a recklessly immoral life, and his or her salvation would be unaffected. Presbyterians had long been anxious about such radicalism, and over the previous forty years had often accused Congregationalists of antinomianism. The tales which reached London about the revival at Rothwell seemed to have enough in common with Crisp's antinomianism to bear investigation.

So it was that far from causing universal rejoicing, Davis's remarkable ministry raised the hackles of some of his colleagues, both Congregational and Presbyterian. The Congregational churches at Wellingborough and Bedworth were divided into pro- and anti-Davis parties, and John King, the minister at Wellingborough did much to rouse local opposition. The real issues at stake were probably not theological but questions of ministerial style. Davis's methods - the use of uneducated lay preachers, his carefree attitude to 'parish' boundaries, and his fervent evangelicalism were precisely the difficult matters which the Happy Union had deliberately avoided. Doubtless there were faults on both sides. Davis was not a man too much concerned with the niceties of professional etiquette, and his tongue sometimes outran his brain. Equally, Presbyterians like the London minister and theologian Daniel Williams (*c.*1643-1716) believed fervently that the way to solve the ministerial crisis was to educate more ministers and were unwilling to see that a new world might demand new ways of being the church.

Davis was summoned to give an account of himself to the London ministers in 1692. Congregationalists caught a whiff of synodical jurisdiction in the air. Davis demanded to know what authority the London ministers had and refused to co-operate. In the middle of all of this Daniel Williams' book *Gospel-truth stated and vindicated*, which he had been working on for a long time, was published. It was a lucid, elegant, point by point refutation of Crisp. It didn't seem like that to Davis and his Congregationalist supporters. They thought it rather an attack on them, using Crisp as a mask. The London ministers eventually published the results of their enquiry into Davis's ministry. They were, as might have been predicted, severely critical.

Relations between Presbyterians and Congregationalists had reached a low ebb. The Congregationalists left the Common Fund to form their own Congregational Fund in 1695. Joint ventures like a shared lectureship at Pinners Hall were dissolved. The Union was at an end. It was not to be resurrected for nearly 300 years, but in 1972 the Presbyterian Church of England could scarcely claim descent from the presbyterians of the 1690s, as we shall see. The dispute was important because it revealed the very real differences of style and theology between the two communions. That was to become all too clear over the next thirty years.

## Occasional conformity

In the meantime all dissenters faced the difficulties of establishing themselves as coherent and viable communities. The Toleration Act had not been met with universal approval. It had received strenuous opposition from the Tories in 1689 when their power was in abeyance. Clouds began to gather on the dissenting horizon during 1697, by which time the Tories were gaining ground again. The Lord Mayor of London in 1697 was Sir Humphrey Edwin (1642-1707), a wealthy wool merchant who was also a Presbyterian. On the Sunday of his election he took communion in his parish church in the morning, but in the afternoon, suitably robed and accompanied, he attended his own meeting-house. Such 'occasional conformity', as it was known, was a perfectly acceptable practice for presbyterians whose whole history was one of seeking a more comprehensive national church. It did not seem so to High Church Tories like Henry Sacheverell (1674-1724) and Francis Atterbury (1662-1732). They were enraged by such a flagrant display of occasional conformity by such 'amphibious' Christians (the phrase is Daniel Defoe's) and their rage was enhanced when another Presbyterian Lord Mayor, Sir Thomas Abney, did the same in 1700.

More ominously, also in 1697, one Joshua Oldfield was cited to appear before an ecclesiastical court for keeping a school without a bishop's licence and without the due subscription described by the Act of Uniformity. The litigation had gone a considerable distance before it was dropped at the king's insistence. Prosecutions against dissenting schools and academies were to recur throughout the early 1700s - even Philip Doddridge was arraigned by the Chancellor of Peterborough diocese as late as 1733.

News of efforts by some West Country dissenters to create national structures in 1697 caused some High Church hearts to flutter, but the scheme came to naught. These were straws in the wind. A new assault was being prepared.

William died in 1702, to be succeeded by his sister-in-law, Anne (1665-1714), the last of the Stuarts. That in itself was a reminder of times dissenters preferred to forget. One congregation at Newcastle-under-Lyme were so apprehensive at Anne's accession that they dismantled their meeting-house. Matters were compounded by a Tory victory in the election in 1702. It was in this new mood of anxiety that dissenters took steps to unite in protection of their civil liberties. Baptists, Presbyterians and Congregationalists came together to form the General Body of Protestant Dissenting Ministers in and about London, and that body set up a permanent Committee of the Three Denominations to monitor their common interests.

Dissenting fears quickly proved themselves justified. The clear aim of the new administration was to try and reduce the dissenting community to nothing. A savagely vindictive bill to control occasional conformity was laid before Parliament in 1702, but it was mauled to destruction by the Whig-dominated House of Lords, and attempts to resurrect it in 1703 and 1704 also met with failure. Daniel Defoe satirised the prevailing mood brilliantly in his *The shortest way with Dissenters*, and suffered the punishment of the pillory for his trouble. The London mob, always fickle and frequently anti-dissenting, responded by garlanding the pillory with flowers. The government finally got their way in 1711, and the Occasional Conformity Act imposed a £40 fine on those who attempted to evade the Corporation Act in such a way. It was a blow to Presbyterians, but less of a problem to Congregationalists who had scant regard for the practice.

They were far more seriously affected by the Schism Act of 1714. The status of dissenting schoolmasters and their academies had been left unclear by the Toleration Act. The law as it stood under the Act of Uniformity of 1661 had been tested in several cases in the late seventeenth century, and it had been found that schoolmasters could not be ejected provided they had been properly appointed by the school's founder or patron, even if they were operating without a bishop's licence. The Toleration Act had not made it clear whether schoolmasters could operate without a bishop's licence. The Schism Act was created to close this loop-hole, with the clear intent of doing the maximum possible damage to the dissenting interest. It declared that no one could keep a school or teach in a school unless they assented to the whole of the Book of Common Prayer and were in possession of a bishop's licence. No licence could be granted unless the authorising bishop had proof that the applicant had received communion according to the rites of the Church of England during the previous year. The Act was due to come into force on 1 August 1714 - and on that day Queen Anne died.

1 August was a Sunday. The preacher at Fetter Lane chapel was Thomas Bradbury (1677-1759). On his way to the chapel he met bishop Gilbert Burnet (1643-1715). Burnet was a Scot who had been Professor of Divinity at Glasgow and a minister in the Church of Scotland before moving to England. He was an ardent advocate of a more inclusive national church, and always a friend to dissenters. He gave Bradbury the latest news of the Queen's condition and arranged that if there should be any change he would send a messenger to the chapel. So it was that in the midst of the service a white handkerchief fluttered from the balcony, and Bradbury ended the service with a prayer for God's blessing *'upon his majesty King George and the House of Hanover.'* It was measure of dissenting feeling about Anne that on the day of her funeral Bradbury preached on the text, *'Go see now this cursed woman and bury her, for she is a king's daughter.'*

## Hanoverian dissent

Hanoverian England was to prove a more benign climate for dissenters. The new dynasty was explicitly pro-Whig. The Tories went into a wilderness. They were to remain there for half a century. Whigs and dissenters were natural allies. The history of the Whigs in the early eighteenth century is complex, contradictory and schismatic. Although they included landowners amongst their number, many were merchants, manufacturers, and men of money. The 'party' had its origins in the Exclusion Crisis - they were those who opposed the Catholic Duke of York

- and their key political values were civil and religious liberty. Ideologically and socially, this was also the world of dissent. The penal legislation and systematic exclusion of dissenters from the mainstream of English life since 1662 meant that only a few aristocratic supporters of dissent remained. The strength of the dissenting interest was essentially mercantile. Although relationships between Whigs and dissenters were good, the Whigs were never in dissenting pockets. They were realistic politicians. They knew the limits of acceptability and the price of power, and had no intention of subverting the ascendancy of the Church of England. Indeed, Walpole's prorogation of the Convocation (the Church's 'parliament') in 1717 meant that parliament became the central legislative body of the Church of England, and this strengthened rather than weakened the bonds which tied church to state. Convocation did not meet again regularly until 1855.

The climate was therefore benign, but not bountiful. Whig concessions to the dissenting interest were limited to a slackening of restrictive legislation. All attempts at its abolition came to naught until 1828. The Occasional Conformity and Schism Acts were repealed in 1719. The Corporation Act was loosened a little in the same year - municipal office was conceded to dissenters against whom no legal proceedings had been commenced within six months of appointment. Dissenters kept up pressure for complete repeal of the Test and Corporation Acts, and as part of this process the Protestant Dissenting Deputies were created by the three denominations in 1732 to spearhead the campaign. In 1739, during the final attempt for over fifty years, one of the Deputies challenged Walpole outright when he demurred yet again that the time was not ripe - *'I trust you will give me leave to ask when the time will come.' 'If you require a specific answer'* Walpole retorted, *'I will give it you in a word - never.'* In the face of such intransigence, the Deputies were consistently unsuccessful and the Acts remained on the statute book.

In 1753 the fortunes of dissent actually took an unexpected and unintended step backwards. The Lord Chancellor, Lord Hardwicke (1690-1764), introduced legislation which was intended to curb the problem of clandestine marriages, thus protecting the landed interest. Unfortunately he did so by decreeing that the only valid marriages were those conducted by banns or licence in parish churches. Dissenters, who had been able to conduct their own marriages under the provision of Common Law, now found themselves faced with the necessity of marrying according to the rites of the Church of England. The difficulties this caused were intensified by the fact that not all Anglican clergy were willing to marry dissenters -

especially if they were Baptists and 'unbaptised'. The Deputies eventually took counsel's opinion, which was that Anglican clergy had no right to refuse those who came to them, even if they were unbaptised.

If parliament was a continual source of frustration for dissenters under the Hanoverians, the monarchy made its support abundantly clear. In 1723 George I granted £500 for the relief of widows of dissenting ministers. The hand of Walpole and the government was clearly visible behind the scenes. The grant was increased to £1,000 annually and was known as the *Regium donum*. It remained in force until 1851, latterly as a government grant. For many it was a welcome, indeed crucial, support, but it was not without its problems. There were intellectual objections from those who thought that all state aid should be shunned because the church should be entirely self-sufficient and financially independent of the state, and pragmatic protests from those who suspected those responsible for distribution of malpractice.

The charity of the monarch to the dissenting interest did not extend to the Corporation of the City of London who were the protagonists in the Evans or Mansion House case, one of the most bitter conflicts between Dissenters and civic authority during the eighteenth century. In 1748 they passed a by-law, obviously aimed at dissenters, which imposed heavy fines on anyone who declined to take the sacramental test after election to a city office. The fines so raised were devoted to the building of the new Mansion House. In 1754, by which time £15,000 had been raised, three dissenters - Sheafe, Streatfield and Evans, who had been elected to the office of Sheriff, all resisted the fine, with the backing of the Protestant Dissenting Deputies. Litigation dragged on for twelve years, before two City courts, a special commission, and eventually the Lords. By the time the Lord Chief Justice, Lord Mansfield, gave his judgement only Evans was still alive, and he was dying. The City's case was ignominiously dismissed, condemned as iniquitous, unjust and impolitic. The judgement was a significant marker in the history of toleration.

However, the City of London's attitude was not mirrored in the provinces. In general life eased for dissenters, and as it did so they began to play their part in civic affairs. Annual Indemnity Acts from 1727 onwards suspended the penalties incurred for refusing the sacramental test, and in some corporations, like Bridgwater in Somerset, the entire civic magistracy consisted of dissenters.

During the reigns of Anne and George I dissenters began to gather information and statistics about themselves as part of their work in protecting their political interests. Dr John Evans (*c.*1680-1730), a presbyterian minister in London and the Secretary of the Committee of the Three Denominations, compiled a list of congregations. This is the main source of statistics about the fortunes of the three denominations in 1715-18:

| | | England | Wales | Total |
|---|---|---|---|---|
| (a) | Congregations | | | |
| | Presbyterians | 637 | 25 | 662 |
| | Independents | 203 | 26 | 229 |
| | All dissenters | 1,845 | 89 | 1,934 |
| (b) | Estimated membership | | | |
| | Presbyterians | 179,350 | 6,080 | 185,438 |
| | Independents | 59,940 | 7,640 | 67,580 |
| | All dissenters | 338,120 | 17,770 | 355,890 |

The figures for Wales are far more suspect than those for England. A recent analysis suggests that dissenters made up 6.2% of the English population and 5.7% of the Welsh population. Presbyterians accounted for 3.3% of the English population, 1.9% of the Welsh population, Independents 1.1% and 2.4% respectively.

The dissenting interest was small but significant. Separated by law from the mainstream of life, dissent developed its own culture and life-style organised around the worship and witness of its chapels and meeting-houses. The spiritual space lent to dissent by the slow creation of toleration began to be walled around by the stone and brick of distinctive meeting-houses - rectangular, plain, modest, elegant, airy. In many a two or three decker pulpit on one of the long walls dominated the chapel. It is evidence of the importance of preaching, of the centrality of the Scripture in the worship and devotional life of dissenters. The precentor (also sometimes called the clerk) used to lead the singing of the metrical psalms and hymns from the lowest level. The minister led the prayers and read the lessons from the second tier, ascending to the dizzy heights of the third to preach. High pulpits were not intended to place a minister twenty feet above contradiction. They were intended to make the preaching accessible to as many as possible because most meeting-houses had a gallery. However, the chapel was much more than a preaching house. In the eighteenth century most dissenters celebrated communion more frequently than their Anglican neighbours. Communion was celebrated in the midst of the congregation, often with a removable table brought in for that purpose. The members used to receive seated around the table. In Presbyterian chapels the congregation used to receive the elements in their pews, and thus a small table raised on a slight dais became a permanent feature of Presbyterian chapels.

Chapels varied from the poor and shoddily built to the exquisite and daring, like the Unitarian Octagon chapel in Norwich and Mary Street in Taunton. Most however, were quiet and inconspicuous, tucked away in back streets, beautiful only in their economy and simplicity with dark wood pews and galleries, white walls, perhaps a grand clock facing the pulpit, and maybe a scarlet pulpit cushion on which the Bible rested. Imagery and colour were deliberately eschewed. What mattered was the beauty of holiness and the majesty of God, beyond the reach of artist's imagination, yet known in the Word read, expounded and lived.

Worship was dominated by the Word, and by many words. Words were as important to eighteenth and nineteenth century culture as visual, video imagery is to late twentieth century society. In a typical morning service a psalm would be sung, followed by a prayer which asked God to be present in the worship that was offered. A lesson would then be read and expounded for about half an hour. A psalm or hymn would follow, after which the minister would lead the people in prayers of confession, thanksgiving and intercession. The climax of the service was the sermon, which would usually last about an hour, followed by a short prayer and a closing hymn or psalm. The entire act of worship was expected to last at least two hours. After a break for lunch, the afternoon service followed a similar pattern. Communion was celebrated monthly, usually following the afternoon sermon, although in the winter at noon so that the congregation could return home before the light faded.

Worship was a serious business. Barely a generation before, dissenters had given freely of lives and livelihood for this right. It was hardly surprising that it flowed from chapel to hearth. Sermons were often taken down in shorthand and repeated in whole or part to the family on Sunday evenings. Week-night sermons and 'lectures' were frequent, so too an evening of preparation for the monthly communion.

The evidence for the social structure of English dissent in the early eighteenth century is sparse, based on a few surviving registers. The conclusion to which scholars are drawn is that dissent counted a few members of the gentry amongst its numbers, and a rather larger contingent of 'labourers', but the bulk of its strength was to be found in the 'middling' sort - tradesmen, merchants, manufacturers and farmers - in other worlds, the economically independent. In urban areas, like Coventry and Norwich though, where dissent flourished, the occupational structure of dissenting congregations differed little from the surrounding locality.

Every Christian denomination is distinctive, yet the very similarities which make Congregationalists Congregationalists rather than Anglicans, should not blind us to the variety which exists within denominations. The common threads of being of the 'middling sort', the disciplines of church membership and a shared spirituality forged from worship bound our forebears into a common 'walk', a mutually supportive way of being Christian, and yet that very unity was forged out of great variety. There was a world of difference between some of the rural chapels of Somerset and Isaac Watts's Mark Lane Chapel in the city of London.

Mark Lane had an honourable pedigree. Possibly founded in 1662, its first minister was the Biblical commentator Joseph Caryl, its second the great John Owen, the third the learned Isaac Chauncey (1632-1712) who left in 1701 to become a tutor at Homerton Academy. During Owen's days, the aristocratic remnants of Cromwellian England had filled the pews. By the time Watts took over that was a fading memory, but still a memory. It lived on in members like Sir Thomas Abney (1640-1722) and John Shute, later Viscount, Barrington (1678-1734). Abney was the scion of an old Derbyshire Puritan family. His first marriage was to Sarah, the daughter of Joseph Caryl, first minister of Mark Lane; his second to Mary, daughter of Sir Thomas Gunston, who brought with her the beautiful manor at Stoke Newington where the Abneys were to live. Abney was a successful businessman, a fish merchant, one of the original directors of the Bank of England and a noted philanthropist, sometime president of St Thomas's Hospital in Southwark, sheriff of London and Middlesex, Lord Mayor in 1700 and, the following year, MP for London.

Jonathan Swift (1667-1745) called Shute '*..the shrewdest head in England*'. In the close-knit world of dissent, he was related by marriage to Abney, and educated at Thomas Rowe's Academy at the same time as Watts. He went on to study at Utrecht, became a barrister, wrote widely on dissenting rights and entered parliament. His political career was cut short when he became the scapegoat for the Prince of Wales in the Harburgh Lottery Scandal (part of the South Sea Bubble speculation scandal of 1720), but by then he had inherited an Irish peerage.

He and Abney were not typical of dissenters socially or intellectually, but their careers illustrate the permeable membrane that existed between some dissenters and the establishment in Hanoverian England. Swift noted that Shute was *'..a moderate man, frequenting the church and meeting indifferently'*. As was noted earlier, Abney's deliberate occasional conformity as Lord Mayor raised the temperatures of High Church Tories. They were men who moved easily in the corridors of power, confident yet not exclusive in their dissent. It would be a serious mistake to read the rigidity of later denominational structures back into the spiritualities of the early eighteenth century. Anglicans like archbishop Thomas Tenison positively encouraged occasional conformity, and in the politics of social reform Anglicans and dissenters made common cause in societies like the SPCK (formed 1699).

The Protestantism which united Anglican and dissenter was in inherent tension with the political protest which had led dissenters to break from the continental reformation principle 'cuius regio eius religio' (the nation's religion is determined by the religion of the ruler). To-day, as in the eighteenth century, the established church finds it easier to relate to continental reformed churches formed on the same political principle as themselves than with the English dissenting churches who share the same polities as the continental reformed communions. Isaac Watts's career is an admirable example of that inherent tension.

## Isaac Watts (1674-1748)

He was born of solid dissenting stock in Southampton in 1674. His father had been imprisoned for his nonconformity the same year. Young Isaac quickly showed himself at ease with words, learning Latin aged four, Greek at nine, French at eleven and Hebrew at thirteen. His mother was astonished by the quality of the poetry he wrote when he was seven. He was educated at the local school, whose master was John Pinhorne, the Rector of All Saints. In later life Watts remained a close and admiring friend of Pinhorne, sending him a portrait on the occasion of his ordination. At the age of 16 he was faced with the decision of either going on to university, and conforming, or of being educated at a Dissenting Academy. Watts chose the latter and proceeded to Thomas Rowe's Academy at Newington Green in London.

The academies were remarkable institutions. They had been forced on dissenters by their exclusion from the universities, principally as a way of educating young men for ministry. At a time when the English universities were at a low ebb, the academies were innovative. The best were at the cutting edge of educational advance, offering liberal, broadly based curricula. The list of those educated in the academies contains formidable names - Samuel Wesley (father of John and Charles), Daniel Defoe, the Roman historian John Horsley, and two future archbishops - Thomas Secker of Canterbury and Josiah Hort of Tuam. Joseph Priestley, the discoverer of oxygen, was a tutor at the Warrington Academy.

Rowe's Academy was noted for its freedom of thought. He was one of the first teachers to introduce Cartesian principles into English education. It was that clarity of thought and diction which guided the young Isaac Watts into a form of sacred poetry which was elegant, economic and uncluttered.

The development of the hymn was one of dissent's greatest gifts to Christianity. The pre-history of the English hymn runs by way of Coverdale's translations of mainly Lutheran hymns which was banned by Henry VIII, Sternhold and Hopkins' 1557 literal translations of the psalms, and the Puritan poet George Wither's *Hymns and Songs of the church* (1623). However, congregational psalm and hymn-singing did not become an accepted part of the life of English dissenting churches until the eighteenth century, and it was not widely practised in the Church of England until the mid-nineteenth century.

Watts was a good pastor and a popular preacher. Called to Mark Lane in 1701, the congregation eventually moved to Bury Street in 1708 because they had outgrown their premises. In 1712 he was taken ill, and Sir Thomas Abney invited him to recuperate at his home near Cheshunt in Hertfordshire. Thirty years later he was still there! The illness had affected his nerves, and he was never able to minister as he might have wished. A co-minister was appointed to Bury Street, and Watts kept in touch with occasional visits and voluminous correspondence. He did, however, assiduously attend meetings of the Congregational Fund Board once a fortnight throughout his career. He might have been one of those ministers who preferred church administration to pastoral work. His own work became the work of the pen. He wrote text-books on logic and the art of reading and writing, children's poetry, devotional treatises, catechisms, works of doctrine, and, of course, 'spiritual poetry', or hymns. Like John Mason Neale in the nineteenth century, he crafted a ministry of hymn writing from the confines of physical weakness and ill-health which re-shaped the spirituality of the nation - 'Give to our God immortal praise', 'I'll praise my maker while I've breath', 'Our God our help in ages past', 'With joy we meditate the grace', 'When I survey the wondrous cross', 'Jesus shall reign where'er the sun', 'Give me the wings of faith to rise' and 'This is the day the Lord hath made' are but a sample of his output.

Watts wrote to be understood, to give voice to what he believed to be the self-evident truths of the faith in a language that was simple, precise and economic. That in itself was a task of some magnitude in the early years of the eighteenth century, for Watts had no models on which to rely. The dignity and restraint of his hymns gave body to an instinctive dissenting aesthetic - simple, structured, disciplined, devoted, classical. It was echoed in the dress of the clergy, the form of chapel worship and the calm, unemotional lines of meeting-house architecture. It was not a religion without feeling, it was a religion of emotion responding to the love of God in Christ and lived out in the disciplined fellowship of the marginalised.

In Watts's hymns the believer is taken up into the cosmic drama of salvation and redemption, and is at once both the subject of God's great work and also the object of it . It is 'I' who survey the wondrous cross, yet 'I' too who would offer all creation in gratitude for the gift of redemption, were that not an offering far too small. There is a sense of vastness and grandeur about Watts's vision, allied to secure sense of worth. In a memorable description of the church in his poem 'The Church the Garden of Christ', he wrote:

We are a Garden wall'd around,
Chosen and made peculiar Ground;
A little Spot inclos'd by Grace
Out of the World's wide Wilderness.

That was the dissenting vision. They were a radical people, chosen and blessed, yet in their very election was to be found the key to the whole drama of redemption, for

Our Lord into his Garden comes,
Well pleas'd to smell our poor Perfumes,
And calls us to a Feast divine,
Sweeter than Honey, Milk or Wine.

Ironically, it was precisely that sense of the particular that caused Watts to transcend the boundaries of dissent. In 1736 he received a letter from an Anglican priest pleading that when Watts reached the Throne of Grace he should pray 'for my soul's health'. In return he promised to pray for the poet as one 'who honour you as a father and brother (though differently ordered)...' In his re-vamping of the psalms Watts thought nothing of replacing 'Israel' with 'Great Britain'. Some divisions were subsumed by greater wholes. Watts the dissenter was also Watts the Protestant, and Protestantism held the disparate parts of the British Isles together.

In his theological writings Watts was suspected of crossing another line of division - that of orthodoxy.

## Presbyterian to Unitarian - the subscription crisis

One of the most perplexing movements of the eighteenth century was the drift of presbyterianism into unitarianism. Colin Morris, the Methodist preacher and broadcaster once quipped that all wise ministers take a holiday on Trinity Sunday! The doctrine of the trinity is one which Christians have always found hard to explain. It gave rise to one of the great controversies of the early Christian centuries, the Arian crisis of the fourth century. Arians thought that there was a time when Jesus was not. That is to say, they accepted his pre-existence in some sense, but denied that he was part of the godhead before creation. During the sixteenth century all the mainstream reformers accepted the trinity without question, but there were some radicals, like Michael Servetus and Fausto Sozzini (or Socinus in Latin), who searched their Scriptures diligently and found there little mention of the trinity. Servetus was tried for heresy in Geneva and burnt. Socinus found his way to Racow in Poland, where he joined a small group of the like-minded and ended his days in peace. Socinians denied both the pre-existence of Jesus and his divinity. Anti-trinitarian ideas surfaced in England in the free-thinking decades of the Commonwealth and Protectorate. Nearly thirty years later, in 1687, Stephen Nye (*c.*1648-1719), the Anglican grandson of Philip Nye (1596-1672), one of the great Congregationalists of Cromwellian England, published *A brief history of the Unitarians, also called Socinians.* It caused scandal and anxiety as much to the bishops of the Church of England as to dissenters. Those who subscribed to Unitarian views were excluded from the provisions of the Toleration Act and were liable to three years' imprisonment under the terms of the Blasphemy Act of 1698. In 1710 William Whiston (1667-1752), the professor of mathematics at Cambridge, was dismissed from his chair for his Arian views. He published them the following year as *Primitive Christianity revised.* A year later Samuel Clarke (1675-1729), the rector of St James's Westminster, undertook the perilous task of explaining *The Scripture doctrines of the trinity*. His critics accused him of heresy, with the end result that lots of people, including many dissenters, read his book. For those who regarded Scripture as the final arbiter of doctrine, and for those who were aware of current trends of thought and therefore valued reason highly, this was dangerous ground. The doctrine of the trinity makes no explicit appearance in the New Testament, although it may be inferred, and reason unconstrained by revelation can lead to novel and sometimes unwelcome destinations.

These books were read in those centres of free-thinking education, the dissenting academies, particularly in Mr Joseph Hallet's Academy at Exeter. Hallet (1656-1722) was also a city minister. In 1713 he was joined by a bright colleague, James Peirce (1672-1726), who had known Whiston whilst he had a pastorate in Cambridge. Over the next three years the Presbyterian ministers of Exeter and those laymen who had responsibility for the financial affairs of the chapels, the so-called Committee of Thirteen, grew increasingly anxious. Rumours had reached their ears that Hallet's pupils were casting doubts on Christ's divinity. In 1718 Hallet, Peirce and two of their colleagues were asked to give evidence of their orthodoxy. Only one complied. In the September the presbyterian ministers of Devon and Cornwall resolved at their Assembly at Exeter that they should express their trinitarian faith in the formula *'That there is but one God; and that the Father, Word, and the Holy Spirit, is that One God.'* In the November the Committee of Thirteen asked that the suspect Exeter ministers should subscribe to this, or the first of the Thirty-nine Articles of the Church of England, or the Sixth Question of the Westminster Catechism. In a neat (and thoroughly Reformed) move, Peirce refused on the grounds that Scripture was the sole test of faith.

No formal structure linked Protestant Dissenters across the nation, but there were informal networks. The Exeter folk were now completely flummoxed, and they wrote to ask the advice of their colleagues in London. The London ministers were cautious and hesitated to interfere. John Shute Barrington, then the spokesman of political dissent, thought the matter should come before the Three Denominations. A General Meeting of the London Ministers was called at Salters' Hall on 19 February to decide what advice could be given. The process revealed a deep rift within dissent. The Congregationalist Thomas Bradbury put forward a motion that a declaration of faith in the trinity should be included in any advice sent to Exeter. He lost, by 57 votes to 53.

The London ministers were now divided into Subscribers and Non-Subscribers. In Exeter meanwhile, the orthodox ministers persuaded the chapel trustees to exclude Hallet and Peirce. With the doors locked against them, they set up their own Unitarian congregation, numbering 300. The controversy continued to rage in London. The ministers met again on 3 March. Those who lost the February vote put their signatures to a trinitarian declaration of faith, and thus became known as the Subscribers. Their opponents became the Non-subscribers by default. There were many reasons for refusing to subscribe, some of which, for example the belief that Scripture alone was the source of doctrine, were deeply orthodox, and the Non-subscribers were at pains to underline their belief in the divinity of Jesus.

The Subscribers remained suspicious and unconvinced. They feared a drift into heresy. Events proved them justified. The figures are interesting. Seventy-eight London ministers subscribed at Salters' Hall - thirty Presbyterians, twenty-eight Congregationalists, fourteen Particular Baptists and one General Baptist. There were seventy-three non-subscribers. The vast majority, forty-seven, were Presbyterians, nine were Congregationalists, the rest Baptists or unaffiliated. By the end of the century the great majority of English Presbyterians had abandoned their belief in the trinity and become Unitarians. If we are to understand what happened, we must first of all appreciate that denominationalism is a product of the late eighteenth and early nineteenth centuries. The subscribers and non-subscribers at Salters' Hall were not drawing up denominational lines of battle; still less were they 'switching' denominational allegiance. Protestant dissent at that time is best understood as a spectrum of beliefs and styles - rational theological free thinking was as much a part of Anglican life as dissenting. It was a response to the prevailing philosophical climate which sought logical order in religious life. Reason, morality and duty were the keys. This was Christianity without crosses and minus the tears. It is not to our taste, but that does not mean it was without effect. The diary of a Sussex tradesman, Thomas Turner, introduces us to a man who drank too often and too well, yet repented and spent sober Sunday afternoon's reading the (to our mind) dry and moralistic sermons of archbishop John Tillotson (1630-1694). Those who castigate the early eighteenth century for its lack of religion actually mean that its religion was not to their liking.

The Subscription crisis needs to be understood in that context. Later, in the early nineteenth century, when battles raged between orthodox dissenters and Unitarians over property rights and trust funds, George Hadfield, sometime Congregationalist MP for Sheffield, calculated that of the 223 Unitarian chapels in England in 1825, 178 were originally orthodox. Most were either Presbyterian or General Baptist in origin. By then it made sense to speak of denominations; a century earlier the model was rather one of diversity of theological opinion within the unity of dissent as a whole.

However, historians are still faced with the problem of explaining why the majority of the chapels which veered to the free-thinking end of the dissenting spectrum were presbyterian. Several reasons have been advanced. None of them are thoroughly convincing, but until more research is undertaken they must suffice. First, presbyterianism as a theoretical system of church government depends on a series of interlocking church councils, local and national, such as there is in the United Reformed Church and the Church of Scotland. The English Presbyterian dissenters were never able to institute such a system. That meant that power which should have been balanced elsewhere became concentrated in the local church. Secondly, unlike Congregational churches, Presbyterian congregations did not have Church Meetings. Power was concentrated in the hands of trustees or managers, and there was no internal check to their power. Ministers had a far freer hand in presbyterian congregations precisely because they were not answerable to Church Meeting. As the Exeter case showed, their fellow ministers only had a moral authority over their fellows, and that could be easily ignored, or contradicted by protestations of the importance of conscience. This illustrates the fact that it was on the whole ministers who were shifting their theological opinions rather than congregations. Occasionally congregations could get rid of an unorthodox minister, but more usually the orthodox members had to secede and form another congregation. It was also a phenomenon more often found in urban areas. Thirdly, it is thought that Presbyterian chapels attracted a constituency of a higher social class than the Congregationalists, and that they were more liable to be impressed by radical theological ideas. Fourthly, the reformation principle of '*sola scriptura*' (by Scripture alone), if rigorously applied, could indeed lead to a non-trinitarian position, as Socinus and the Exeter ministers had discovered.

Fifthly, the history of Presbyterianism in England was one of gentle moderation. Originally a pressure group within the Elizabethan church for a more reformed establishment, presbyterians constituted the national church under Cromwell. They were reluctant dissenters, more attracted to Baxter's 'Middle Way' of modified Calvinism than the more severely orthodox forms embraced by the Congregationalists. They were naturally inclined to toleration. The movement from presbyterianism to unitarianism was a gradual evolution. It was by no means clear cut. As the eighteenth century continued, 'presbyterian' became a label attached to a liberal way of being Christian while 'congregationalist' became a sign of orthodoxy. Some chapels, like Aston Thirrold in Berkshire, changed their name according to the stance of their minister at the time.

## A time of decline ?

The first part of the eighteenth century was a trying time for dissent. The persecution which had been a mark of dissenting life before 1689 had given way to irascible, yet unpredictable, threat. Social apartheid was biting. The cost of an alternative, voluntarist way of being Christian was rising. Buildings had to be paid for, ministers supported, academies maintained. The unity lent to dissent by national policy was a mask for serious divisions, glimpsed over the Richard Davis affair, but made all too apparent in the wake of Salters' Hall. The mood was caught by an anonymous pamphlet of 1730, *An enquiry into the causes of the decline of the dissenting interest.* It was the work of Strickland Gough, a young man who had just left a dissenting academy. His analysis (if such it can be called) was based on a mis-reading of dissenting history. He was the first, but by no means the last, to suggest that the kernel of dissenting life was liberty of conscience. The Subscription crisis, and the consequent unsettlement of 'unorthodox' ministers by their congregations disturbed him. It seemed to him a decline from the heady days of Puritanism. Ministers should pay less attention to their humble congregations, and more to the educated opinions of polite society. The number of congregations should be reduced. Those causes which were not viable should be shut and the money saved be re-directed to increase stipends to a level proper for gentlemen. The most amusing suggestion in the pamphlet was that dancing masters should be employed in the academies to erase the inherent clumsiness of dissenting ordinands. Gough was soon counted amongst the fifty of so dissenting ministers who conformed to the Church of England between 1714 and 1731.

It was a facile performance, but a telling one. Even unintended caricature reveals an element of truth. Statistics for the period are unavailable, yet no one doubts that dissent was in a slough of despond. The sieve of toleration had achieved what its creators had intended - dissent was markedly second-rate, and no-one enjoys being second-rate. Gough's analysis was a thinly veiled lament that dissent was the world of the 'middling sort' and as such distinctly unfashionable. Little did Gough know that England was on the verge of a religious movement which was to discover that the gospel was not only for the 'middling' sort but for the poorest of God's poor. His pamphlet caused a young Congregationalist minister to take to print for the first time with an anonymous reply, *Free thoughts on the most probable means of reviving the Dissenting Interest.* The principle cause of dissenting decline, he propounded, was dissent's ability to fragment into sectarian dog-fighting. The most probable means of reviving it was to discover a unity based on an evangelical ministry, and he issued a rallying cry, *'that all who sincerely wish well to it* [the dissenting interest,] *should express their affection by exerting themselves with the utmost zeal for the revival of practical religion amongst us.'* That young minister was Philip Doddridge, minister at Northampton, where he also ran what was to become one of nonconformity's most revered academies.

## A time of revival ?

### Philip Doddridge of Northampton (1702-1751)

A reading of the history of dissent which makes a divide between the 'decline' of the early years of the eighteenth century and its resurgence in the wake of the Evangelical Revival is too simplistic. No doubt dissenting life was in need of revival, but so too was the life of the Church of England. It is equally clear that the spirituality of deep personal encounter with God which was to be the hall-mark of the Revival was also to be encountered amongst the members and ministers of dissenting congregations, and indeed in the Church of England long before Wesley took to field preaching in 1739. The evidence of journals kept by lay people and funeral sermons of ministers and lay people make that plain. So too does Philip Doddridge's career. He was born in 1702. He died too young some 49 years later. His life bridges the worlds of old dissent and new, the world of Queen Anne and the world of John Wesley and the Evangelical revival. A man of theological moderation and ecumenical generosity and openness, his greatness lies not in originality so much as in the creative energy with which he synthesised the work of others, held together a enormous network of correspondents and friends of different spiritual hues, and encouraged the growth of 'practical' religion through his devotional writings and hymns. The love of God, and an earnest desire to translate the gospel into the realities of everyday discipleship were the golden threads which held Doddridge's diverse interests together.

He was a man whose vision of the catholicity of the church caused him to be friends with Wesley, yet also to invite Whitefield to occupy his pulpit, to dedicate sermons to the Countess of Huntingdon and to share in informal conversations about church unity with archbishop Herring at Lambeth. Doddridge was widely respected and loved. His educational work at his academy was so appreciated that he found himself a welcome guest on the high tables of Oxford and Cambridge colleges, and when Hertford College Oxford was re-founded, its Principal, Dr Richard Newton sought his advice on the college's new statutes prior to their publication. Doddridge, it sometimes seems, knew everyone, and knew about everything! However, his importance to dissenting history lies not just in busyness and all-round abilities, but in his devotional writings. His *Rise and progress of religion in the soul* has been described as one of the most important devotional books of the first part of the eighteenth century. By the end of the nineteenth century over one hundred editions of it had been produced and it had been translated into almost all the European languages, as well as Syriac and Tamil. Almost equally influential was his *Family Expositor*, a massive Bible commentary which was intended to be used in family worship. It was meant to enhance people's appreciation of the New Testament as *'the grand instrument of reforming a very degenerate world'* by forming the mind in *'manly devotion, diffusive benevolence, [and] steady fortitude'*. In other words, it was a work of 'practical' religion. By that term Doddridge meant religion which makes a difference, which bears the fruits of the Spirit, which can be measured on the pulses of human emotion and experience.

It was an emphasis which was to reach full flower in the Evangelical Revival, but the shift of sensibility which is most commonly associated with the Wesleys was pre-figured in the writings of Doddridge and in the spiritual experience of some dissenters of his day. Older Puritan literature tended to distrust feeling as part of the fallenness of human nature. Although it would be wrong to exaggerate Doddridge's originality, there is something new here, a new tenderness and awareness of pain and sorrow, joy and delight, and of their relation to God's love in Christ. Research has shown that Doddridge's works were read by all kinds and conditions of people. Analyses of the subscription lists for *On the rise and progress of religion in the soul* shows aristocrats, clergy, merchants, college heads, and a remarkable number of women amongst his readers, as well as the 'middling' sort of Dissenters who would be expected to be his natural audience. His work crossed the barriers of class and religious culture, and that in itself was a crucial factor in the creation of a milieu for the broad impact of the Evangelical Revival in England.

## The Evangelical Revival

The Evangelical revival was an international movement. It began in Eastern and Central Europe, and then spread westwards. A recent study has suggested that the roots of the revival are to be found in rebellion against the state regulation of religious life. The religious division of Europe in the wake of the reformation was carried out by political leaders. Whether a country was Protestant or Catholic depended on the decision of rulers, whether individual kings (as in England) or city councils (as in the cities of Switzerland). Nations have a natural inclination to increase their power and influence, and to try and impose their wills on less powerful neighbours or on fringe groupings within their own boundaries. That was what happened across Europe - for example, Sweden sought to master Bremen and Verden, its territories on the south side of the Baltic, in Lapland and Greenland. In the United Kingdom successive monarchs and governments strove to unite England and Scotland, quell the Irish and maintain control of the American colonies.

National, state churches were made part of the process of political control. To be a good English citizen was to be a member of the Church of England. Churches were part of a wider political process of teaching, civilising and redeeming. This process of imposing political unity and religious orthodoxy on disparate peoples was, then as now, fraught with difficulty. The problem can be seen most clearly in languages. In the United Kingdom English religious societies made well-meaning attempts to assimilate Wales into an English language culture, and in Scotland the Kirk tried to eradicate Gaelic in the Scottish Highlands. Revival, it is argued, was a reaction against this process. It began amongst the Protestant minorities of Central and Eastern Europe, most of which were under pressure from hostile Catholic or Lutheran states. As it spread westwards, its character began to change. Rather than being used against the state churches, it was harnessed by them to solve previously intractable pastoral problems. It became a method of breaking up old-style paganism in the Baltic lands, and of combating the odd mixtures of Christianity and antique paganisms in West Wales and the Scottish Highlands. As we shall see, its end result was subtly different in England.

During the eighteenth century the Protestant world was linked by letter and journal. Doddridge's prodigious correspondence was but the tip of an iceberg. News of conversion and Protestant victory was eagerly awaited and devoured across the world. The Revival was truly international. It linked Britain with America in new, and (as far as Protestantism was concerned) mutually beneficial ways. Many of modern America's roots are to be found in English Puritan soil, particularly in the experience of the 'separatists' of Elizabethan and Jacobean England who found in 'New England' freedom to create the church and society they felt God calling them to create. By the time of the Revival, America was cosmopolitan - Europe transposed into a brave new world through emigration. America's uniqueness is that it is a melting pot, juxtaposing cultures and nationalities which were separated by linguistic and geographical barriers in Europe. The American revival was marked by a fluid interchange of traditions.

The English revivalist George Whitefield said that 'the great beginner of the work' was Theodorus Frelingshuysen (1692-1747), who became pastor to four predominantly Dutch churches in the Raritan valley of New Jersey in 1719. He was a German who had ministered in the East Friesland and the Lower Rhine, a part of Germany which had close contacts with the Netherlands. He brought with him the Lower Rhine tradition of 'discriminating preaching' - that is of preaching to different parts of the congregation according to their supposed spiritual state, and he developed into a revivalist. His evangelical preaching began to produce frequent converts, and the revival spread to neighbouring English speaking presbyterians. Their minister, Gilbert Tennent (1703-1764), was an Irishman of Scottish descent. He and Freylingshuysen formed a close friendship. By 1729 Tennent and his father and brothers found their ministries producing many converts. Then, five years later, in 1734, Jonathan Edwards (1703-1758), the Congregational minister of the remote town of Northampton in West Massachusetts preached a sermon on 'justification by faith alone'. The effect was electrifying. Edwards recorded that 300 people *'were savingly brought home to Christ...in the space of half a year'* and the revival soon spread to neighbouring towns. Edwards was to become America's first great theologian, a thinker overwhelmed by the majesty and glory of God, exploring the twin themes of the greatness of God and the utter dependence of sinful humanity on God for salvation.

## George Whitefield (1714-1770)

The transatlantic nature of the revival was epitomised in Whitefield, an Anglican minister, who was probably the best known Protestant in the world in the eighteenth century. He had visited America in 1738 to help found an orphanage at Bethesda in Georgia. He was to cross the Atlantic thirteen times in all. When he returned in 1739 his reputation as a preacher preceded him, and his visit became a sensation. In the autumn of 1740 in New England he preached to crowds of up to 8,000 nearly every day for a month. This was the key event in the Great Awakening which swept across America. In New England it brought new life to the Congregational churches which had been established by the Pilgrim Fathers a century before. In the middle colonies it brought rapid growth to the Presbyterians and Dutch Reformed. In the South it galvanised the Baptists and prepared the way for the great Methodist movement of the post-Revolutionary period. It also bridged the cultural divide between black and white.

Whitefield's personal evangelical awakening occurred in 1735 in the heartland of the English establishment, the University of Oxford. A small group of graduates and students had been meeting together for study, prayer and mutual support since 1729. They were nicknamed 'Methodists' by their contemporaries 'from their custom of regulating their time and planning the business of the day every morning.' Whitefield became a member of that little group during his undergraduate career (1732-6). The son of the keeper of the Bell Inn in Gloucester, he worked his way through Oxford as a 'servitor', waiting on the gentlemen undergraduates. So eager a Methodist was he that his fasting and mortifications threatened his health. He was converted soon after Easter 1735, found his spiritual journey helped by various Puritan writings (which may explain his later Calvinism), and was ordained deacon in 1736. Whilst he was at Oxford, Doddridge was praying for him, and Whitefield knew it. When his 'enthusiasm' made him an unwelcome visitor in some pulpits around Gloucester and Bristol, he found encouragement from the dissenting minister of Gloucester, Thomas Cole. Turned away from many pulpits, Whitefield took to field preaching, beginning in the colliery area of Kingswood. Possibly for the first time since the Franciscan friars, the love of God was proclaimed in the open air to all who would hear. It was probably illegal under canon law, but as Whitefield said,

*I thought it might be doing the service of my Creator, who had a mountain for his pulpit, and the heavens for his sounding board; and who, when the gospel was refused by the Jews, sent his servants into the highways and hedges.*

Unconventional it may have been, but Whitefield found a ready response amongst the less sophisticated, even if at the expense of alienating some of the respectable. He graphically described the Kingswood colliers:

*Having no righteousness of their own to renounce, they were glad to hear of a Jesus who was a friend to publicans, and came not to call the righteous, but sinners to repentance. The first discovery of their affectedness was to see the white gutters made by their tears, which plentifully ran down their black cheeks as they came out of their coal pits.*

Throughout 1737, before his departure for Georgia, he attracted huge, excited crowds in Gloucester, Bristol and London. Whitefield was an extraordinary man of commanding presence and bell-like voice. Like many great preachers he had all the gifts of the actor. By all accounts he was an hilarious mimic, with a telling command of gesture and quiverful of rhetorical devices. He was ebullient, polemical, supremely quick-witted, sentimental, romantic, vulgar, a fine story-teller with a fund of jokes and puns, but above all he combined a passion for the gospel with an overwhelming sympathy for the weak and the poor. Whitefield was the source of the English revival. He turned the spiritual eccentricities of a few Oxford intellectuals into a mass movement.

Whitefield's chief patroness and supporter was the formidable Selina, Countess of Huntingdon, the Margaret Thatcher of the Evangelical Revival, a lady definitely not for turning. She threw her considerable energy into bringing Methodism, particularly Calvinistic Methodism, into drawing room society. Whitefield was her favourite, and he became her private chaplain. She catapulted him into café society - Daniel in the pit of port and card tables. Despite the droll amusement of some members of upper-class society, Lady Huntingdon met with some success, and she had the organisational ability that Whitefield so lacked. She gave the movement some degree of permanence by founding a series of proprietary chapels in such fashionable places as Bath and Brighton, staffing them with handpicked Evangelical clergy. By 1790 there were sixty-four chapels in her Connexion, and she had founded a theological college at Trevecca in Wales. She was a committed Anglican, and made every attempt to remain within the Church of England, but in 1778 the Consistorial Court of the diocese of London ruled that it was illegal for her domestic chaplains to officiate at worship in other people's parishes, so she took the grave step of registering all her chapels as nonconformist chapels. Those of her leading preachers who wished to remain in the Church of England resigned, and from that point onwards her chapels came to have a closer connection with Congregationalism than with the established church. That, in a way, was a parable of the Evangelical Revival's relationship with the establishment, for later the new wine of Methodism was also to burst the wine skin of the Church of England.

It was Whitefield who linked the worlds of the American, Welsh and English revivals. He stands at the beginning of the English revival, an astonishing Anglican blend of Bernard Manning and Billy Graham. He was a wonderful communicator, but a dreadful administrator, in marked contrast to both Howell Harris and John Wesley (1703-1791). It is a telling statistic that by 1750 Harris had founded over 400 societies but Whitefield a mere twenty-nine in England, and twenty-three preaching stations. Had he been more interested in organisation, the Evangelical revival might have had a very different shape. As it was, English Methodism was almost entirely the creation of John Wesley, and its theology Arminian rather than Calvinist.

## Howell Harris (1714-1774) and the Welsh revival

Harris, an Anglican layman, was the lynch-pin of the Welsh revival. One Sunday in 1735 in Trevecca in Breconshire, the 21 year old Harris was alarmed by his vicar's warning, '..*if you are not fit to come to the Lord's table... you are not fit to live, nor fit to die.*' He was thrown into spiritual turmoil until Whit Sunday when:

*I felt suddenly my heart melting within me, like wax before fire, with love to God my Saviour: and also felt not only love and peace but a longing to be dissolved and be with Christ. There was a cry in my soul, which I was totally unacquainted with before - 'Abba, Father!' I could not help calling God my father. I knew that I was his child and that he loved and heard me.*

He immediately felt a responsibility to share his good fortune - began family worship, invited the neighbours in, and then took off for the surrounding villages '*exhorting all those with whom I had formerly sinned.*' By the end of 1726 he was organising his converts into religious societies.

Meanwhile, independently of Harris, Daniel Rowland, the curate of Llangeitho in Cardigan attended a service conducted by Griffith Jones, the rector of Landdower in Carmarthanshire whose work in founding Welsh language circulating schools is intertwined with the history of the Revival in Wales. Jones was struck by Rowland's vain appearance and offered a prayer on his behalf. Conversion was instant and Rowland became a compelling revivalist preacher. Harris and Rowland met for the first time in 1737 and agreed to work together for the conversion of Wales. Harris worked himself into the ground evangelising throughout Wales and England. In 33 days early in 1747 he wrote,

*I travelled about 600 miles and have visited 5 counties of Wales, and have been through the West of England, through Bristol, Bath, Exeter, Plymouth dock and Cornwall, and came home at 2 in the morning last Sunday after travelling last week about 250 miles.*

By 1750 there were over 400 religious societies or *seiadau* ('soul-clinics') in Wales and the borders, although one estimate suggests that the total number of Methodists in Wales was then no more than 8,000. They were organised into an almost presbyterian form of government, and unlike English Methodists, were strictly Calvinist in theology. That in itself created close links with Welsh nonconformity, although Harris was clear that his movement was a renewal of the established church. Some of the tensions which existed between old dissent and Methodism in England were also apparent in Wales, but Harris's work changed the tone of Welsh nonconformity, and prepared the way for its remarkable growth in the nineteenth century.

## English dissent and Methodism

Dissenting attitudes to the Revival and the burgeoning of Methodism were more ambiguous. As we have seen, the revival was not a Methodist preserve. It was a universal movement, and its influence could not but be widely felt. Congregationalism was slowly transformed between 1760 and 1815. Many of the Countess of Huntingdon's congregations were to swell its ranks eventually, including some of those founded by Whitefield like Moorfields and Tottenham Court Road in London, and the Tabernacle at Bristol. A fair number of the students trained at her college in Trevecca, and later at Cheshunt, found themselves called by Congregational churches. In Yorkshire the work of other leaders of the Revival like the Anglicans William Grimshaw at Haworth and Henry Venn at Huddersfield, and Benjamin Ingham, the founder of the Inghamites, led to the formation of local churches which eventually found their home in Congregationalism. The Countess's preachers were also active in Lancashire and the Midlands, where once again Congregationalism was the long-term beneficiary. One of the most remarkable was William Roby - briefly a student at Trevecca in 1787. He soon became irritated by the Countess's habit of moving her preachers around the country, and was relieved to be ordained as assistant-minister of her chapel in Wigan. Irritation soon turned to disillusion with the Connexion, and he accepted a call to Cannon Street Independent Church in Manchester in 1795, which became Grosvenor Street in 1807. He ministered there until his death in 1830, during which time the congregation grew from 150 to 1,200. His deep commitment to evangelicalism did much to transform the fortunes of Congregationalism in Lancashire, for he and his congregation were eager itinerants. His hand can be discerned behind the birth of Congregational churches in Leigh, Hulme, Rochdale, Ashton-under-Lyme, Oldham, Dukinfield and Salford. He persuaded the Lancashire churches to join together in supporting the work of itinerancy, and between 1803-8 ran an academy for training ministers which was to be one of the precursors of the present Northern College in Manchester.

An itinerant evangelistic ministry which drew on the talents of ministers and lay people alike but which distinguished between their roles was not unknown in the earlier history of dissent - it had been a hallmark of the Richard Davis affair. Prior to that it had been part of the experience of the ejected ministers of 1662 and those who followed immediately after them, including Francis Holcroft in Cambridgeshire and John Bunyan in Bedfordshire. Nor was it confined to Roby's ministry in the eighteenth century. Recent studies have pointed to its existence in the West Country, in parts of London, Essex and the Midlands amongst Baptists as well as Congregationalists. In tone and style it was subtly different from the Methodist idea of itinerancy. For those in the tradition of older dissent, itinerancy was a pattern of outreach from an established congregation served by a settled minister. As such, it depended on co-operation between churches, and it is not surprising that associations of ministers and churches, which were the precursors of County Unions, grew up alongside the itinerant movement.

The new mood of evangelicalism which old and new dissent shared did not mean that Congregationalists and Baptists were uncritically welcoming to Methodism. Old dissent was noted for its discipline and structure. Revivalism, in the eighteenth century and to-day, has a tendency to cut across structures. Methodism seemed disorderly to many, and even such a mature and sympathetic critic as Isaac Watts was severely doubtful about Wesley's irregularity. The age was also deeply anxious about 'enthusiasm'. Although those at the more rational end of the dissenting spectrum tended towards Unitarianism, there remained a distrust of emotionalism in religion which was heightened by the more extreme spiritual manifestations of the Revival. Those who have experience of the charismatic movement in our day may well be better placed to discern the spiritual from the hysterical than were the dissenters of the 1740s and 1750s. Fanaticism seemed just around the corner. As Thomas Morgan, the minister of Morley, put it in 1769, *'Religion at Low Ebb crucified between Enthusiasm and Infidelity.'*

Perhaps the hardest objection for us to understand is theological. To those bred in traditional Calvinism, Wesley and the Methodists seemed to be offering the hope of eternal life too lightly. One reason why the Reformation did not give birth to a missionary movement was the conviction that the elect were not numerous, that they were known to God, and that God in his mercy would guarantee their salvation. There was therefore no need for evangelistic preaching. In our day, when the preaching of God's love as freely available to all seems the only option, it is hard to reconstruct the lost world of our predecessors in the faith. However, to some in our traditions, Wesley seemed to be genuinely misleading people. A shift in theological consciousness can be detected in the growth of itinerancy. The times were changing, the population growing. Election remained God's prerogative, but perhaps the elect were larger in number than had been commonly perceived. A new optimism was abroad, expressed rather cheekily almost a century later by the prayer of the great Baptist preacher C H Spurgeon, *'Oh Lord, bring in thine elect, and then elect some more.'!*

The Revival changed the face of English religion. It burst the confines of class, spawned the Sunday School Movement (possibly the only true form of liberation theology ever seen on British soil), lent dissenting worship warmth and dynamism (particularly through hymnody) and brought about a quiet theological revolution as the old stringent Calvinism was laid aside in favour of a 'Modern Calvinism' which firmly denied that God had predestined anyone to damnation but claimed that he had influenced the hearts of some to respond to the free preaching of God's limitless grace. If those developments lay behind the increase in what became known as 'home missions', they also inspired the most significant movement in modern Christianity - the missionary movement.

The Baptist Missionary Society of 1792 was the first denominational missionary society to be founded. It was followed three years later by the London Missionary Society. In origin the Society was avowedly and actually non-denominational, uniting Welsh, Scots and English, dissenters and episcopalians, declaring in famous words *'that our design is not to send Presbyterianism, Independency, Episcopacy, or any other form of Church Order and Government...but the Glorious Gospel of the blessed God to the Heathen.'* By default and within a generation the LMS was fundamentally a Congregationalist Society and under its auspices Congregationalism played its own significant part in the heady brew of Christianity and imperialism which was to have such a formative role on the development of the political and ecclesiastical structures of modern Africa and Asia.

In 1794 David Bogue of Gosport, one of the founders of the LMS, wrote to *The Evangelical Magazine*,

*We all know that it is the supreme end of our existence to glorify God. But can we suppose that though we endeavour personally to live to His honour, our obligations are fulfilled, while we have employed no methods as a Christian body to lead our brethren in Pagan lands to glorify Him also, by making them acquainted with His nature, government and grace? We profess 'to love the Lord Jesus Christ in sincerity.' But are we not bound thereby 'to shed abroad the sweet odour of His name in every place', till it be diffused throughout all the dark paths of the earth, the habitations of ignorance and cruelty?*

It was a richly symbolic moment. A new vista could be seen. The impetus was rooted in the formative Calvinism of the dissenting tradition. The language and imagery of the supreme end of life as the glorification of God was that of the Westminster Confession. But here was no 'Garden wall'd around'. Here was rather the vision of men and women who had learnt that 'were the whole realm of nature mine / that were a present far too small.' These people knew that the whole expanding world, discovered and yet to be discovered, was God's world. Drawing on a tradition of openness and catholicity seen in Baxter and Doddridge, tempered by the love of God which had broken down barriers of class and communion during the Evangelical Revival, the founders of the LMS opened their arms and hearts to their fellow Protestant Christians for the sake of God's world. The Toleration Act was over a century away. Memories of Queen Anne had faded. The irritation of social apartheid remained, but the wave of factories and merchant houses which was creating new prosperity carried dissenters on its crest. As the ancien régime began to crumble, there was a new confidence in the air.

## The formation of the Congregational Union

The LMS was one of many religious societies formed in the wake of the Evangelical Revival. Between 1780 and 1850 religious life became steadily institutionalised. Dissenting academies were becoming theological colleges. Missions at home and overseas stimulated the growth of societies designed both to raise funds and deepen understanding of humanitarian and evangelical needs. Interdenominational societies like the British and Foreign Bible Society (1804), the Religious Tract Society (1799), and the British and Foreign Sailors' Society (1818) came into being to deal with specific concerns. This was partly a consequence of the steady growth of institutionalised life in British society at large, and partly a reflection of the growing sophistication of the Christian community. Nonconformists were people of business, growing in affluence and organisational skills. It was only natural that they should seek to use those gifts in the service of the church.

During the latter half of the eighteenth century county and district associations began to be created which provided fellowship and counsel for Congregational ministers and churches. The Essex Ministerial Association was formed in 1776 to provide *'Christian fellowship, conversation and public worship among its members'*. Later County Unions added home mission to those objectives. The Lancashire Union of 1806 was established *'to promote the spread of the Gospel'* in the county, and the Hertfordshire Union of 1810 was created for *'the diffusion of religious knowledge through the towns and villages of Hertfordshire.'* Slowly but surely Congregational churches were expressing a sense of common purpose and mutual support. *The Congregational Magazine* appeared for the first time in 1818. The following year the Home Missionary Society was formed. Originally undenominational, it soon took on the flavour of Congregationalism, and by 1830 was supporting twenty-eight preaching stations, and its twenty-eight missionaries were holding services in 172 villages.

There were unsuccessful attempts to create a national Congregational Union in 1806 and 1816, but it was not until 1830 that the matter began to receive serious attention. In that year a number of like-minded Congregational ministers took the lead in circulating a subscription list for the creation of a Congregational Library and Denominational Home. They were immediately successful, and secured a building in Blomfield Street, Finsbury Circus. It was opened in May 1831. It was, as it were, a home for an institution which did not yet exist. In the meantime a group of interested lay people and ministers promoted the ideas of a Union of County Associations and an annual General Assembly. They were careful to proceed with caution and moderation, and were greatly surprised to find that the Dorset Association had simultaneously prepared a vast and detailed document which supported the same aims. They were, however, concerned that such a detailed plan would raise the hackles of staunchly independent local churches. They were right, and a furious debate raged in the pages of the denominational press during 1831. However, the promoters kept their heads and moved forward with courage and discretion, and in 1833 the Congregational Union came into being. Its early years were difficult, dogged by financial difficulties, but as the century progressed the Union and the annual May Meetings gained a higher profile, until by the end of the century it was hard to imagine how Congregationalism had existed without it.

# 1832-1914 - a time-chart

| Date | Politics / National | Congregationalism | Presbyterianism | Churches of Christ |
|---|---|---|---|---|
| 1833 | Irish Temporalities Act<br>Oxford movement f. | | | <br>Peyton Wyeth visits England |
| 1836 | | *Congregational Hymnbook* | | |
| 1837 | | Algernon Wells first Secretary of Congregational Union | | Wallis f. *Christian Messenger* |
| 1838 | People's Charter | | | |
| 1841 | | Miall f. *The Nonconformist* | | |
| 1842 | | | | Churches of Christ in being in Britain |
| 1843 | | | The Disruption in Scotland | |
| 1844 | | Miall f. Anti-State-Church Society | *Declaration of Independence* of the Presbyterian Church in England | |
| 1847 | | | United Presbyterian Church f. | Alexander Campbell visits Britain |
| 1848 | Revolution in Europe | | | |
| 1851 | Religious Census<br>Great Exhibition marks Britain's industrial ascendancy | | | |
| 1853 | Crimean War (to 1856) | R W Dale to Carrs Lane, Birmingham (to 1895) | | |
| 1854 | | | | David King's first general evangelistic tour |

| | | | | |
|---|---|---|---|---|
| 1857 | | Samuel Davidson resigns from Lancashire Independent College | *Paraphrases and Hymns* | |
| 1858 | | | Organ debate | |
| 1859 | Charles Darwin *Origin of Species* | | | |
| 1863 | | | Formation of the English Synod of the UPC | |
| 1868 | Gladstone's first administration (to 1874) | | | |
| 1869 | Matthew Arnold *Culture and Anarchy*<br>Disestablishment of Irish church<br>First Vatican Council | | | |
| 1870 | Forster's Education Act | | | |
| 1871 | University Tests Act | | | |
| 1874 | Disraeli Prime Minister | | | |
| 1876 | | Alexander Mackennal to Bowdon Downs (to 1904) | The union of the PCIE and the English Synod of the UPC to form the Presbyterian Church of England | |
| 1880 | Gladstone's second administration (to 1885) | | | |
| 1881 | | | | Christian Association formed |
| 1886 | Home Rule split | | | |
| 1889 | | Mansfield College opened | | |
| 1890 | Parnell case - 'nonconformist conscience' | | | |
| 1892 | Gladstone's last administration (to 1894) | | | |
| 1899 | Boer Wars (to 1902) | | | |
| 1901 | Victoria d.<br>Edward VII to throne | | | |
| 1902 | Balfour's Education Act - 'passive resistance' | | | |
| 1904 | Evan Roberts and the Welsh revival | | | |
| 1906 | Liberal landslide | | | |
| 1914 | Ourbreak of war | | | |

*John Laski, the minister of the Strangers' Congregation in London, receives his licence from Edward VI.*

# The Epistle of S. Paul the Apostle to the Romayns.

## The fyrst Chapter.

A 

Paul the seruaunt of Jesus Christ/ called to be an Apostle/ put a parte to preache ỹ Gospell of God / whiche he promysed afore by his prophetes in the holy scriptures that make mencion of his sone/ the whiche was begottẽ of the sead of Dauid/ as pertaynynge to the fleshe: and declared to be the sone of God with power of the holy goost that sanctifyeth/ sence the tyme that Jesus Christ our Lord rose agayne frõ death/ by whom we haue receaued grace and Apostleshippe/ to brynge all maner Hethen people vnto the obedience of the fayth/ that is in his name: of the which Hethen are ye a part also/ which are Jesus Christes by vocation.

To all you of Rome beloued of God & sayncttes by callynge. Grace be with you and peace from God oure father/ and from the Lorde Jesus Christ.

B Fyrst verely I thanke my God thorow Jesus Christ/ for you all because your fayth is published throughout all the worlde. For God is my witnes/ whõ I serue with my sprete in the gospell of his sone/ that without ceasynge I make mencion of you alwayes in my prayers/ besechynge that at one tyme or other/ a prosperous iorney (by the will of God) myght fortune me/ to come vnto you. For I longe to se you/ that I myght bestowe among you some spirituall gyfte/ to strength you with all: that is/ that I myght haue consolacion together with you/ through the commen fayth/ which both ye and I haue.

I wolde that ye shulde knowe brethren / howe that I haue often tymes purposed to come vnto you (but haue bene let hytherto) to haue same frute amõge you/ as I haue amõge other

t   of the

*The first page of the Epistle to the Romans in the Countess of Huntingdon's copy of the William Tyndale's New Testament.*

*Thomas Cartwright (1535–1603) – the first thinker to give a systematic exposition of presbyterian ideas in England.*

*Richard Baxter (1615–91). Puritan devotional writer and 'mere nonconformist' (from a 1702 abridgement of his life)*

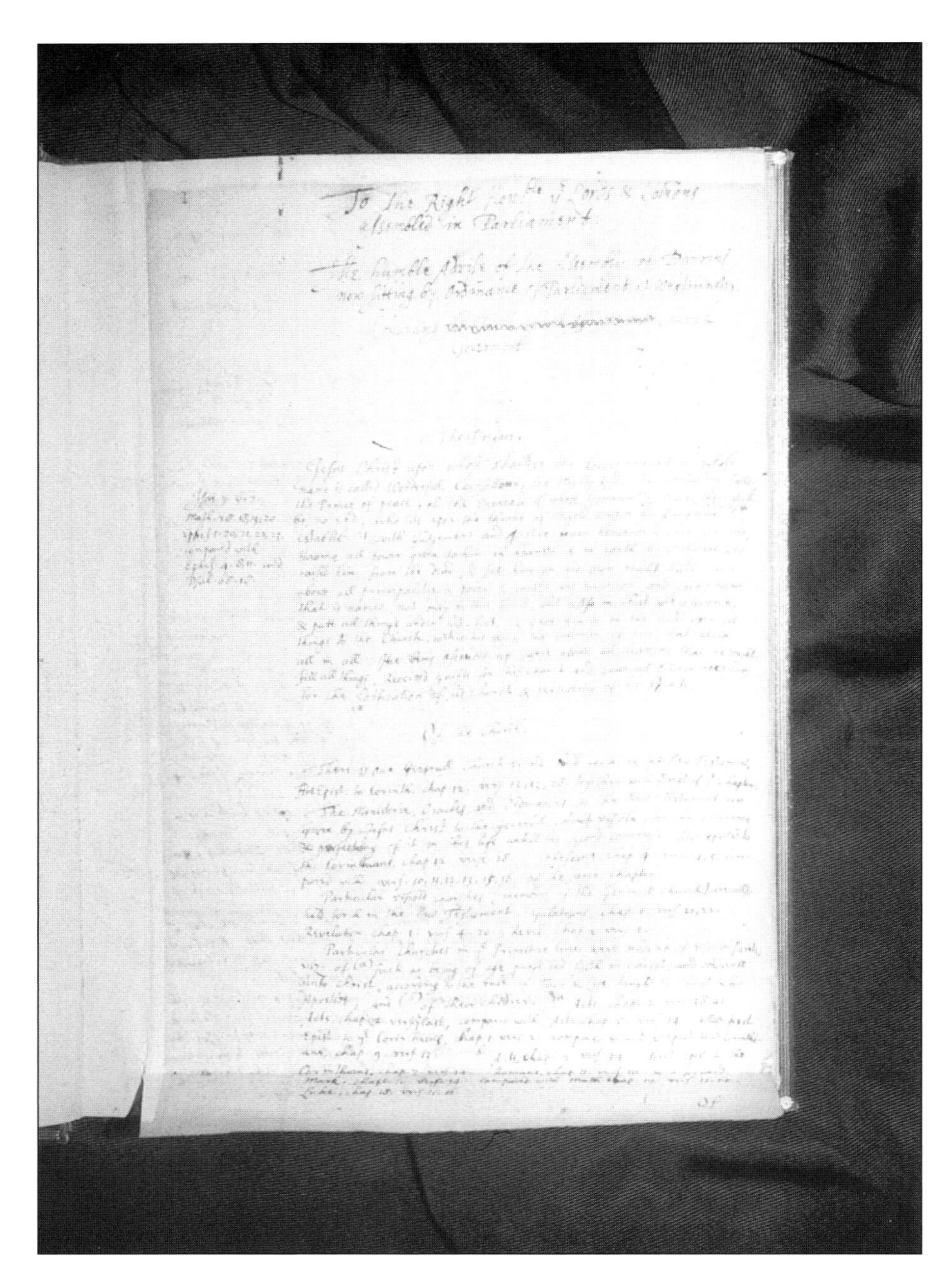
To the Right Hon.ble ye Lords & Commons
assembled in Parliament.

*The first page of the Westminster Confession.*

*John Owen (1616-83)*
*Congregationalist thoelogian.*

*Isaac Watts (1674-1748)*
*Congregationalist minister,*
*hymn writer and poet.*

*Philip Doddridge (1702-1751)*
*Congregationalist Minister, hymn writer and author.*

*Selina, Countess of Huntingdon (1707-1791) and her family.*

*Robert Barbour (1797-1856) Mancunian merchant, Presbyterian elder: one of the great lay benefactors of English Presbyterianism.*

*Hugh Campbell (1803-55) - the 'architect' of the Presbyterian church in England.*

*James Hamilton (1814-1867) minister of Regents Square presbyterian church, and prolific writer. [from the March 1897 edition of The Monthly Messenger]*

*R W Dale (1829-1895) Congregationalist theologian, and minister of Carr's Lane, Birmingham 1853-1895.*

*David King (1819-1894)*
*Part-time evangelist for the Churches of Christ.*

*The chapel of Mansfield College Oxford, designed by Basil Champneys.*

*John Wood Oman (1860-1939)*
*Presbyterian theologian, Principal of*
*Westminster College, Cambridge 1922-35.*

*William Robinson (1888-1963).*
*Churches of Christ theologian,*
*and the first Principal of*
*Overdale College, Birmingham*

*The Rt Revd John Huxtable addresses the uniting Assembly October 8th 1972.*

*Archbishop Michael Ramsay greets the Rt Revd John Huxtable at the thanksgiving service for the formation of the URC October 8th 1972, and pledges the Church of England's support for the further quest for visible unity.*

# REV. CONSTANCE M. COLTMAN, M.A., B.D

COWLEY ROAD CONGREGATIONAL CHURCH, OXFORD.

Mrs. COLTMAN is the elder daughter of Mrs. E. M. Todd and the late Mr. G. Todd, I.S.O., of Greenock. She was educated at St. Felix School, Southwold, subsequently becoming an Exhibitioner at Somerville College, Oxford, where she read Modern History for her Honours M.A. Degree. After a short period of social work she returned to Oxford in 1913 and entered Mansfield Theological College as its first woman student of Theology. Here she took the full three years' course of study, receiving the Certificate of the College and also taking the Degree of B.D. in the University of London.

The question of the ordination of women in the Congregational Church first came up some twenty years ago, when Miss Hatty Baker, for many years in charge of the Horsted Keynes Congregational Church, Sussex, applied to the Congregational Union for official recognition. The Union considered the subject and finally passed a Resolution that, other things being equal, there was no sex-distinction in spiritual matters. Though Miss Baker's own position remained the same as before, because she had not received the necessary training, she continued her work, and the question of recognition was dropped for the time being. The leaven was working, however, for when, in 1917, Mrs. Coltman applied not only for recognition but for full ordination her application was granted. She is thus the first ordained wcman in the Congregational Ministry.

She then became assistant Minister to the Rev. W. E. Orchard, D.D., at the King's Weigh House Church, London. The Rev. Claud M. Coltman, M.A., B.Litt., who studied at Mansfield College at the same time as Mrs. Coltman, was ordained with her at King's Weigh House, and the two were subsequently married. During their period in London they were in joint charge of the social and religious work at the Darby St. Mission, Wapping, undertaken by the King's Weigh House Church.

In 1924, after a brief period as co-pastors at Greville Place Congregational Church, Kilburn, London, Mr. and Mrs. Coltman were called to the co-pastorate of Cowley Road Congregational Church, Oxford, where they still officiate. They share together in the entire work of their ministry, including preaching and the administration of the Sacraments. They have two children.

Mrs. Coltman collaborated with Miss Maude Royden in writing "The Church and Woman" (James Clarke & Co., 6s.), and she has translated the books of *Ruth, Jonah* and *Obadiah* for the Adult School series of translations of the Bible into modern speech.

Mrs. Coltman is deeply interested in the prospects of women in the Ministry, and believes that very many women have a vocation to the cure of souls. She and her husband intend to further the Movement in every possible way. When the Fellowship of Women Ministers was founded in 1927 (see page 6), she was elected its President and remains in this capacity.

4

*A description of Constance Coltman , the first woman to be otrdained a Congregationalist Minister, from D M Northcroft's pamphlet Women Free Church Ministers (1926)*

# Chapter 5

# The nineteenth century

The nineteenth century was an age of massive expansion. From roughly the 1780s to the 1860s the British economy changed from an agrarian to an industrial base. The industrial revolution brought about an unprecedented demographic switch. In 1750 15% of the population lived in settlements of over 5,000 people. That rose to 50% by 1851 and to nearly 75% in 1901. The alteration in the country's economic base caused a shift in political power from the land to manufacturing industry and commerce. The new transport system of the railway linked cities and urban developments together, and from the 1860s onwards cities and suburbs were knit together by tram lines. The entire structure of living was altered for the majority of the population. Time began to be regulated by the factory hooter and transport timetables rather than the rhythm of day and night and the movement of the seasons. Gas light, and later electric light aided and abetted the process. Intellectually this was an age of excitement, unsettlement and possibility. The achievements of science applied by the genius of Victorian technologists and engineers like Brunel helped create a world in which anything seemed possible. The human ability to harness the forces of nature seemed limitless. It was a world of improvement, growth and optimism. The myth of progress swept all before it until it was shattered by the blood and mud of the trenches of the first world war.

Such expansion was costly. The wealth of the few was built on the labour of the many. Laissez-faire capitalism led to astonishing achievement, but also to the misery and squalour of the chaotic city with its filthy tenements and oppressive factories. The churches, like the rest of society, were caught up in the cruel and perplexing ambiguities of Victorian Britain. On the surface the life of the churches seems much like the life of the world that surrounded it. Church membership increased in numerical terms until the early years of the twentieth century, but the surface hid one of the most telling sea-changes in the history of western Europe. Historians have long noted that the ratio of Christians to the total population began to fall around 1840. In 1854 when the report on the only religious census ever to be taken in Britain was published, all churches had to face the sobering news that only 40.5% of the population were in worship on Census Sunday. There are arguments amongst historians and sociologists about the precise interpretation of that evidence, but it is clear that secularism had become a serious part of British life. People might still believe in God, might still view the world through Christian spectacles, but many no longer felt the need to belong to a Christian community and worship corporately.

The reasons for that are many and complex, and beyond the scope of this book, but it forms an essential back-drop for any understanding of the contemporary church. The sea of faith was beginning to ebb. The serious questioning of the nature of human knowing which had been raised by the philosophers of the Enlightenment, the development of history as a science which led to a re-evaluation of the Bible as an historical source, the discoveries of geologists about the age of the world and of biologists about the nature of human evolution, undermined old certainties and created an agenda with which thoughtful Christians still have to wrestle. The latter half of the century saw all denominations involved in a work of theological re-evaluation which frightened some and liberated others. Our own traditions were not immune. In 1857 Samuel Davidson (1806-1899) was forced to resign from the Lancashire Independent College because of the way in which he used historical science in his study of the Old Testament, but by the 1880s most Congregationalist scholars had abandoned their belief in the inerrancy of Scripture. In 1876 R W Dale (1829-1895) noted that one of the more striking features of theological life was the abandonment of Calvinism. Ideas of election and hell were being replaced by a new stress on the universal love of God which could brook no defeat. The Presbyterian Church of England, generally more conservative than the Congregationalists, revised its attitude to subscription to the Westminster Confession during the 1880s. New ways of doing theology and expressing the faith were struggling to birth. Our traditions made their own significant contributions. The work of Dale on the atonement and the nature of authority, of A M Fairbairn (1838-1912) in the philosophy of religion, and later of John Oman on the relationship between the grace of God and the workings of the human personality had a significance far beyond denominational boundaries.

The nineteenth century was of crucial significance in the shaping of all three denominations which came together to form the United Reformed Church. That slippery word 'denomination' is a nineteenth century construct. Its origins lie in the work of nineteenth century historians and sociologists, and refers to a religious organisation which is somewhere between a 'sect' and a 'church'. Those terms are used in specific and technical ways by sociologists. A sect is easily recognisable. It has hard edges. It is very clear about who can belong and who cannot. It demands allegiance to a clearly defined set of beliefs and practices. A 'church' is easily identified. The classical examples are national churches, like the Church of England and the Church of Scotland. They 'belong' to the nation, and all citizens are prospective members. Everyone who lives in a parish has the right to expect certain things from its parish church, like the right to be married within it. A 'denomination' lies in the middle. It has beliefs and conditions of membership, but it also has structures, and its edges are more of a permeable membrane than a brick wall. Believers can pass through the membrane - even in the nineteenth century Methodists could become Congregationalists and vice versa. Denominational structures as we understand them are the products of the early nineteenth century. In the eighteenth century the relationships between dissenting communions were far more fluid, and less centralised. Each of the strands which makes up the URC became a denomination in the nineteenth century. Each was shaped in significant and different ways.

Congregationalism, with an honourable history reaching back to the reformation in ideology and to 1662 in structure, was part of, and was shaped by, the dynamic resurgence of nonconformity in the wake of the Evangelical Revival and the Industrial Revolution. Presbyterianism, which had almost faded from the English scene in its orthodox form, spilled over the border from Scotland, and became a distinctive part of the panorama of Victorian Christianity, a reluctant form of dissent, pitched between establishment and voluntaryism. The Churches of Christ, founded to foster unity in the 1820s, ended the century a distinct denomination.

## Congregationalism and nonconformity

The report on the 1851 religious census was published in 1854 by the civil servant in charge, Horace Mann. Historians and sociologists have pored over his work and analysed its strengths and shortcomings, which are many. Most are agreed that if it is used to show the relative strengths of denominations, it is fairly reliable. A detailed recent study has suggested that it might be marginally unfair to nonconformity by 1-2%. The census showed that 7,261,032 people attended a place of worship on Census Sunday, out of a total population of 17,927,604 - 40.50%. Of that 40.50%, 3,773,474 (17.58%) were Protestant nonconformists, and 21.05% attended the Church of England. The religious affiliation of the English people was divided roughly into two - about 51% of church attenders were to be found in the pews of their parish churches. 44% were in chapels of varying kinds, but principally Methodist, Baptist and Congregationalist. The remaining 5% were Catholics (about 4%), Jews (less than 1%), Presbyterians, and members of small and statistically insignificant denominations.

Mann's report revealed some interesting contours on the nonconformist map. First, rather mundanely, it showed that nonconformity was an intensely varied experience. It contained churches which traced their ancestry to 1662 and earlier - Baptists, Quakers, Congregationalists. Then there was Wesleyan Methodism, the institutional result of the Evangelical revival. Methodism had shown a distinct ability to fragment in the aftermath of Wesley's death. The census revealed that denominations had different demographic patterns - for example, Methodism was to be found *'in its greatest force'* in Cornwall, Yorkshire, Lincolnshire, Derbyshire, Durham and Nottinghamshire, whereas *'the Independents (Congregationalists) flourish most in South Wales, North Wales, Essex, Dorsetshire, Monmouthshire and Suffolk.'* Secondly, his statistics showed how rapidly the denominations had grown since 1801.

More detailed work on the census returns produced even sharper lines. It showed that nonconformity provided the majority of churchgoers in the larger towns. That continued to be the case for the remainder of the century. An analysis of twenty-eight large towns in the 1880s has revealed that 58% of churchgoers were nonconformists. Catholics were the largest grouping in Liverpool. In London, Birmingham and Portsmouth church and chapel were equals, but in most other cities nonconformity was dominant. In rural areas the census showed that, broadly speaking, the Church of England was numerically dominant in the agrarian south, from east Devon to Kent, but in west Devon and Cornwall, in some of the Midlands belt, in east Lancashire, Yorkshire and the north-east, varying types of nonconformity predominated.

If Mann's figures are set beside an earlier set of figures produced by Dr John Evans, a Presbyterian minister, in 1715, the growth of all sections of nonconformity, but particularly of Methodism, becomes clear.

| | 1715-1718 | % of population | 1851 | % of population |
|---|---|---|---|---|
| Congregationalism | 59,940 | 1.10 | 655,935 | 3.88 |
| Baptists | 59,320 | 1.09 | 499,604 | 2.95 |
| Arminian Methodism | | | 1,489,194 | 8.80 |
| Calvinistic Methodism | | | 19,270 | 0.11 |
| All nonconformists | 388,120 | 6.21 | 2,878,543 | 17.02 |

There was a remarkable shift in religious behaviour in England between 1718 when dissenters made up just over 6% of population and 1851 when they accounted for 17.02% of a population which had grown by 67% over the same period. The most dramatic change was that Methodism didn't exist in 1718. It was a product of the Evangelical Revival, and by 1851 its various brands made it by far the largest part of nonconformity. The second obvious feature is that the Congregationalists and Baptists had grown exponentially in the same period. Nonconformity as a whole had grown by an astonishing 751%!

For comparative purposes, presbyterianism has been omitted from the table. Evans was a Presbyterian minister. In 1718 the Presbyterians were by far the largest nonconformist grouping - just over half English dissenters in 1718 called themselves 'presbyterians', but by the time of the 1851 census they had almost disappeared - a generous 'guesstimate' would be that there were *c.*20,000 presbyterians in England in 1851 (there are no definite statistics). That bald statistic reflects the transformation of presbyterianism into Unitarianism during the eighteenth century. From the middle of the eighteenth century some Scots migrated south, principally to London, the North East, the cotton towns of the north west, and Merseyside, and they brought their own very Scottish brand of presbyterianism with them. They are the presbyterians mentioned in Mann's census, and they were eventually to form the Presbyterian Church of England, which became part of the United Reformed Church in 1972.

That points to the second major factor in the growth of nonconformity - population movement. Scots came south from the mid eighteenth century onwards because there were jobs - in London, in the shipbuilding yards of the north-east and (much later) the south coast, and in the merchant houses and factories of 'cottonopolis' - Manchester, Liverpool, Cheshire. That was symptomatic of the much larger population shift from village to town occasioned by the industrial revolution. Some students of nineteenth century nonconformity speak of it 'baptising' the industrial revolution. They mean that nonconformity was able to respond to the movement of the population. Nonconformity was voluntaryist. It was financed by its members, and all it needed to do to found a chapel was raise the money and employ a builder. It had a geographical, legal and economic freedom which the Church of England simply did not have. So, as the vast parishes of the north, which contained such manufacturing villages as Halifax and Huddersfield and Ashton-under-Lyme and Leeds, grew, nonconformity was flexible enough to be able to move with the people. It was these places that provided the context for the Victorian chapel and its rich and frequently misunderstood culture. As nonconformity moved with the population flow, it caught the hopes and aspirations of those with whom it moved - artisans and entrepreneurs, new industrialists and local capitalists who both created and benefited from the industrial revolution. Chapel was the natural milieu for Titus Salt, the Bradford alpaca prince, for the carpeting Crossleys of Halifax, and the shirt manufacturing Bannermans of Manchester. But it wasn't just a northern world. In Norwich, the Colman mustard dynasty was solidly nonconformist, as were the Courtaulds in Essex, the Prentices whose gun-cotton factory dominated Stowmarket, and the jam making Chivers' of Histon near Cambridge.

The industrial revolution had created a new class. Economic power had shifted from the land to the factory. That was the economic reality behind the break up of the ancien régime of the long eighteenth century. Society had changed dramatically. The growth of dissent was mirrored, albeit rather more palely, in the growth of Catholicism, whose numbers seem to have risen from about 1720, accelerating rapidly from 1770 onwards - prior, be it noted, to the massive influx of Irish immigrants. Local studies would suggest that this too was because a higher proportion of Catholics were concentrated in areas of the country most affected by socio-economic changes - for example, Lancashire and Durham.

Nonconformists and Catholics were both dissenting communities. Their growth was part of the undermining of an established order criticised by radicals and acutely anxious of the threat of revolution. The two 'arms' of English dissent had much in common, not least a shared exclusion from the heartlands of the civil, political and educational life of the nation. The Corporation Act, passed by the Cavalier Parliament of 1660 had decreed that all mayors, aldermen and councillors and borough officials should swear loyalty to king and take the sacraments according to rites of the Church of England. It effectively excluded nonconformists from the political life of the nation. The Test Acts of 1673 and 1678, passed during the Exclusion Crisis, stated that all civil and military office holders should accept the royal supremacy, receive communion according to Anglican rites, and forswear the

Catholic doctrine of the mass. Those were the acts that marginalised Roman Catholics. The severity of these laws had been slightly assuaged in 1719 and 1727, but dissenting campaigns to have them repealed had been rejected in 1736 and 1739, and in 1753 Lord Hardwicke's Marriage Act had tightened restrictions on dissenters by requiring them to be married according to the rites of the Church of England.

At the beginning of the nineteenth century then, dissenters were unable to play their part in the civil and political life of the nation. They could not sit as magistrates. They could not be members of municipal corporations. Their children could not be educated in grammar schools. They could not enter Oxford University - subscription to the Thirty-Nine Articles was demanded at matriculation, and although they might be educated at Cambridge they could not graduate because subscription was demanded at graduation. Those were England's only two universities, so exclusion from them effectively stopped them joining any of the learned professions. They were unable to be married according to the rites of their own churches, and they had to be buried according to Anglican rites, albeit in their own churchyards from 1809. Their own chapels were voluntaryist, but they also had to pay for the upkeep of their parish churches and sometimes the building of new Anglican churches through the payment of church rates.

This was part of the panoply of measures which protected the Establishment. Clearly, it could not last. As the Chiverses and Courtaulds and Colmans became people of power and influence, it was clear that religious disabilities could not continue. By the end of the century all disabilities had been erased from the statute book. That was a considerable achievement. It began in 1828 when Wellington's Tory government repealed the Test and Corporation Acts, and the following year passed the Catholic Emancipation Act. It was a legislative sign that the old order was passing, even if it produced protests from the reactionary. W F Hook, the High Church vicar of Leeds wrote in 1831, *'I refer our calamities to the repeal of the Test Act; for then the state virtually renounced any connection with religion'*. J H Newman, one of the leaders of the Oxford Movement, wrote to his mother in 1829 listing the enemies of the church - the uneducated masses, the Utilitarians, useful knowledge people, the schismatics, the Baptists, the high circles in London, the political indifferentists. A few years later when much needed reform of Oxford University was mooted, Newman railed against the foundation of University College London - *'It does seem too bad that the dissenters are to take our titles. Why should they call themselves MA except to seem like us ? Why not call themselves licentiates & c ?'* The economic, social and religious revolution of the late eighteenth and early nineteenth centuries seemed full of threat. Regicide and abomination was only an English Channel away in France.

The great reforms of 1828-1832, culminating in the Reform Act, decisively fractured the ancien régime. Nonconformity lived with the consequences, one of which was the breakdown of the rigid class structure of eighteenth century England into a more subtly differentiated but none the less real and difficult set of social mores. It has been estimated that all but 8.6% of nonconformist strength came from the 67% of society which fitted between the professional classes and the unskilled - the godly poor who might become the better rich. Writing in 1937 towards the end of his life the Liberal MP Augustine Birrell, the son of a Baptist minister, looked back to the 1860s:

*...in those days to have been a nonconformist in England entailed many consequences of a separatist nature. Like Offa's dyke, it marked a boundary, hard to jump over. Not only different places of worship - but different friends, different schools, different books, different habits of life. The great public schools, the Universities, Scholarships, Fellowships etc. lay as much out of the ordinary track of the Nonconformists as the Opera House in Paris, or a Court Ball at the Palace of St James, or other suchlike places.*

Nonconformity cannot be understood apart from that background. It was that common experience of being second class citizens that welded the disparate dissenting community into an homogeneous whole in the nineteenth century. Neither the differences between chapels nor their unity should be exaggerated. Nonconformists were held together by the common political agenda of the fight for their civil rights, but chapel culture was scarcely the same in rural Suffolk as it was in suburban Manchester. Congregationalism had considerable rural strength, often in areas where the Church of England was equally strong. In such areas a nonconformist chapel could become the focus of a counter-culture, for the influence of the squire and the vicar did not reach so readily within its walls. The 'church-chapel conflict' which was such a marked feature of Victorian life was often at its sharpest in villages. Rural chapels provided the space for an independent voice, the chance of free expression, and an arena for responsibility. Skills learnt in such places were easily transferable to the world of politics. Historians of rural dissent have pointed particularly to the close relationship between Primitive Methodism in Norfolk and Suffolk and the rise of the early Agricultural unions. Other studies have highlighted the survival of folk-religion and superstition in more isolated areas. Some chapels managed to support a minister, others relied on lay-preachers. Few were wealthy, and the financial plight of some ministers in the days of a market economy in ministry could be heart-rending. William Whitehouse (1780?-1847), the minister of the small Presbyterian chapel at Spittal on the banks of the Tweed, whose stipend was £80 per year, wrote in the last months of his life to thank a benefactor who had sent him £10 - *'..it is of double value by comming (sic) so opportune - when it is now about two months before we receive any thing of salary, and when we had no other resource, but to beg of our creditors to supply us with food; when they have already too much in their books against us...'* His was an extreme case, but it was not untypical.

What united the extremes of wealth and poverty, city and village was nonconformity's common agenda. The community was simultaneously rising to respectability and campaigning for justice. If respectability required elegance, taste and learning, the fight for rights demanded brashness, political nous and an insistent voice. The cultured, like Thomas Binney (1798-1874) the minister of Kings Weigh House Congregational Church, protested that their dissent was purely religious. Binney thought differences in church government to be a secondary concern, and continually argued that the role of dissent was to call the Church of England back to its true mission. Throughout the 1830s, he was an advocate of joint communion services as the first step on the road to unity. However, the voice of the provinces had a very different tone.

We turn first then, to political nonconformity. In 1841 Edward Miall (1809-1881), Congregational minister turned journalist and later Liberal MP for Rochdale, founded *The Nonconformist.* Through its pages he campaigned relentlessly for an end to religious disabilities and the disestablishment of the Church of England - *'a Counterfeit Church - an image carved with marvellous cunning, tricked out in solemn vestments, a part woven by human fancy, a part stolen from the chest of truth.'* Hidden behind the rhetoric was the principle of voluntaryism - the belief that all religious organisations should be supported by the people, not state aid. Miall pursued it relentlessly. His Anti-State Church Society of 1844 became the Liberation Society, the most successful pressure group in Victorian England. In the 1850s and 60s it spearheaded the campaign for civil liberties and disestablishment. Congregationalists were by no means united in their support of Miall. In 1841, the same year that Miall founded *The Nonconformist*, the Congregational Union (which had been formed in 1833) put out a statement protesting that its dissent was religious, not political, and in 1848 a speaker at its Leicester meeting was told that only a few Congregational ministers had joined the Anti-State Church Society. However, the mood was swinging in Miall's direction.

The nonconformist political voice was the voice of the disadvantaged, its method concentration on issues rather than party loyalty. Given their agenda, it was only natural that nonconformists should find the Whig and Liberal tradition congenial. There was a clear correlation between religious affiliation and political activity in Victorian England. The secret ballot was not introduced until 1872, and analysis of poll books prior to 1872 reveals the overwhelming preference of dissenting ministers and Catholic priests for Liberal candidates. The number of nonconformist MPs rose steadily throughout the latter part of the century. When Miall became MP for Rochdale in 1852 he was one of thirty-eight nonconformist MPs. After the Liberal landslide of 1906 there were 180. An analysis of the religious affiliations of the candidates in the 1900, 1906 and 1910 elections shows that 64% of Anglicans stood either as Conservatives or Liberal Unionists, whereas 91% of nonconformists stood for the Liberals or Labour. Again, there was denominational variation - Baptists, Congregationalists, Quakers and non-Wesleyan Methodists were almost invariably Liberals, but Wesleyans, Unitarians and Presbyterians counted a larger proportion of Unionists in their number.

The history of the nonconformist-Liberal alliance between 1830 and 1914 was neither smooth nor uniform. Wesleyan Methodism had an ambivalent relationship with the Church of England which made it more sympathetic to the Tory cause than the generality of nonconformists. The Liberals and the nonconformists fell out in the late '30s over education policy, and disillusion set in again in the early '60s. It was not until William Gladstone's (1809-1898) administration between 1868-86 that nonconformity began to have a modest influence on national party policy, and their revolt over the 1870 Education Act showed once again how easily they could slip back from party solidarity to denominational defensiveness. Gladstonian Liberalism was an alliance of conflicting interests, of which nonconformity was just one, albeit a powerful influence. Irish campaigners for home rule were another. Their political muscle and their willingness to use it ruthlessly made them far more significant. The 1874 election returned 58 Irish Home Rule MPs, and their influence rose steadily in the late 70s and early 80s under the leadership of Charles Parnell. By 1886 he had convinced Gladstone of the rightness of Home Rule, and Gladstone was returned with a mandate to deliver it in 1886. It split the Liberal Party. Joseph Chamberlain (1836-1914), president of the Board of Trade, a Birmingham based Unitarian, led a secession of Liberal Unionists. It was a tragedy for Liberalism, but also for nonconformity, for it divided its political base and sounded the death knell for serious hopes of disestablishment.

Most nonconformists remained true to Gladstone, who was revered almost to the point of worship. Most supported his continued attempts to produce Home Rule, although prior to the 1886 split Ireland had not been a major nonconformist concern. The Methodist leader, Hugh Price Hughes (1847-1902), then turned the Irish question into a moral crusade. Gladstone eagerly took up the tune, telling a Congregationalist audience in Nottingham in 1887 that Home Rule was a cause which *'the Prince of Peace it may be hoped will recognise and bless'*. The cracks were showing though. Anxiety rippled through the denominational assemblies of 1888. The Conservatives accused nonconformists of politicking. They were debasing religion in the arena of party politics. In 1890 political naïvety led to political tragedy. Nonconformists regarded politics as a branch of morality rather than an exercise in statecraft - an attitude *The Times* christened 'the nonconformist conscience.' In 1890 two moral crusades collided. Charles Parnell (1846-1891), the great leader of the Irish Home Rule Party was cited as the co-respondent in a messy divorce case, and nonconformist passion for sexual purity met the campaign for Home Rule head on. The Baptist leader John Clifford (1836-1923) stated the problem succinctly - *'Men legally convicted of immorality will not be permitted to lead in the legislation of the Kingdom.'* In an attempt to save Home Rule, Gladstone ditched Parnell. It didn't work. Parnell's Irish supporters deserted him in droves, and with Parnell's fall went the main chance of solving the Irish problem in nineteenth century politics. It was not that the nonconformists were hypocritical - they were never that. They were naïve. Cut off from the political life of the nation for nearly two centuries, they did not understand the meaning of expediency, nor the plain truth that in politics the end sometimes does indeed justify the means. The Parnell case laid that bare. It was the legacy of 'second-classness', of expressing life in negatives because that was the only way to produce positive action - against oppression, against the establishment, against Anglican influence in education and so on.

Political nonconformity fell with Home Rule, and like Humpty Dumpty, it couldn't be put back together again. Ironically, the roots of the downfall lay in the very success of the campaign mentality in removing disabilities. It was a legacy that sat at odds with the rise to respectability. If we are to catch the flavour of chapel culture, we have to appreciate that paradox. In 1869 Matthew Arnold (1822-1888), poet, school-inspector and lingerer on Dover Beach launched a famous attack on nonconformity in *Culture and Anarchy*. He gently mocked the strident tones of provincial nonconformity. He took up the motto of Miall's *The Nonconformist, 'The dissidence of Dissent and the Protestantism of the Protestant religion'* and mocked with elegant, measured distaste:

*There is sweetness and light, and an ideal of complete harmonious human perfection... 'Finally, be of one mind, united in feeling' says St Peter....do not let us fail to see clearly that their idea of human perfection is narrow and inadequate, and that the Dissidence of Dissent and the Protestantism of the Protestant religion will never bring humanity to its true goal...Look at the life imagined in such a newspaper as* The Nonconformist *- a life of jealousy of the Establishment, disputes, tea-meetings, openings of chapels, sermons; and then think of it as an ideal of human life completing itself on all sides, and aspiring with all its organs after sweetness, light and perfection.*

His poet's ear had caught to perfection the shrill, campaigning voice of provincial dissent. What he missed was the quieter cultured tones of the rise to respectability, the subtle melodies of suburbia. Congregationalism was changing. A measure of the change is to be found in its attitude to worship. The Evangelical Revival had lent a new immediacy to preaching and prayer, but in the average chapel in the early nineteenth century the sermon still lasted on average an hour and a half, and prayers were extempore and expected to last about half an hour. In 1846 the Congregational Union pleaded that the 'long prayer' should not include every subject under the sun! Ordinations were great feasts, and expected to last five hours with two good sermons. All the evidence suggests that hymn-singing in the early years of the century was not good, and it was not until 1836 that *The Congregational Hymnbook* appeared, taking congregations into realms other than Watts and metrical psalms. However, this was the age of the word, of the newspaper and the serial novel. Thousands thronged to hear their favourite preachers. What was telling and disturbing was the low ratio of communicants to hearers. Preaching was a hair's breadth from religious theatre, and the idea of the church as a disciplined company gathered together under God's Word was in danger of drifting away.

In the latter half of the century worship underwent a transformation. A new awareness of the beauty of holiness was abroad in all the churches of England, reflecting both the prevailing 'romanticism' and pseudo-medievalism of Victorian art, and the influence of the Oxford movement which had radically challenged existing styles of liturgy within the Church of England. Psalm chanting was adopted in some churches. The number of hymnbooks multiplied, as did the catholicity of the hymns sung. By the end of the century Congregationalists sang the hymns of the Unitarian James Martineau and the Roman Catholic J H Newman with as much gusto as those of Watts and Wesley. Unaccompanied singing was slowly replaced by the use of organs, although not without much trouble and anxiety in the process. Ministers experimented with new forms of worship. Some, like

Thomas Binney and John Hunter at King's Weigh House, explored the use of set liturgies. Anthems, creeds and collects began to find their place. Others exploited 'new' festivals - church and Sunday School anniversaries, flower Sundays and so on, all in the quest for relevant and accessible worship. Worship was becoming much more than a sermon. The plain meeting house style of architecture was swept aside by an all-consuming passion for Gothic. Congregationalism was re-discovering itself not as dissent, or nonconformity (both of which are negative - definitions of 'what we are not') but as a Free Church - free of state control, yet part of the church universal. The transformation of worship, architecture and style co-incided with the drift of urban populations from the city to the suburb.

Suburbia depends on the urban, distanced from the smoke yet unable to wriggle free into rural idyll. It is a landscape of paradox, yet undeniably, at its best, it was a place where those Arnoldian virtues of sweetness and light were readily to be found. In late Victorian and early Edwardian England suburban culture was chapel culture. In the last twenty years historians have deepened our understanding of this frequently misunderstood and easily dismissed world. Research into families and cousinhoods that stretched across England and beyond has enhanced our appreciation of the way nonconformity challenged the existing order, and brought a new class into power and influence. We will borrow one example from that wealth of work.

The William Armitages of Manchester were members of a large and influential Congregational family, woven together (inevitably) by cotton. The family had established themselves in Mancunian religion and politics in the 1830s. William Armitage lived in Bowden, the most genteel and relaxed of Manchester's suburbs. In spite of splendid parish churches, it was chapel country, its streets full of Wesleyan, Presbyterian and Congregational Gothic. The William Armitages went to Bowden Downs Congregational, set well back from the road with a sweeping gravel drive to accommodate the carriages of the cotton kings. It was a well-crafted, stylish building with tasteful stained glass and a stone pulpit, which was complemented by a communion table of cedar from Lebanon and olive wood from the Mount of Olives. Its minister from 1876-1904 was Alexander Mackennal. He was a Cornishman of Scottish descent, educated at Glasgow and the Congregationalists' Hackney College. Powerful, energetic, cultivated and polished, he became an ecclesiastical statesman of international repute during his ministry at Bowden - Chairman of the Congregational Union of England and Wales in 1887, Secretary of the International Congregational Council in 1891, a leading advocate of Free Church Union, and the drafter of the constitution of the National Free Church Council which he served as

Secretary for six years. He was a force to be reckoned with in the councils of Congregationalism. His conduct of worship was thoughtful, incisive, tasteful, even artistic. A suburban minister of a suburban people, his salary reached the astonishing heights of £1,000 a year (the same as that of a cathedral canon). His son was educated at Rugby. His sister was headmistress of an exclusive girls' school in the Midlands.

Most of William Armitage's eleven surviving children married into other cotton dynasties. One, Elkanah, equally predictably, was called to ministry, but had the good sense to marry the daughter of a Liverpool cotton-broker. A Trinity graduate with a first in Moral Science (philosophy), he noted in his diary in 1874, *'Went up to Cambridge for the opening of the new chapel there on the 19th. Dr Raleigh preached. Lady Reed and many more were at Cambridge. Annie and Amy and Caroline Bulley at Merton.'* It is a diary entry which is worth exploring in detail, for it takes us to the heart of the obverse of Miall's strident, shrill provincialism and gives the lie to Matthew Arnold. Raleigh was a London pulpit giant whose son, Sir Walter Raleigh was to become Professor of English at Oxford. Lady Reed was the wife, daughter and sister of Liberal and Dissenting grandees. Annie was Elkanah's sister, Amy and Caroline his sisters-in-law. They had been pioneers at what became Newnham College Cambridge, and his wife Ella had been one of the first 5 students there. The chapel was Emmanuel Congregational Church in Trumpington Street, an eloquent symbol of barriers being broken, a stone sacrament of the abolition of university tests. Its architect was Cubitt, its scale grand, a University Free Church, a Puritanism renewed and refined. In 1906 Oliver Cromwell arrived in stained glass. Fifteen years on Elkanah, now minister of Rotherham, was in Oxford to witness more barriers being broken. Ever since the abolition of university tests, Congregationalists had wanted a college at Oxford. In 1889 they achieved it, and Spring Hill College, Birmingham became Mansfield College, Oxford. Provincial Congregationalism had taken on Oxford, the Arnoldian dream, and won. Almost a tenth of the £50,000 raised came from the Armitages. The architect was the then little known Basil Champneys, preferred in competition to Alfred Waterhouse, but best admired for the delightful Dutch revival buildings of Newnham. Mansfield, in the best Gothic style, was a quiet triumph. The chapel at Mansfield, a bold fugue in stained glass, statues and wood, was described by a German visitor as *'the most catholic place in Oxford'*. And Catholic is absolutely right. In the stained glass Christ enthroned in glory rules above the saints, and the saints include Wiclif and the Edwardine reformers, but nowhere is there a hint of the reformation of Henry VIII. Here is a different heritage, a new catholicity. Hidden away in a side aisle even Plato has a window for himself. It was impressive.

Enrique Rylands, third wife of John Rylands, and now his widow, a generous contributor to Mansfield, was deeply impressed by Champney's work, and she decided to employ him to build a fitting tribute to her husband in his native Manchester. He did, and the result, John Rylands University library, was a fitting union of mercantile endeavour and religious vision, reformed and liberated by education. And so it all fits together - the suburban villas of Bowden, the warehouses of Ancoats, the olive wood and cedar of Lebanon, the Word preached and applied by the Mackennals and Elkanah Armitages, Emmanuel Congregational Church, Newnham and Mansfield. Nonconformity had become the Free Church. The alternative society had come of age. It is perhaps fitting to add a footnote. In September 1879 Elkanah's younger brother married Josephine Melland, daughter of the local doctor, in Rusholme Congregational Church, Manchester. Two years previously Josephine's elder sister had married, in the same church, a rising young barrister called Herbert Henry Asquith.

The history of that suburban Congregational family lays bare the dynamics of change which were operating in nineteenth century nonconformity. The social structure of the country was changing. Industrialisation had moved power from the land to the factory, the population from the country to the town. Congregationalism played its part in bringing the new industrialised class to power.

## Reluctant nonconformists - the re-birth of English Presbyterianism.

English Presbyterianism almost died out in eighteenth century. All that remained were a few isolated congregations. In the far north, however, between the Tyne and the Tweed were some indigenous English *classes* or presbyteries, served mainly but not entirely by Scottish ministers. The religious boundary between England and Scotland would have been better drawn at the Tyne than the Tweed. Nonetheless, those congregations in small towns like Wooler, ports like Berwick and villages like Crookham nestling under the Cheviots, were a reminder of and link with the presbyterianism of Baxter and 1662. Tradition says that is their root. Documentary evidence demands that we be more circumspect - we have no evidence before the early eighteenth century.

An earlier historian of English presbyterianism once described the denomination as a threefold cord. What were the strands and how were they woven together to form one rope? The first strand was formed by the indigenous presbyterianism of the far north. The other two strands are Scottish.

Historians have made much of the Irish contribution to the expansion of Catholicism in England during the nineteenth. Less well known, but of considerable significance, is the Scottish contribution to English church life. In 1801 0.6% of the population of the English counties had been born in Scotland. By 1891 that figure had risen to 1% - something like 250,000, and the total population of Scotland was only four million. The Scottish contribution to theology is well known. Two of English Congregationalism's finest thinkers - A M Fairbairn, the first Principal of Mansfield, and P T Forsyth, Principal of Hackney College and the most significant British theologian of the early twentieth century, were both Scots, but neither were presbyterians. Less appreciated is the Scots general contribution to English nonconformity, for many chose to attend free churches, which were closer to the ethos of their homeland, than their sister establishment church with its prayer book and bishops.

Others were denominational tortoises, bringing their religious homes on their backs, and because they did that they brought the divisions of Scottish presbyterianism into English ecclesiastical history. The second strand of English Presbyterianism was made up of congregations in connection with the Church of Scotland. Between 1820 and 1840 emigré entrepreneurs, engineers and financiers came south to 'cottonopolis' (Manchester, Liverpool and the North West) and London. They brought their church life with them, and it was their dynamism and passion that brought new presbyterian structures into being in London and the North-West initially. The third strand of English Presbyterianism has its roots in Scottish dissent. During the eighteenth century the Church of Scotland suffered two secessions over patronage - the right of patrons to appoint ministers versus the rights of congregations to choose them - in 1731 and 1751, creating the Secession and Relief Churches. The Secession church showed a marked tendency to split, and did so twice more before the fragmented bits began to re-unite in 1820. Scottish dissenting churches were to be found in England. They too were emigré communities. Most eventually gathered into one church, the United Presbyterian, in 1847.

The emigré churches shared a common cultural agenda. The Scotch Church, London Wall in the city of London, wrote to '*..the Scottish people, residing in and about the city of London*' exhorting them to '*..try and forget that we are in London where there is no neighbourhood, and fancy we are back again in Scotland where everybody knows everybody else.*', and James Hamilton (1814-1867), minister of Regent Square, rebuilding the ministry there after the heretical crash of Edward Irving (1792-1834), wrote with journalistic romanticism, '*let us here in this busy, tumultuous Babylon, sit down for a while* *and remember our Zion.'* They gathered together to form small kirks, to bring a little bit of Scotland into the busy squalor of industrial England. As such, they were similar to other churches of exiles - the Huguenots, the Welsh speaking chapels - and yet they were distinctively different. Scotland and England shared the same language (just!). The Scottish population of England was large, and presbyterianism had at least some English roots - the Westminster Confession and Westminster theology were English productions, albeit with Scottish prodding and help. That lent a studied ambiguity to English presbyterianism. Was it to be, as one of its eminent ministers suggested to a Scottish Assembly, *'a nursing mother to your orphan children'*, or should it be part of a concerted Protestant mission to the English cities? The history of modern English presbyterianism can be told in terms of that tension between Englishness and Scottishness.

Until 1844, the second strand of English presbyterianism, that in connection with the Church of Scotland, considered itself part of the Scottish establishment. There had been a synod in England between 1826-1831, consisting of nineteen congregations in the far north. It was small, unsanctioned by the Kirk, and weak - a federation of individual churches rather than an organic synod. In 1833 Lancashire presbytery was formed in the vestry of St Peter's Square Church, Manchester. It was a decisive moment because prior to that the churches of south Lancashire had been the responsibility of the unwieldy presbytery of the North-West of England, whose centre of influence was in Cumberland. The switch represented the birth of a new style of presbyterianism - urban, dynamic, mercantile, vigorously pro-Scottish. It was exemplified by Robert Barbour (1797-1885), partner in Barbour brothers, merchants, later High Sheriff of Cheshire and the greatest and most generous benefactor of English presbyterianism. The Clerk of the North-West of England presbytery, Walter Fairlie (1787-1856), the minister of Carlisle, had written to Barbour lamenting that:

*...our Liverpool friends are either so indifferent about the prosperity of the Established Church of Scotland in their kingdom, or they are so engrossed in their own affairs that they will not enter into the work with activity and zeal. But I trust that once you good people of Manchester get your congregation properly formed and your temporalities finally adjusted, we may find in you...firm, generous and zealous advocates for the Presbyterian Interest in this Kingdom, in connexion with the Established Church of Scotland.*

His trust was not misplaced. The first act of Lancashire presbytery was to petition the General Assembly to alleviate the anomalous position of the Presbyterian churches in England by granting them representative status.

The 1835 Assembly responded by suggesting that the English presbyteries form themselves into one or more Synods. The process did not run smoothly. The indigenous *classes* of the far north felt that their trust deeds would not permit their Trustees and Elders to enter into such a relationship with the Kirk. More perceptively, they doubted the Kirk would allow such a relationship. However, Mancunian orthodoxy prevailed, and an English Synod was formed in 1836. It hid severe divisions, and might have been more successful if Barbour and his friends had been less determinedly myopic and more statesman-like. Barbour's new minister, Alexander Munro (1796-1869), used all his diplomatic skill later in the decade to bring the English presbyteries together into one Synod. Relations with the Kirk remained problematic in the late 1830s and early 1840s. English presbyterianism was a side-show in Scottish ecclesiastical affairs, which were dominated by the 'Ten years conflict'. The issue of patronage, a running sore in Scottish church history since 1690, which had been the prime cause of the secessions of 1731 and 51, erupted again. There were two protest movements in the 1830s against the power of the state in church affairs. Parliament's perfectly sensible attempt to reform the Anglican church in Ireland, the Irish Temporalities Act of 1833, led to the Oxford movement in England, a high-church re-definition of the nature and spiritual independence of the Church of England. In Scotland, the Evangelicals concentrated their attention on patronage. The underlying difficulty was that the right of patrons to appoint ministers was enshrined in law. In two celebrated cases it became clear that church and state were on a collision course. The eventual result was the disruption of 1843, which split the Church of Scotland in two, the continuing establishment and the Free Church of Scotland. These were not good years to be running a campaign for the inclusion of the English churches in the Scottish establishment. However, the English presbyterians pressed the great and the good north of the border. It was all to no avail.

Assembly put up the constitutional argument. They had no authority to act in England. It would be an abrogation of their duty to the state to sanction two establishments in England. However, sharp legal minds pointed out that there was no foundation to this thesis in the acts of parliament which governed the affairs of Kirk. The root of the problem was that the English case had been subsumed in the wider battle for freedom from English interference in Scottish affairs.

There was though, one voice in England raised consistently against the all-powerful Mancunian orthodoxy of Scottish unity. Hugh Campbell (1803-1855), minister of Ancoats, a pernickety, precise scholar and church lawyer, was a clear minded observer of the church scene. He had been the first in Scotland to predict publicly that the Oxford movement would result in conversions to Catholicism. He was later to become the English Synod Clerk, the architect of the English church's independence and the Professor of Church History and Jurisprudence at the English Presbyterian College. At the 1838 Synod he insisted that his dissension from the motion to seek union with the Church of Scotland on the grounds that it would be '..*unconstitutional of the Church of Scotland to grant and injurious to this church to accept of, the union prayed for.*' His vision was of an English future for the church. Between 1838 and 1844 he virtually invented the concept of English Presbyterianism. He distinguished sharply between presbyterianism and its Scottish manifestation, a distinction which eluded most of his contemporaries. He saw clearly that English presbyterianism could only live in England by becoming an English institution.

*You will have noticed Moderator,* (he told the Free Church Assembly in 1845), *I desire to be recognised in this house distinctively as an English Presbyterian, a descendant and representative of the English Puritan divines. Scotchman though I be by what has been termed the accident of birth, - attached though I am to my native land with all the enthusiastic affection of a Scottish Highlander, yet, as an ecclesiastic, I am in heart and soul with all the warmth and devotion of my nature, a member of the English Presbyterian Church.*

Such a view gained in popularity after the disruption. In 1838 though, he had been a voice crying in the wilderness.

The disruption spelt the end of establishment dreams for the English presbyterians. South of the Tweed the disruption produced a united church. There were seventy-two congregations in England in 1843. Of the seventy-two ministers in pastoral charge, thirty-six left for vacant parishes in Scotland, and one was dismissed on a disciplinary charge. Thirty-three remained to serve the English church. In 1844, meeting in Synod at Berwick, the English Presbyterians declared their independence and the Presbyterian Church in England came into legal existence. Hugh Campbell drafted the declaration. At roughly the same time he was the catalytic thinker in the process that produced the English Presbyterian College in 1844, for an English Church needed English ministers, and English ministers should be trained in England, not Scotland. The following year he was one of the founders of the *English Presbyterian Messenger*, a further attempt to consolidate the English future of presbyterianism.

In 1844 the Presbyterian Church in England was a small church with a large vision, full of confidence about its possible place in the English scene. Just as the Free Church was an alternative establishment in Scotland, so English presbyterianism could be a bulwark against the rising tide of Popery and Puseyism which was infecting the Church of England. That was absurdly unrealistic - England was not Scotland, and the tide of financial generosity which swept the Free Church into permanence and pervasiveness in Scotland could not be matched in England. The church grew rapidly though, from *c.*15,000 members in 1850 to 29,351 in 1875, some 153 congregations. However, in spite of the fact that the umbilical cord had been severed by the disruption, the English child still looked anxiously to its Scottish parents, and it remained a Scottish church. There is, as one would expect a rough correlation between the curve of the graph of Scottish emigration to England and the growth of the church. The evidence is difficult to measure precisely. Census figures only give details of the place of birth. But are children born in England to true-blue Scottish presbyterian parents English or Scottish - spiritually and emotionally rather than legally that is? A moment's reflection on the passion of the New York Irish shows the subtlety of the question.

From independence in 1845 until union with the English Synod of the United Presbyterian Church in 1876, the Presbyterian Church in England lived in the tension between 'Scottishness' and 'Englishness'. Every aspect of church life was affected, from the supply of ministers to the provision of hymnbooks, from the use of organs to schemes for union. The tale is worth tracing.

Barely two months after the disruption a meeting was held in Scotland to celebrate the bi-centenary of the Westminster Assembly. A book of papers, *Essays on Christian Union* was published as a result. After reading the book Dr Patton of New York suggested a convention of Protestant churches to take a stand against Catholicism. After much discussion, a preliminary meeting was held in Liverpool in 1845 which brought together the cream of British Evangelical church leadership. It explored two visions of union - that between individual Christians, and co-operation between denominations. The first strand resulted in the Evangelical Alliance, which became polemical and defensively anti-Catholic. What has rarely been noted is the presence at Liverpool of presbyterian leaders, north and south of the border, dissenting and Free Church of Scotland. Amongst them was James Hamilton, who was to convene the Presbyterian Church in England's union committee 1854-7 and 1862-7, and Thomas M'Crie (1797-1875), who brought his Original Secession church into union with the Free Church of

Scotland in 1852, and later, as Primarius Professor at the English Presbyterian College, was to have a significant influence on the ecumenical direction of the Presbyterian Church in England. The missionary task in the godless city of London demanded an ecumenical future, Hamilton told the Liverpool conference. Hamilton was a remarkable man. He allowed Arminian Wesleyans and even Anglicans to occupy Regent Square's pulpit - scandalising his more conservative brethren, including M'Crie.

In 1849 the presbytery of Cumberland transmitted an overture to Synod to take steps towards union with the fifty-eight Presbyterian dissenting congregations in England. Synod divided into 'pro-English' union liberals, and 'pro-Scottish' anti-union conservatives. Hugh Campbell, perceptive as ever, noted that the main hindrance was that the United Presbyterians had no body with which the Presbyterian Church in England could negotiate, for they were a Scottish church. The result was compromise, and the creation of a committee to look generally at union. However, the question was eclipsed in the 1850s by liturgical storms about the introduction of hymnbooks and the use of organs. To introduce a hymnbook was a departure from the purity of the Westminster standards which demanded that only the divinely inspired psalms of David be used, and the denomination was divided between those who felt that introducing a hymnbook would alienate faithful Scottish members, and those who felt that their peculiar Scottish liturgy was a grave hindrance to their English mission. Hamilton put it with characteristic wit:

*When the Englishman comes to hear my sermon, the first thing that he meets is a collection plate, which he regards as a phenomenon. He concludes he has been so fortunate as to arrive on the day of the annual collection, and puts a sovereign in - for the whole year, as he supposes. But he is somewhat taken aback when he returns next Sabbath and is again met by a collection plate. Then he hears the opening psalm, and imagines it is the dead march from Saul, or some funeral dirge, till he makes out the words:-*

*All people that on earth do dwell,*
*sing to the Lord with cheerful voice*

*And he thinks that the gravity of the people of Scotland must be something very awful if this is their cheerful voice.*

The debate raged on until the hymnbook *Paraphrases and Hymns* was introduced in 1857. The fury switched to the use of organs, and in 1858 the church was threatened by disruption. That jolted them back to their senses, and church unity found its way back on to the agenda. It was not a simple question, because the partners in the conversation were the United Presbyterian Church, the Presbyterian Church in England and the Free Church of Scotland. For a short while, it seemed as if a united British presbyterian church might emerge, and the Presbyterian Church in England was inevitably divided into those who looked for a wider British union, and those who thought the way forward should be an English union. The matter was actually solved by the cavalier way that the Free Church of Scotland treated her English little sister, and the end result was the union of the English congregations of the United Presbyterian Church (which had come together in an English Synod in 1863) with the Presbyterian Church in England in 1876.

At union the third strand in English Presbyterianism had 104 congregations in England, with a membership of 20,679. Because they were dissenters, the United Presbyterians had been the first to modify subscription to the Westminster Confession on the rôle of the civil magistrate in upholding religion because they naturally did not think that the state had a rôle to play. That modification, made in 1796 by the Antiburgher Synod, led to a new *Narrative and Testimony of Faith* which was made a condition of communion in 1804. This was probably the earliest instance of theological liberalism in nineteenth Scotland. Although trenchantly orthodox, the United Presbyterians and their ancestors had admitted the fallibility of the Westminster Confession, and not been afraid to alter it. The Secession churches spread rapidly through the Lowlands, and with commercial wealth came religious respectability, until by 1830, roughly one third of the Scottish population were dissenters. Its tone was distinctly liberal. The United Presbyterian tradition produced remarkable ministers like John Cairns (1818-1892) of Berwick - a theologian fluent in German and conversant with the flow of the continental debate as early as the 1840s, and William Graham (1823-1887), a lively, witty church historian who had studied under Neander, a man who wept at the beauty of the music of a Catholic mass at the Votif Kirche in Vienna when he visited it in 1879, and danced delightedly shouting *'Eureka, eureka, I've found it'* when he discovered Mozart's grave - a man of culture, catholicity and spiritual depth. From that liberal tradition eventually came English presbyterianism's finest theologian, John Oman.

A minor theme in the symphony, since 1845, was ecumenism. Hugh Campbell had predicted the union of English Presbyterians and English Congregationalists by 1900. He was seventy-two years out, but it is nice to think he would have rejoiced at the formation of the United Reformed Church, and at the distinctive contribution of Congregationalists and Presbyterians to the world church in the twentieth century.

## The Churches of Christ

One historian of the Churches of Christ began his study by pointing out how difficult it was to write a 'denominational' history of that part of Christ's church, for the Churches of Christ never set out to be a 'denomination', although, inevitably, they became one. In origin they are best understood as a 'movement', committed to the search for unity. The Churches of Christ, like the Congregationalists and the Presbyterians, do not look back to one founding figure as Methodists, for example, look back to John Wesley.

The early history of the movement revolves around the career of an Irish presbyterian minister, Thomas Campbell (1763-1854). Scottish presbyterianism suffered many schisms in the mid eighteenth century, and those schisms were exported to Ireland and England, where they made little sense. Campbell was a minister of one of those dissenting presbyterian churches - the Anti-Burgher Secession Presbyterian Church in Ireland, at Ahorey, near Armagh. He was an open-minded man who tried to heal the rifts between the presbyterian churches of Ireland, but his efforts met with little success. Thomas's son Alexander (1788-1866) eventually followed him into the ministry in America. Like many ministers in the early nineteenth century, they combined ministry with school-teaching. Thomas opened a school in Rich-Hill, near an Independent church, which was closely associated with Scottish Congregationalism through the work of the Haldane brothers, the founders of Scottish Congregationalism. The Campbells developed friendly relations with their Independent neighbours. In 1807 Thomas emigrated to America. Alexander was set to follow him, but by the accident of shipwreck, he found himself in Glasgow the following year where he was deeply impressed by the ministry of Greville Ewing, the minister of the Independent congregation at Glasgow Tabernacle, particularly by the congregation's practice of weekly communion. He became steadily more disillusioned with presbyterianism, and in 1809 he and his family set sail for America, to join his father. To his amazement and delight he found that his father's spiritual journey was leading him in the same direction. Thomas had continued his ecumenical ways, allowing all presbyterians to receive communion in his congregation. He had been censured by the Secession Presbytery of Chartiers in Western Pennsylvania for so doing, and had left the church to continue an independent ministry. In the same year Thomas Campbell and his sympathisers formed the Christian Association of Washington, Pennsylvania.

It was at this point that he produced his *Declaration and Address*, which set out the principles which had led him to forsake his church. It is rather a long document, but at the heart of it were thirteen moving and prophetic propositions, the first of which determines the structure of the rest:

*That the Church of Christ upon earth is essentially, intentionally, and constitutionally one, consisting of all those in every place that profess their faith in Christ and obedience to Him in all things according to the scriptures, and that manifest the same by their tempers and conduct, and of none else, as none can be truly and properly called Christians.*

Disunity, he stated in proposition ten, was '*..a horrid evil...It is anti-Christian, as it destroys the visible unity of the Body of Christ; as if He were divided against Himself, excluding and excommunicating part of Himself.*' Churches, he claimed, must obviously exist locally and separately, but there '*ought to be no schisms, no uncharitable divisions between them.*' Such unity could only be accomplished by an agreement that nothing '*..ought to be received into the faith or worship of the Church, or be made a term of communion amongst Christians, that is not as old as the New Testament.*' Unity was to be found in Scripture.

Alexander Campbell was deeply impressed and decided to devote himself to the work of this new movement. Such vision was ahead of its time. It soon became clear that the other churches were not interested, and in 1811 the Association became a church. Between 1811 and 1833 Alexander Campbell's thinking developed in two important directions. First, he became convinced that Christians were not bound by Mosaic law, and that weakened his understanding that paedo-baptism was analogous to circumcision. That led towards a belief in believers' baptism, and to closer relationships with the Baptists. Secondly, he became more doubtful of the value of creeds because it seemed to him that the Bible should be the only source of Christian doctrine because God's revelation was to be found there and there alone. At this point in British and American church history most Baptist churches were Calvinist in theological tradition, and they valued creeds. They therefore became suspicious of Campbell's position, so the Campbellites and the Baptists drifted apart.

In the summer of 1833, a member of Campbell's congregation, Peyton Wyeth, a young artist, visited a Scotch Baptist church in Finsbury Square in London. He explained to one of the elders afterwards that he was looking for a church like the one he had come from in Pennsylvania. He felt he had found it in that Scotch Baptist congregation, and he was admitted to membership. That leads us to the second source of the 'movement'. The Scotch Baptists were unlike the English Baptists. Their roots are to be found in one of the many secessions from the Scottish presbyterians of the eighteenth century. In 1730 John Glas (1695-1773) was deposed from the ministry of the Church of Scotland because he doubted the Scriptural basis of the Kirk's understanding of civil polity. The Glasites (also known as the Sandemanians after Glas's son-in-law, Robert Sandeman (1718-1771), who shared in the work with him) set up churches in Scotland on independent, congregationalist principles. It was never more than a small movement. In 1763, Archibald McLean and Robert Carmichael left the Glasite congregation in Glasgow, of which they had been members, over a point of church discipline. As they studied Scripture, they too became convinced of the believers' baptist position, and formed the first Scottish Baptist chapel, in Edinburgh.

The Scotch Baptists were a distinctive group. Like all Scottish Protestants, they were deeply influenced by the Calvinism which was enshrined in the Westminster Confession, but they were opposed to any idea of a national, established church (like the Glasites) and organised their churches on a congregational basis. Their ideas of church practice were similar to Campbell's - Scripture was the only possible source for that. They therefore had a number of elders or pastors in each congregation, rather than a single minister (which was the English dissenting pattern), practised believers' baptism and celebrated communion weekly. The movement expanded gradually in Scotland, but also spread to North Wales and England.

The Scotch Baptists and the Campbellites were clearly very similar. Both were 'restorationist' - that is to say, they sought a revival of New Testament Christianity. Wyeth acted as the intermediary who brought the writings of the Campbells to the attention of the Scotch Baptists, in particular to William Jones, a bookseller who was one of the elders of the Finsbury Park congregation. There were, however, significant differences. Like their American fellows, the Scotch Baptists were perplexed by Campbell's joyful rejection of creeds, and their doubts about his orthodoxy made the relationship short-lived.

However, Campbell's ideas continued to be influential in a variety of disparate places. The Scotch Baptists were severely exercised over the question of the Lord's Supper in the early nineteenth century. Could the Lord's Supper be celebrated if the elders were not present? It was a particular instance of a debate which has recurred often in church history - the relationship between church order and holy communion. Alexander Campbell had clear views about this. In his mind the Lord's Supper came first, and the community of believers should not be deprived of its benefits simply because the elder (or minister) was not present. Some of his writings setting out this position came to the attention of James Wallis, a member of the Scotch Baptist chapel in Nottingham. In 1836 that chapel was having a serious and divisive debate about the meaning of baptism, and their minister was so upset that he refused to attend worship on 18 December, and he instructed the church not to celebrate communion because of their disunity. That led to a split. Fourteen members, led by Wallis, met separately in the upper room of a warehouse and broke bread together in defiance of the minister. It was from that root that the first congregation of the Churches of Christ was created.

Campbell's influence was not limited to the Scotch Baptists. In Dungannon in Northern Ireland, a church was founded in 1810 by Robert Tener on the simple principle that all that was required of believers was a confession of faith in Jesus and baptism by immersion. His wife had been one of Thomas Campbell's pupils. John Davies, an unaligned preacher, who founded two congregations at Mollington in Cheshire was in correspondence with Campbell from 1835.

All these tiny groups in the almost unknown underworld of undenominational early Victorian nonconformity were held together by the thread of 'restorationism' - the belief that the life of the primitive church could be recovered and become the pattern for contemporary Christian living. That thread was turned to print in 1837 when Wallis published the *Christian Messenger or A Voice from America*, and it was this journal that brought together the disparate groups who had been captivated by Campbell's thoughts. His first publishing venture was Henry Grew's *A tribute to the memory of the Apostles* in the previous year. It was a book commended by Campbell, and condemned by William Jones of Finsbury Park. Wallis exploited the subscription list for that book and the network of Scotch Baptist chapels in his promotion of his new magazine. It was deliberately created to publicise Campbellite views. Wallis also undertook the publication of Campbell's works in England. The magazine brought the various congregations into a network, and largely through its auspices they grew together over five years to the point where they were able to hold a meeting in 1842 for fifty congregations. They met at South Bridge Street Hall, Edinburgh for business and the proclamation of the gospel. The congregations reported a membership of 1,233, and eight congregations did not submit statistics. The probable total membership would have been in the region of 1,600. They agreed that co-operation was justified, and, conscious of their evangelistic duty, passed a resolution that '*..this meeting deem it binding upon them, as disciples of Jesus Christ, to co-operate for the maintenance of evangelists to proclaim the gospel.*' By the end of 1842 the Churches of Christ were in being, although the name was not yet in wide use. It was at its inception a union of those who had been Scotch Baptists, and those who had not, and although transatlantic in inspiration, its ethos was British rather than American.

By the end of the century there were 176 Churches of Christ in Britain, and the total membership had risen to just over 11,000. The early years were ones of struggle. None of the movement's members could be called wealthy. Most were poor, some on the lower edge of the middle class, tradesmen and small manufacturers. Opposition was frequently encountered. This was a lay movement and clergy of various denominations were suspicious, if not hostile. In 1847 Alexander Campbell paid his only visit to England when he met with John Davies, James Wallis and other leaders of the infant British movement. The climax of his visit was the second Co-operation Meeting in Chester on 1-2 October. Twenty-six congregations were represented by messengers (delegates / representatives) and two by letter. In his address Campbell called their attention to the importance of co-operation in proclaiming the gospel, and the meeting agreed unanimously to support a general evangelist. They resolved to meet again in Glasgow the following year, thus establishing a pattern of annual meetings.

Between 1848-50 the movement was weakened by the activity of Dr John Thomas, an American doctor of adventist views, who thought that the revolutionary activity in Europe that year was a sign of the coming End. He attended the Glasgow meeting in 1847 as the delegate of the Lincoln church, and although the Cooperation Meeting judged that the congregation had acted injudiciously, the publicity strengthened his cause, and his writings and lecturing around the country undoubtedly weakened the Campbellite movement. Thomas's followers eventually adopted the name Christadelphians during the American Civil War. Spasmodically, for the rest of the century, the two groups tried to convert each other.

Between 1861 and 1892 the Churches of Christ experienced rapid growth - half the churches that were part of the Association of the Churches of Christ in the 1970s were founded during these three decades, and the centre of gravity of the denomination became firmly settled in the Midlands, Lancashire and Cheshire. Scotland, which had been of such significance in the early years, declined relatively in influence. The total proportion of the membership living in Scotland fell from just over a quarter in 1861 to about a fifth in 1892.

Numerical growth was inevitably accompanied by the development of denominational traits. A district association structure had begun to emerge in the late 1840s, and by the 1850s the church was able to support two full-time evangelists, J B Rotherham, an ex-Baptist minister, and David King (1819-1894), an ex-Wesleyan Methodist layman. That in turn produced a more aggressive policy of church planting. King, energetic, committed and inherently conservative on most issues, was a dominant figure in the Churches of Christ for the next thirty years. The Cooperation Meeting (the Annual Meeting) spawned committees. The General Evangelist Committee, which dealt with home mission, was the most significant. A Reference Committee was created in 1871. It acted almost like an executive committee, sifting requests for evangelistic help, dealing with communications to the Annual Meeting and handling matters between Annual Meetings. An official Yearbook appeared in 1886. The number of full-time evangelists multiplied from three to fifteen between 1861-92, and their work therefore became regionalised, and in some cases almost localised. It was a telling moment when King resigned in 1861 because the Annual Meeting asked him to work for a year in Liverpool, preferring to localise his work with the Birmingham District Association which had been created for that purpose. The long journey of peripatetic evangelist to settled minister had begun. As a growing church, the Churches of Christ played their part in the chapel-building bonanza of mid and late Victorian Britain, setting up a Chapel Building Committee in 1871 and the administrative machinery to finance it. They resisted the temptation of a theological college until Overdale was founded in 1920, but the pressure for professionalised training which led the Presbyterians to found Westminster and the Congregationalists to aspire to the dizzy heights of Arnoldian Oxford, led to the creation of a training course for evangelists which used secular educational institutions and the sharp and thoughtful mind of David King. Sunday Schools flourished, as elsewhere. By 1887 the denomination boasted 100 schools, over 1,000 teachers and 9,000 students. A Sisters' Meeting and a Temperance Meeting appeared alongside the Annual Meeting in 1880, although the Sisters' Committee didn't gain equal status to other committees until 1937, and women were not admitted to the ministry until 1973.

The British Churches of Christ in the late nineteenth century developed differently from the American Disciples (which is what the Campbellite movement became in America). During the 1850s rumours reached the British churches that the Americans were admitting the unbaptised to communion. They wrote to Alexander Campbell to seek clarification in 1859. He replied that there was no such custom, but not all believed him, and the question came to the fore in 1860 when an American evangelist, Henry Earl, arrived in Britain, with letters of recommendation from Campbell and other leading Disciples, practising open communion. An offer of further help from America was declined in 1865, when, under King's guidance, the British churches came down firmly (but not unanimously) on the side of closed communion.

The British also felt that the American church was slowly but surely departing from true restorationism in its attitude to ministry and church order. As G Y Tickle put it in a paper 1872, *'The college-educated pastor is fast assuming a sort of presidency over the elders as well as over the church.'* In 1875 the Americans formed a Foreign Missionary Society, and Henry Earl let it be known that he would like to return to England as a missionary. Unfortunately the British churches had not been consulted. He began his work in Southampton, and was remarkably successful. His methods came under scrutiny from his British colleagues, whose noses were not a little out of joint. David King and others led the opposition. It had little effect and in 1878, Marion Todd, another American evangelist, arrived in Chester. There had been no Church of Christ in Southampton, but there was in Chester. It was on its last legs, and it scented the possibility of new life and threw itself behind the new work. That encouraged Timothy Coop, a Wigan clothing manufacturer and one of the few truly wealthy members of the British churches to lend his support to the American effort, and he promised to add £1,000 to every £2,000 raised by the Americans for missionary work in England. W T Moore, minister of one of the most influential American congregations, returned to England with Coop, who established him as minister of Mornington Road, Southport. To other members of the British church, this seemed like direct competition, because there was already a church in Southport. The end result was that the American-founded churches formed themselves into a separate Christian Association in 1881, and for the next thirty five years the two organisations developed along parallel but separate lines. The irony of two restorationist movements, both pledged to the quest for unity on New Testament lines, yet refusing to have communion one with the other, was not lost on observers.

At the Jubilee Conference in 1892 King delivered a paper on the lessons of the previous fifty years. He was not slow to emphasise that the British churches had upheld the views of Alexander Campbell with faithfulness. It was a paeon to the past which he had done so much to create, but times were changing, and although his contribution to the movement had been incalculable, the future lay in different directions. He died two years later, and the Churches of Christ entered a new era.

## The Welsh experience

Nineteenth century Welsh nonconformity was the child of revivalism. It is possible that older dissent would have died out in Wales without the work of Howell Harris and Daniel Rowland in the Evangelical Revival. Their work caught the imagination of ordinary people, and they created a pattern of revivalism which was echoed in both local and national revivals in the late eighteenth and early nineteenth centuries, in David Morgan's great 1859-1860 campaign, in Richard Owen's work in north Wales in the 1880s, and finally in the extraordinary events of the 1904 revival which is associated with the name of Evan Roberts.

Revivalism expressed itself in itinerancy - 1800-1850 was the golden age of the Welsh itinerant preacher. Some, like the Independent William Williams (1781-1840) were men of astonishing rhetorical ability who attracted thousands of listeners. Others were pale imitations. The success of the itinerants was remarkable, and their work was given permanence in the chapel-building bonanza which changed the Welsh landscape in the early nineteenth century. By the time the 1851 religious census was taken there were 2,813 chapels in Wales. It has been estimated that one chapel was completed every eight days between 1800-1850. Chapel had become an expression of Welshness.

It did so because the growth of nonconformity co-incided with the industrialisation of Wales. As in England, nonconformity was mobile and adaptable to population shifts. The census also revealed a clear correlation between nonconformist strength and Welsh-speaking areas. Welsh was the language of many of the working classes, and the chapel was the creation of the people, a place where they could be themselves, linguistically, socially and politically, as well as spiritually. 83% of the population were in church on Census Sunday, and four in every five were to be found in chapels. One distinguished scholar of world missions has noted that Christianity was more successful in Wales than in any other European country.

In the latter half of the century nonconformity exercised a considerable influence on the nature of Welsh language publications. Numerical growth continued until 1907, when nonconformist membership peaked at 750,000. At least two-thirds of the Welsh-speaking populace were church members, so that in the early years of the twentieth century Welsh culture and chapel were virtually synonymous, although outreach to English speakers and English immigrants was also part of nonconformity's missionary drive. It had been deliberate policy in the Congregational church since 1853. Historians are divided in their interpretations of the intimate relationship between chapel and culture. Some consider it an expression of the essentially Christian nature of Welsh civilisation. Others argue that nonconformity effectively hi-jacked Welshness, thus preventing the emergence of a secular Welsh-language culture, making the English-language world the only escape for those who could not accept the values of nonconformity.

The identity of chapel and culture was so close that there was anxiety within the denominations about the distinctiveness of the Christian witness. That was the background to the remarkable events of Evan Roberts' 1904 revival which began in south Cardiganshire amongst the Calvinistic Methodists. Roberts was a twenty-six year-old ex-collier. His meetings were accompanied by the classical signs of charismatic renewal, eagerly chronicled by the South Wales press. Its effects were felt by all denominations, and its impact on society at large was telling - some rugby clubs disbanded, in many quarries and collieries the working day began with prayer, and in Glamorgan convictions for drunkenness almost halved between 1903 and 1906. The Apostolic Church and the Elim Movement both trace their origins in part to the revival, and its reach was international.

The chapels experienced a rapid growth in membership - about 80,000 - but most had fallen away by 1912. However, nonconformity was at the peak of influence in Wales at the time of the revival, and the campaign for disestablishment which had failed so lamentably in England in the 1880s was successful. The Royal Commission of 1906-10 discovered that the ratio of nonconformists to Anglicans was about three to one. A Disestablishment bill was introduced to parliament in 1912. After many twists and turns it received royal assent in 1914, but it was not implemented until 1920 because of the war. Ironically, disestablishment was liberation for the Church in Wales which has since made every effort to develop a clear Welsh identity. Welsh nonconformity, divided by language as well as denomination, has shared the same experience as English nonconformity - gentle but unremitting decline. However, the influence of chapel on the general life of the community was to remain a significant factor in Welsh culture until the 1950s.

## Conclusion

Victorian England had given decisive form to all three of our traditions. The Churches of Christ had come into being. They were a small denomination of just under 12,000 members in 173 churches at the turn of the century. The Presbyterian Church of England had a decidedly Scottish accent, yet it was determinedly part of the mission to England. They had just over 76,000 members in 318 congregations. The Congregationalists had 257,616 members in England and 147,513 in Wales. This was the golden age of nonconformity. The long decline of the twentieth century was not visible to contemporaries, although its roots are obvious to historians who have the benefit of hindsight. Ironically, the root of nonconformity's decline lay in its very success.

The campaign for justice and the rise to respectability had both been extraordinarily successful. By 1900 the civil disabilities which had made dissent a second-class sub-culture were a thing of the past. Arm in arm with liberalism, nonconformity had penetrated the centres of power and influence. Congregationalism in England reached its membership plateau between 1908-1916. It almost reached its 1908 height again in 1927, but thereafter it declined and has continued to do so. By 1914 it was clear that the confident predictions of nonconformity's bright future in the wake of the 1851 census were hopelessly off-centre. The reasons are many. Nonconformity was by nature a loose alliance of the disparate, often in competition rather than co-operation. Their political unity had been shattered by Home Rule. Secularisation was taking its toll. Anglicanism had recovered its poise and its mission, but perhaps too the social rôle of nonconformity was over. The traumas of industrialisation were fading. Society had been entirely re-aligned, and once you start sending your children to Rugby and Oxford, they show a marked tendency to become Anglicans. Nonconformists no longer, but Free Churches, heirs to the catholic faith, the future was to be one of healing the divisions of the past. Ecumenism beckoned.

# The twentieth century - a time chart

| Date | National / political | Church Affairs | URC traditions |
|---|---|---|---|
| 1901 | Victoria d. Edward VI to throne | | |
| 1902 | Balfour Education Act | | 'passive resistance' |
| 1904 | | Evan Roberts & Welsh revival | |
| 1906 | Liberal landslide | | |
| 1907 | | Formation of United Methodist Free Church | R J Campbell *New Theology* P T Forsyth *Positive preaching and the modern min* |
| 1910 | Edward VII d. George V to throne | Edinburgh Missionary Conference | |
| 1914 | First World War (to 1918) | | |
| 1917 | | | Constance Coltman ordained John Oman *Grace and Personality* |
| 1919 | Versailles Agreement | Barth' s commentary on Romans | Congregationalists introduce Moderators |
| 1920 | Disestablishment of the Welsh church | Lambeth Conference - *Faith & Witness of the church in this generation* | Overdale College f. William Robinson Principal |
| 1921 | | International Missionary Conference formed | |
| 1922 | BBC formed | | Sidney Berry Secretary of CU (to 1948) William Robinson *Essays on Christian unity* |
| 1924 | First Labour government formed | COPEC | |
| 1926 | General Strike | | |
| 1927 | | First World Conference on Faith and Order (Lausanne) | |
| 1928 | Prayer Book revision | | |
| 1929 | Wall Street crash | | |
| 1932 | | Methodist Union | Talks between Congregationalists and Presbyterians |
| 1935 | | | C H Dodd Norris-Hulse Professor at Cambridge |
| 1936 | George V d. Edward VIII to throne Abdication crisis | | |
| 1937 | George VI to throne | | |

| | | | |
|---|---|---|---|
| 1938 | | World Council of Churches formed | C J Cadoux *The case for Evangelical Modernism* |
| 1939 | Second World War (to 1945) | | |
| 1940 | | Formation of Free Church Federal Council | |
| 1941 | | | Churches of Christ Commission on ordination reports |
| 1942 | Beveridge Report | William Temple archbishop of Canterbury<br>Formation of the British Council of Churches | |
| 1944 | Butler Education Act | William Temple d.<br>Geoffrey Fisher archbishop of Canterbury (to 1961) | |
| 1945 | Dropping of atomic bombs<br>Atlee PM | | V2 rocket destroys Presbyterian offices<br>Joint Conference of Congregationalists and Presbyterians |
| 1946 | | Fisher's University Sermon | |
| 1947 | | Church of South India formed | Scheme of Union Congregationalists and Presbyterians |
| 1948 | | World Council of Churches constituted | Churches of Christ begin discussions with Baptist Union (to 1956) |
| 1949 | NATO formed | | |
| 1952 | George VI d.<br>Elizabeth II to throne | | |
| 1953 | | | Approval of Churches of Christ report on Work and Status of Ministry |
| 1954 | | Billy Graham's first visit to Britain | |
| 1955 | Beginning of commercial television | | |
| 1956 | Suez crisis | | |
| 1957 | MacMillan PM (to 1963) | | |
| 1958 | First race riots (Notting Hill) | | |
| 1961 | | Michael Ramsey archbishop of Canterbury (to 1974)<br>New English Bible New Testament | |
| 1962 | | Vatican II (to 1965) | |
| 1963 | | John Robinson *Honest to God* | Joint Committee of Congregationalists and Presbyterians meets |

| | | | |
|---|---|---|---|
| 1964 | | British Council of Churches Faith & Order Commission at Nottingham<br>Paul report on clergy pay and deployment | |
| 1966 | | Failure of Anglican-Methodist union | |
| 1967 | | Keele Conference of Anglican Evangelicals | |
| 1968 | Start of Troubles in Northern Ireland | | |
| 1969 | | | Scheme of Union Congregationalists and Presbyterians |
| 1970 | Edward Heath PM (to 1974) | New English Bible (OT and Apocrypha) | |
| 1972 | | | United Reformed Church formed<br>Conversations between URC and Churches of Christ |
| 1973 | Britain joins EEC | | |
| 1974 | Harold Wilson PM (to 1976) | Robert Runcie archbishop of Canterbury<br>Churches Unity Commission for England | Permission given for Churches of Christ Scottish congregations to negotiate with Scottish Congregationalists |
| 1976 | James Callaghan PM (to 1979) | | Proposals for union URC & Churches of Christ published |
| 1978 | | Churches Council for Covenanting formed | Dissolution of the Association of Churches of Christ |
| 1979 | Margaret Thatcher PM (to 1992) | | |
| 1981 | | Church of England turns down covenanting proposals | Union of Re-formed Association of the Churches of Christ and the United Reformed Church |
| 1982 | Falklands' War | | |
| 1989 | | Mrs Thatcher's speech to the General Assembly of the Church of Scotland | |

# Chapter 6

# The twentieth century

The history of the church in the twentieth century must be seen in an international context. This has been an international century. The two wars which divide the century into three convenient periods were world wars. The emergence of a communist state in Russia in 1917 would eventually lead to the polarising of world politics into 'East' and 'West' after 1945. The development of air transport, and the telecommunications revolution of radio, telephone, television and now the computer have shrunk the world, and lent a technological unity to cultural diversity. Seeing our planet from the moon has changed perceptions irrevocably. It has made us newly aware of the fragile and beautiful ecosystem which supports life on earth, and which binds the nations together in geographical and economic interdependence. Such major shifts in human culture have also affected the churches. As we shall see, the ecumenical movement pre-dated the growth of secular internationalism, but it was part of the same international vision which produced the League of Nations and the United Nations.

The missionary movement of the nineteenth century, caught in the inevitable ambiguities of empire and imperialism, made Christianity a world faith. Its legacy, one in which we can rejoice, is that the centre of gravity of world Christianity has moved from north to south during the twentieth century, to the churches of Africa and Asia. Our missionary societies played significant parts in that expansion, and in the development of indigenous churches. However, the growth of the faith in the south has been matched by its decline in western Europe. No amount of statistical massaging can disguise the massive decline of church attendance and church membership in the Protestant west during this century.

If internationalism and the communications revolution have been formative influences on the twentieth century, so too has war. Twentieth-century Christians have been confronted with the heart of darkness on a scale that Christians of 1850 could scarcely have begun to imagine. The American Civil War had marked the end of warfare as a localised, gentlemanly affair, confinable within specific theatres, obeying relatively well-defined rules of engagement. The Great War of 1914-1918 was the first truly European war, and the first technological war - for the first time in British history, an officer could enjoy breakfast in London and be in the trenches by dinner time. Innocence died at the Somme and on Flanders fields. The statistics are numbing even in the nuclear age - 60,000 dead on the first day of the battle of the Somme; overall the Central Powers lost 3.5 million men, the Allies 5 million. It was the systematic slaughter of a European generation. In 1911 there were 155 men aged between twenty and forty-five per thousand population in England and Wales. In 1921 there only 141. The number of women over fourteen per thousand population correspondingly rose from 595 to 638, and the number of widows per thousand population from thirty-eight to forty-five. Facile philosophies and theologies of the inevitable progress of humanity were rightly rendered speechless.

Twenty years later the Second World War unleashed destruction on a scale which we can still barely comprehend. This was total war. There were no 'civilians' who were beyond the reach of the power of destruction. The twisted horror of the Third Reich and the sheer ordinary, mechanical inhumanity of the holocaust stretch the historian's language to breaking point. Statistics have their own eloquence. Nearly six million Jews - almost the entire Jewish population of Europe - perished in the unspeakable violence of the holocaust. The gas chambers of Auschwitz were designed to dispose of 2,000 bodies every twelve hours. The atomic bomb had the capacity to obliterate a city in seconds. One of the American scientists who worked on the project, Robert Oppenheimer, did so for fear that Hitler would develop one first. On 16 July 1944 when a prototype was exploded in New Mexico, Oppenheimer quoted from the Bhagavad-Gita, '*I am become as death, the destroyer of worlds.*' On 6 August and 9 August 1945, the Allies dropped atomic bombs on Hiroshima and Nagasaki. Nearly 300,000 died. The world could never be the same again.

The experiences of war, genocide and the bomb have been powerful contributory factors in the failure of confidence in all forms of authority, political, social, and religious which has been such a marked feature of the post-war world. These have not been easy years for the churches of Western Europe.

For British Christians, whose churches were forged on the anvil of nineteenth century success, decline has been a new and sobering experience. Numerical decline, the growth of non-Christian and anti-Christian understandings of the universe, and consequent marginalisation from the centres of political power and intellectual influence have been profoundly difficult experiences. Decline and decay are not synonyms though. A loss of membership does not mean a loss of vitality, nor does it mean retrenchment. The twentieth century has seen remarkable achievements in theology, in Biblical study, in ecumenism and in social and political involvement. Our traditions have contributed markedly to those developments. "

## The 'silver' age

The churches of our traditions entered the century on the crest of a wave. Great preachers attracted huge crowds, and absolute church membership continued to increase. In 1900 the combined membership of our three traditions in England was 345,285. There were also 147,513 Congregationalists in Wales. 2% of the total population of Great Britain belonged to our traditions. Methodists accounted for another 1.83% of the population. 7.7% of the population took communion on Easter Sunday in England's parish churches.

There was, of course, considerable regional variation, and the strengths of the three traditions were different. In 1903 Richard Mudie-Smith's census of churchgoing in London showed that a tenth of London churchgoers went to one of the capital's 345 Congregational churches. 7,008 attended the two services at the City Temple alone on Census Sunday. However, London was not typical of the country at large. Congregationalism's great strength was also its underlying structural weakness. It boasted a huge number of churches, 1,980 of them outside the London and the Kent metropolitan area in 1903, 61% of which had a membership of less than 100. Only 3% of Congregational churches outside London had a membership of over 400. It was a denomination of small churches. Presbyterianism, on the other hand, had a carefully structured approach to church extension. It was mainly urban, and in 1903 only sixty of its 329 congregations (18.23%) had memberships of under 100, and most of them were either in the villages of Northumberland and Durham or were new charges. In 1903 the Churches of Christ had 183 congregations on its list, and a membership of 12,841. Forty congregations had a membership of more than one hundred. 78% were smaller than that.

Nonconformity was at the height of its power and influence. The old alliance between nonconformity and the Liberal Party had been grievously wounded by the split in the Liberal Party over Irish Home Rule in 1886 which had led to the defection of Joseph Chamberlain and the formation of the Liberal Unionists. It was not what it was, but it still had strength, as the 1902 Education Act showed. That was, as it were, the last battle of the Victorian 'war' between church and chapel and it was thoroughly anachronistic. Voluntaryism, the belief that the church ought to be independent of the state, was an essential part of the creed of Free Churchmen and women in the nineteenth century. All state support for churches was theoretically wrong. It was up to believers to pay for the facilities they needed. That belief lay behind the campaign for the disestablishment of the Church of England, and in nonconformity's resistance of compulsory church rates which had only been abolished in 1868.

Although all the churches were involved in the provision of education in the nineteenth century, the Church of England was by far the major player. Most Free Church people accepted that, and expected their own churches to provide schools for their children. Forster's Education Act of 1870 had made elementary education available to all, and after 1876 local authorities were able to make it compulsory in their areas. After 1891 it was provided free. Forster's bill envisaged state support for church schools where they existed, and the provision of Board schools (schools responsible to a local Board) where there were none. The bill was eventually carried against nonconformist opposition, largely thanks to the Cowper-Temple clause which ensured that no denominational catechisms would be used in religious education. Nonconformists, thereafter, developed a passionate enthusiasm for Board schools.

In 1902 the Conservative administration introduced an education bill (eventually known as the Balfour Act), which proposed the thoroughly sensible ideas of creating a new secondary school system and bringing all elementary education under the control of newly-created Local Education Authorities. Board schools were to be abolished, and church schools were to receive support from the rates. The bill also provided for local authority representatives on the management bodies of voluntary (church) schools.

The Act touched a raw nonconformist nerve, for it conjured up the spectre of the old world of social apartheid. Their vision of the educational future was that state provision would expand steadily whilst the voluntary sector diminished. Instead of that they were presented with an Act which made church schools permanent. It meant that Anglican, Methodist and Roman Catholic schools would be supported by their rates. As Robertson Nicholl, the editor of *The British Weekly* put it, it was *'Rome on the rates.'* The Act became law in December 1902. It was vigorously opposed by the Liberals and by the Free Churches who launched the Passive Resistance movement, which only commanded the support of a minority of members. Passive resisters refused to pay their education rates. In consequence some had goods distrained, and others were imprisoned. The force of feeling unleashed was a contributory factor in the return of a Liberal government in 1906, which included 185 nonconformist MPs. However, the new administration was unable to solve the schools' issue.

In 1910 the Liberals went to the country again to gain a mandate to curb the power of the Lords, which was solidly Conservative and had refused to pass both educational legislation and Lloyd George's budget. The old alliance between nonconformity and Liberalism had new heart whipped into it by David Lloyd George, the son of an intensely religious Welsh Churches of Christ home. His religious belief had largely evaporated into the steam of rhetoric, but it was a steam that powered the nonconformist machine. He channelled its energy with masterful touches, and for the last time nonconformity's support was an essential part of a Liberal victory. One of the new MPs was Sylvester Horne, minister of Whitefield's Tabernacle, London, who was returned for Ipswich. Not since the seventeenth century had a minister in pastoral charge sat in parliament. However, he made little impact on the House, and he resigned from Whitefields in 1913, dying suddenly the following year. The war spelt the end of what Lloyd George called 'the holy alliance' between nonconformity and Liberalism, although he did his best to resurrect it during his premiership, fêting the leaders of the Free Churches at Downing Street breakfasts in 1920. By then both he and they were fading shadows of a passing age.

Liberalism never recovered from the division between Lloyd George and Asquith in 1916. As the fortunes of the Liberal Party waned, those of the Labour Party waxed, and the 1920s saw a decisive change in the structure of English politics. 158 Liberal MPs were returned in 1923; forty in 1924. Nonconformity's political days were over. The 'old alliance' had long been disintegrating as nonconformity had developed. The political base of nonconformity split three ways. Some remained faithful to Liberalism. It is no accident that the predominantly Methodist county of Cornwall has a long history of returning Liberal MPs. In the south and the Midlands the suburban drift of Methodism and Congregationalism found its political home with the Conservative party of Bonar Law, Austen Chamberlain and Baldwin. That was only natural given Birmingham's support for Joseph Chamberlain in the Home Rule split. Others found their faith led them to the Labour Party. There was now no 'nonconformist interest'. The furious church-chapel battles belonged to a chapter of history that was closed.

All that remained were the theological grounds for nonconformity - a theological rejection of establishment (state 'control' of the church), a commitment to the freedom of God's people and a belief that the church should be ordered in particular ways. Those were important issues. They still are, and yet they were eclipsed by a new and overwhelming agenda - the mission of the church in what was fast becoming a post-Christian world.

## A theological excursus - Campbell, Forsyth and Oman

The far-sighted in Edwardian England had noted the underlying trends - the questioning of religious authority, the historical critique of Scripture, the advance of secularism, the rise of socialism, the quiet decline of working class church attendance, but given such growth and influence, optimism was still in the ascendant. The sea of faith might have begun to ebb in universities and intellectual circles, but that was not apparent to the ordinary Christian. Britain was still a Christian country, and this was the silver age of nonconformity. The large questions of the Enlightenment about the nature of human knowing, and the relationship between faith and reason, and the implications of new scientific knowledge about the nature of the universe for Christian orthodoxy, were receiving answers as Liberal Theology came to dominate the theological world of the late nineteenth century. Under the influence of Ritschl and Harnack, theological attention centred more and more on the quest for the teaching of the historical Jesus, and the recovery of the 'pure gospel' of love which he preached. Liberal theology is difficult to categorise. It was more of a mood than a movement, but it would be fair to draw attention to some dominant themes in late Victorian and Edwardian theological thought. It was rational. Liberal theologians therefore found themselves embarrassed by the supernaturalism of the miracles, and the doctrines of the incarnation and the trinity. They considered them to be the accretions of the early centuries of the church which obscured the beauty of the 'pure gospel'. Allied to rational method was a genuine belief in progress. Things were getting better all the time. Human beings were getting better all the time, growing into the mould of Jesus, the perfect human being. Sin was therefore a concept which was at worst redundant, or at best in need of radical re-definition. The role of the church was to strip away all the barnacles which clung to the ship of the gospel. What was needed was a return to the elegant simplicity of the gospel. Find out what Jesus believed, and believe it yourself. Liberal Theology could be summarised, in a classic phrase, as '*The fatherhood of God and the brotherhood of man.*'

Liberalism was an important factor in the theological development of our traditions. The careers of three ministers illustrate both its diversity and its impact. In 1907 R J Campbell, the handsome, charming minister of the City Temple, Congregationalism's foremost pulpit, published *The New Theology*. Campbell had gone up to Oxford a high Anglican, but discovered there a penchant for preaching, and under the influence of A M Fairbairn (1838-1912), the first Principal of Mansfield, he entered the Congregational ministry. After a wildly successful ministry in Brighton, he was called to the City Temple in 1903 as successor to the great Joseph Parker. He brought to that pulpit a blend of Christian socialism and philosophical idealism (idealism is a way of doing philosophy which emphasises the primacy of the mind, understanding and reason rather than experience) which he had imbibed at Oxford. He was a member of the Labour Party, and a friend of Keir Hardie (1856-1915) the founder of the Independent Labour Party and later leader of the parliamentary party. Campbell once refused an invitation to become the Labour candidate for Cardiff.

Theologically Campbell was an eloquent lightweight. In 1906 he addressed a group of Congregational ministers on *'The changing sanctions of popular theology'*. Somehow there was a press leak, and the *Daily Mail*, then the largest selling daily paper, picked up the scent of a story and sent a reporter round to Campbell. Campbell's eloquence was fired by the sight of the reporter's poised pencil, and he delivered himself of a tirade against traditional theology that was printed at length the following day:

> *..the New Theology brushes aside many of the most familiar dogmas still taught from the pulpit...We reject wholly the common interpretation of the Atonement - that another is beaten for our fault. We believe not in a final judgement but in a judgement that is ever preceding. We believe that Jesus is and was divine, but so are we. His mission was to make us realise our divinity and our oneness with God. And we are called to live the life which he lived.*

'Buddhism', said one correspondent to the *Mail*, 'spiritualism' said another. The Free Church press were incensed, and a campaign was unleashed against him, and there were dark mutterings of heresy trials. The book emerged the following year. It was slender, and its ideas can be fairly concisely stated. God and the Universe were one. Humanity was *'climbing the steep ascent towards universal brotherhood'*. Jesus was divine only in the sense in which everyone is divine. Sin was simply the failure to realise the potential within each person, and the church has no unique rôle because God is at work wherever people are trying to improve the human condition, most notably within socialism.

The book whipped up a storm within Congregationalism, and within weeks a series of essays, *The Old Faith and the New Theology*, edited by C H Vine, provided a response. The most telling critique came from the pen of P T Forsyth (1848-1921). Forsyth was Principal of Hackney College, and he was the greatest of twentieth century Congregationalist theologians. An Aberdonian, he had studied under Ritschl (1822-1889) in Göttingen, had a profound admiration for F D Maurice (1805-1872), and was all set to become an outstanding exponent of liberalism. However, his spiritual pilgrimage was eventually to take him in a profoundly different direction. Forsyth's theology was formed by eighteen years of pastoral ministry, in Manchester, Leicester and Cambridge:

*I could not contemplate conclusions'*, he wrote, *'without asking how they would affect these people, and my word to them in doubt, death, grief or repentance. In a word, I was driven to a change of front, though not of footing - to the preacher's and pastor's treatment of the situation, which is also the New Testament view, and which is different from the scholar's.*

Forsyth took on his journey the best of the liberal tradition - the demand for intellectual openness, the valuing of Biblical scholarship, the conviction that each generation had to do its theology afresh. He allied that to a breathtakingly perceptive analysis of the spiritual condition of the Western world. Whilst Campbell and others were confidently proclaiming the inevitability of progress and the goodness of humanity, whilst England was bathing in long, hot summers and there was honey still for tea at Rupert Brooke's Grantchester, Forsyth diagnosed a desperate sickness in western society, and in the western church. The question for him was one of authority, and he found that true authority in the gracious love of God seen in Christ's cross.

*God did not come'*, he wrote, *'to be seen but obeyed. The Christian answer is the cross of Christ. The nerve of Christianity is expressed in such a great and sweeping word as "Ye are not your own, ye are bought at a price."*

Forsyth's theology was an elaborate fugue on a few major themes - the holiness of God, the seriousness of sin, and the centrality of the cross. If liberalism was a programme devoted to getting behind Paul to re-discover the Jesus of history, Forsyth was devoted to showing that Jesus could not be properly understood apart from Paul. If liberalism believed that human beings were getting better all the time, and that sin was simply the failure to harness all human potential, Forsyth knew that the fundamental truth about humanity was sin, that canker of corporate corruption which creates the heart of darkness. Christ, said Forsyth, came to reveal not only God but sin.

The theology of its cure lay not in an unhealthy obsession with guilt, but in the vision of God's holiness. It was, after all, the holiness of God which convicted Isaiah of his sin. God cannot abide sin. God must judge it. That judgement is his wrath, which is but the obverse side of his limitless love. And to those who were bemused at the very idea of the anger of God, Forsyth replied, *'The love of God is not more real than the wrath of God. For he can be really angry only with those he loves. And how can Absolute Love love without acting to save ?'*

Forsyth's theology was a theology of the cross, for there he saw God intervening in history, precisely because of his holiness, to deal with the nature of sin. *'God did not punish Christ, but Christ entered the dark shadow of God's penalty upon sin.'* The world's reconciliation and its future flows from that work. It was the business of the church to proclaim that, and he was therefore a fierce critic of any church which trivialised its task and preferred the world's busyness to the language of Christ:

*The minister's study becomes more of an office than an oratory. Committees suck away the breath of power. Socialities become the only welcome sacraments. The tea-meeting draws people together as the communion table does not.*

The church was the great missionary to humanity - and the rôle of the individual preacher was to enable the church to preach. He had a profoundly high doctrine of church and sacraments - a deep sense of being part of the Great Church. He was scathing about the obstinate independence of some churches within his own Congregational tradition who did not see that the preacher's task was the integration of the small church into the great *'that he and it together may swell the transmission of the Word in the world. That is true Catholicism, the universalising of the universal Word.'* - and this was two years before the Edinburgh Missionary Conference of 1910 which is generally considered the start of the modern ecumenical movement.

In the years before the first world war, Forsyth was a voice crying in the wilderness. His writings were difficult, and not widely read. Only since the enormities of the Second World War have theologians come to realise his true stature, for in a remarkable way he anticipated the whole development of neo-orthodox theology which is associated with the name of the Swiss theologian Karl Barth (1886-1968).

The generous, optimistic belief in progress and the 'brotherhood of man' turned to ashes, or more precisely mud, on the battlefields of France. The first world war sounded the death knell for 'the New Theology'. However, liberalism was made of more sinew and muscle than is apparent in Campbell's writings. Its true stature can be seen in the work of John Wood Oman, who taught at Westminster College, Cambridge from 1907-35, and served as Principal from 1922-35. If Forsyth moved from his liberal roots to emphasise once more the holiness of God and the centrality of the cross, Oman's writings sought to explore the way in which God interacted with human life, accessible to human knowledge and experience, but never exhausted by it. - *'Laboratories and experiments for testing truth are various'*, he wrote, *'but the greatest laboratory is the world and the greatest experiment life. In them alone can we demonstrate God'*. Oman was the English translator of some of the work of Friedrich Schleiermacher (1768-1834) who is regarded by many as the 'father' of liberal theology. Schleiermacher argued that true knowledge of God began with a person's awareness or consciousness of being dependent on God. Oman's own work arose out of his engagement with Schleiermacher's thought, and developed in a highly individual way.

Oman has been described as a great 'religious' or devotional writer as well as a great theologian. Like Forsyth, his theology was rooted in the realities of pastoral experience - he had served as minister of Alnwick from 1889-1907 - and the realities of human living and the Christian pilgrimage are never far below the surface of his writing. Unlike Forsyth, his interest was not in the classical doctrines of the faith - the nature of Christ, the Trinity, and the atonement - but with how the work of God interacts with human experience. For Oman the natural and the supernatural, the sacred and the secular, were an indivisible whole. Religious truth was to be found in ordinary living. Like many liberal theologians Oman was captivated by the Christ of the synoptic gospels who illustrated the truth of God from *'..a varied secular procession of kings and slaves, and bailiffs and debtors, and farmers and fisher-folk, and housewives and children...'*

In his finest, last and most difficult book, *The Natural and the Supernatural* (1931), he laid out the two fundamental assumptions which underlay all his work. The first was the belief that the environment in which we live is both supernatural as well as natural. The supernatural environment cannot be 'proved', but it bears witness to itself and *'shines in its own light.'* The second, allied, belief is that human beings have the innate ability to understand that environment. The supernatural is, as it were, the part of reality which is God's realm, and it is as we encounter that part of reality that we learn more of God. If those assumptions receive their profoundest defence in this last work, they received their most popular and lasting treatment in *Grace and Personality* (1917). A distinguished contemporary reviewer called it *'one of the greatest treasures of theological literature'*. It is a remarkable and courageous investigation of the workings of God in the human heart. Grace, for Oman, was not a display of irresistible power over-riding the human will. As he pondered the realities of living, he concluded in a memorable picture that *'..what all life does say is that God does not conduct His rivers, like arrows, to the sea...'* Human water-engineering produces straight canals, nature *'with a picturesque circumambulancy...produces the river.'* If that was true of God's workings in the natural world, should it not also be true in the world of the human heart ?

The true nature of grace was like the relationship of a father and his children. At the heart of his theology is the belief that God is personal, and that people matter to God. That is why human freedom was so important for him. The parable of the prodigal son was one of Oman's favourite passages of Scripture, for in it he saw an image of God's parental care and attitude. Superficially, the father would have been wise not to give the younger son his inheritance, but the deeper wisdom was to acknowledge the son's right to be responsible for himself even if that responsibility was misused. The son has to realise his own folly, and make his own decision to return to his father.

Oman's God is a personal God, a God who deals with all his children as persons, not an absolute Ruler. Each one is valued and precious in God's eyes, and God chooses to exercise his power in care for each person in the crowd. That care, he suggests, is mediated through the whole of creation and all the experiences of life. He speaks of the *'curve of [God's] patient, personal wisdom encircling and embracing us and all our concerns.'* That is the nature of grace. Oman's God will never force an individual, or indeed the world, to forsake evil ways and turn to him. Rather, God will wait with infinite, patient love for the person to discover him and his will. In an arresting and moving phrase he explains, *'Power can only create a vast plaything, love can create a Kingdom of God.'* Evil and sin are not cauterised by the cross, as in Forsyth's theology. In Oman's thought, only a change in the human heart can change the world by freely accepting the divine order of love. The cross of Christ is therefore the supreme revelation of God's love. It is a laying bare of God's grace. The love of God cannot be defeated, even by the worst of human sin and evil. The resurrection is the great confirmation of God's power manifest on the cross.

Oman was not an easy thinker. Lesslie Newbigin remembers his lectures as 'obscure to the point of opacity', and F G Healey recalls a visitor saying that listening to him lecture was like 'watching a football match in a fog.' Great minds are not always easily understood as they grapple with the ultimate realities of life. What is heartening as our century draws to a close is that both Oman and Forsyth have recently been the subjects of new and appreciative critical studies. That in itself is tribute to the enduring significance of two of our traditions' finest thinkers, and to the depth of their thought and faith which still speaks to the human condition when so much else has perished in the fires of oppression and misery which have raged in our century.

## The First World War and its aftermath

The story of the churches and the first world war is not a glorious one. In 1914 the young poet Rupert Brooke (1887-1915) wrote, *'Now God be thanked who has matched us with this hour...'*. Most Christians shared his innocent euphoria. Many church leaders thought the war an opportunity to show a patriotism and a selfless love close, if not identical, to the Christian ideal of sacrificial love in the service of one's neighbour. When war was declared the Baptist leader John Clifford told his congregation that he had prepared a letter for the press advocating neutrality, but that he could not send it because this war was a fight between *'the forces of freedom and those of slavery...The progress of humanity in my judgement hinges upon this war...We were forced into it.'* That was in August 1914. The following month he was on the recruiting platform at the London Opera House. The nonconformist political tradition had been formed by specific issues - the fight for civil rights, one at a time. Their métier was hyperbolic political rhetoric, and it was a style which lent itself easily to the promotion of the war effort. Robertson Nicholl, leading Liberal, Free Church of Scotland minister, long-standing editor of the prominent Free Church journal *The British Weekly*, in his leading article of 3 September 1914 *'Set down my name, Sir'*, managed to invoke the two favoured gods of the nonconformist pantheon, Cromwell and Bunyan, on the side of the war effort, for *'Cromwell and his like [had] protected both culture and religion in their hour of direst need.'* That theme received a surprising twist in 1915 when the Primitive Methodist A T Guttery told the Primitive Methodist Conference that *'our fathers suffered at Smithfield...and slew the Stuart Kaiser at Naseby and Marston Moor.'* Quite apart from the spiritual gymnastics involved in a Methodist (even a Primitive) claiming the history of old dissent for his own, it was a mythic salving of conscience, a catharsis of jingoism - if the Kaiser was a version of Charles I then naturally all good nonconformists should rally to the flag.

There were, of course, those who had a sadder, more sober estimate of the necessity of war. Campbell Morgan, the minister of Westminster Chapel and the leading expository preacher of Edwardian England, had preached peace for years but supported the war effort because not to have intervened would have disregarded *'the obligations of national morality.'* The sign of the cross, he told his congregation, *'is on every man that marches to his death'* - that from a pacifist who wouldn't allow toy soldiers in the nursery. The war broke his health. P T Forsyth explored the theme that the war was God's judgement on a generation who had ridiculed his grace. His deep sorrow at the war was intensified by his love of Germany and his friendship with German theologians. John Oman sadly admitted that it was sometimes necessary to defend ideals by violence. Some younger ministers were firmly pacifist - W E Orchard (1877-1955) at the King's Weigh House was probably the best known. His sermons aroused questions in Parliament. Nathaniel Micklem (1888-1976), later Principal of Mansfield College, resigned from Withington, and so did his colleague Leyton Richards (1879-1948) at Bowden. Henry Carter resigned from Emmanuel Congregational Church, Cambridge, but was called back. Richards and Orchard were leading activists in the Fellowship of Reconciliation which was formed in December 1914. The Churches of Christ were also divided in their analysis of the war. There was a small but committed pacifist group of about 125, some of whom were imprisoned and ill-treated. They were almost all lay people, and were either self-employed or employees, and were clearly distinguished from the middle-class and employers in the Churches, most of whom supported the war effort.

Looking back in 1926, the Presbyterian historian S W Carruthers (1866-1962) summed up the feelings of many when he wrote,

*The Church had not been blind to the coming danger, though she, no more than the world, had anticipated the full horror and tragedy of it, and must ever look back with regret to the fact that she did so little to avert it. Of course she was on the side of peace and arbitration; but how mild her protests against the war spirit.*

The disruption of war, the grief of mass bereavement, the dreadful memories, all took their toll on the churches. The chaplains and the poets struggled to find a way of expressing faith, of re-formulating theology in the face of the horrors they encountered daily. Back home ministers and members cared faithfully, trying to find words where words were inadequate. Innocence had died. Naïve optimism and faith in the essential goodness of humanity had been found hollow, but above all the churches now realised that a yawning chasm had opened between them and the mass of the population. 1919 was a new world. It was, however, a world which the churches faced with a developing sense of being part of a common mission.

## Ecumenism 1910-39

The roots of the modern ecumenical movement reach back into the history of the nineteenth century. The missionary movement was fertile soil, for there was something absurd about exporting British denominational divisions into Islamic or Hindu cultures, and missionaries quickly realised that. The 'new' nation of America was forged in part from English Puritanism and European Protestantism, both of which provided ready cultures for the growth of revivalism and mission. Revivalism was brash and expansionist. It was the spiritual style of the American dream, a frontier religion of camp meetings and movement, based on the God-given task of civilising, creating godly communities from the raw material of forest and wilderness. The idea of mission as extension and expansion was deep in the American consciousness, and that is why American Christians were deeply committed to world mission in the later decades of the nineteenth century. Moody and Sankey's missions to England in the 1870s and 80s continued the transatlantic tradition of Whitefield. A group of their converts, students from Cambridge, who went on a mission to America in 1882, played a seminal part in helping a young Cornell student, John R Mott (1865-1955), decide the direction of his life. Mott was to be the founder of the Student Volunteer Movement and later the World Student Christian Federation. Those organisations were to play critical parts in the development of world ecumenism. Mott himself became the foremost ecumenical statesman of the early twentieth century.

Other roots are to be found in Britain. The Evangelical Alliance, formed in 1846 as a Protestant bulwark against the increasing power of 'Romanism' in the Church of England, provided a vision of Protestant unity. Although the Alliance was individualistic rather than corporate in its understanding of union, it is certainly possible to trace a continuity of personnel within English Presbyterianism from the initial creation of the Alliance to the union of 1876 and then on to Edinburgh 1910.

A new international awareness was developing in the latter decades of the nineteenth century - the Lambeth Conference began to emerge as a serious force in 1888, and issued a call to reunion based around the historic episcopate, the 'Lambeth Quadrilateral'. If Anglicanism was developing a new international understanding and a new sensitivity to the nature of catholicity, so too did the Free Churches. Negotiations to produce a united British presbyterian church ran into the sands of nationalism in the 1870s, but did at least result in the union of two English presbyterian bodies in 1876 to form the Presbyterian Church of England. Some ten years later, in the wake of the Home Rule debacle of 1886, the English Free Churches began to draw closer to each other. The Congregational Union and the Baptist Union held a joint meeting in 1886. In February 1890 the Congregationalist minister Guiness Rogers (1822-1911) published an article in *The Methodist Times* entitled *'A congress of Free Churches'*. He felt it would be *'..a striking illustration of a Catholic Church including various sections, each with its own form of development and with distinctive features of doctrine and ritual, but all one in Christ Jesus.'* The article received a warm reception. The following year a young Methodist minister and doctor, Henry Lunn (1859-1939) launched an audacious idea. He invited an auspicious array of distinguished church leaders to be his guests at the beautiful Swiss village of Grindelwald. It was an impressive gathering, including bishops Perowne, Moule and Chavasse from the Church of England, the Baptists Richard Glover and C F Aked, Charles Berry, R F Horton, Alexander Mackennal and Joseph Parker from the Congregationalist fold, Munro Gibson, Lindsay and Oliver from the Presbyterians and Percy Bunting and H P Hughes from his own Methodist denomination. It is difficult to overestimate the significance of the Grindelwald meetings, not in subject matter which was mainly discussion of the fourth point of the Lambeth Quadrilateral about episcopacy, but in the meeting of minds and the prevailing spirit of unity. Perowne celebrated a joint communion, an event which caused a storm in England, but which seemed perfectly natural in the tranquil surroundings of the Alps. Lunn's initiative was a powerful factor in the creation of what eventually became the National Council of Evangelical Free Churches in 1896.

Methodism itself, which had splintered so spectacularly in the aftermath of Wesley's death, began the long process of healing its own divisions in 1907 when the Methodist New Connexion, the Bible Christians and the United Methodist Free Church came together to form the United Methodist Church - a significant step on the road to the wider union of 1932 (involving the Wesleyan and Primitive Methodist Churches).

All these strands came together in the Edinburgh World Missionary

Conference of 1910. There had been world missionary gatherings before, but none matched Edinburgh in significance. Its chairman was John R Mott and his careful diplomatic skills brought the archbishop of Canterbury, Randall Davidson (1848-1930) to Edinburgh, along with representatives of the Anglo-Catholic Society for the Propagation of the Gospel. That in itself was an important achievement given the tensions between the Free Churches and the Church of England, and the partisan wariness of Evangelicals and Catholics within the Church of England.

It was intended as a consultative assembly of representatives of missionary societies working amongst non-Christian peoples to plan the next steps in bringing the gospel to the whole world. It had no legislative powers, but acted as a forum to enable the societies to form a common mind and prepare joint strategies. Great conferences often peter out. Edinburgh didn't. It is often referred to as the start of the modern ecumenical movement because it stimulated co-operation between churches both internationally and nationally as never before. One of the reasons for that was Mott's organising genius. He saw to it that a Continuation Committee was appointed to maintain links between the missionary societies. Its secretary until 1938 was J H Oldham (1874-1969), an elder at Free St George's, Edinburgh until he moved to England in 1921 and became an Anglican layman. Under his guidance the Continuation Committee did sterling work in protecting and enhancing the work of missionaries and the indigenous churches. Oldham guided a whole series of conferences in the 1920s and 30s which were to lead to the formation of the World Council of Churches in 1938. (The World Council was not officially constituted until 1948, but the General Secretariat was in operation in Switzerland throughout the Second World War). In 1921 the Edinburgh Continuation Committee became the International Missionary Conference which was one of the 3 bodies which eventually formed the World Council. Oldham was succeeded by Bill Paton (1886-1943), a Presbyterian Church of England minister and a highly capable diplomat and organiser who became an associate General Secretary of the provisional World Council of Churches in 1938. If the International Missionary Conference was one strand that grew from Edinburgh 1910, another was the Faith and Order movement. It was nurtured, indeed almost created, by two Americans, Peter Ainslie of the Disciples of Christ and bishop Charles Brent (1862-1929), an American episcopalian who had been a missionary bishop in the Philippines since 1901 and had seen the vision of world Christian unity at Edinburgh.

Nathan Söderblom (1866-1931), the Lutheran Primate of Sweden since

1914 was not at Edinburgh, although as Professor of Religions at Uppsala, he was aware of its significance. War broke out in Europe almost as soon as he took up his primacy. From neutral Sweden he sought to persuade all Christians to seek peace and work for a just society built on Christian principles. In 1917 he sought to bring about an international conference of Christians to stop the self-destruction of Europe, and in the immediate post-war years he worked unceasingly to create an international representative Christian Council to consider the Life and Work of the churches.

Quite independently of Söderblom's initiative, English church leaders had planned a similar national gathering - the really rather dull COPEC (Conference on Political and Economic Citizenship) of 1924, under the chairmanship of the brilliant young bishop of Manchester, William Temple (1881-1944). The Deputy-Chairman was A E Garvie (1861-1945), the Principal of Hackney (and later New) College. Garvie was an accomplished linguist and theologian. Söderblom, who was almost unknown in Britain, was invited to address COPEC. Life and Work met for the first time in Uppsala the following year - the Universal Christian Conference on Life and Work. Planning had begun five years previously. The conference report was edited by another outstanding Anglican leader, George Bell (1881-1958), an Oxford don turned chaplain to archbishop Randall Davidson, newly appointed Dean of Canterbury and later bishop of Chichester. The third strand of what was to become the World Council of Churches had been born. Garvie was again a key player, and it was in part his work that ensured the continuation of Life and Work. His contribution to world ecumenism was not limited to Life and Work. It is a measure of his stature that bishop Brent insisted that he be elected the deputy chairman of the first World Conference on Faith and Order which met at the University of Lausanne in 1927.

Ten years later Faith and Order and Life and Work held conferences at Edinburgh and Oxford respectively. Both accepted the resolution that they should work towards the formation of a World Council of Churches. A provisional committee met at Utrecht in 1938. William Temple, then archbishop of York was appointed chairman, the Dutch theologian W A Visser't Hooft (1900-1985) as secretary. The second world war interrupted planning, and the World Council was not constituted until 1948.

Edinburgh was also a catalyst in national ecumenism. It deepened Congregationalism's concern about union. W B Selbie (1862-1944), appointed Principal of Mansfield College in 1909, was at Edinburgh as a London Missionary Society delegate. During 1911 he organised a series of lectures at Mansfield College which were later published as *Evangelical Christianity:*

*its history and witness*. The lecturers included Oman on Presbyterianism and F J Powicke, the pioneer historian of early Congregationalism, on the Congregationalists. Selbie intended the volume to promote *'the real spiritual unity of Christendom.'* Mansfield's own particular brand of 'catholic' Congregationalism was of singular value as Congregationalism sought to define its ecumenical stance in the interwar years. Vernon Bartlet, a New Testament and patristic scholar on the staff of Mansfield, analysed the nature of ministry in early Christianity in the Selbie volume, arguing that although there might be *'continuity of apostolic order'* in the early church, there was *'no doctrine of succession to apostolic grace.'* In a series of conferences between Anglicans and the Free Churches between 1918-20, and in the published papers from those conferences the views of the two communions were helpfully clarified, and Bartlet's work was to bear fruit some twenty-five years later in the reconciliation of ministries in the Church of South India.

The Mansfield conferences of 1918-20 were part of a flurry of post-war ecumenical activity which gave rise to the 1920 Lambeth Conference's consideration of *'The Faith and Witness of the Church to this generation'*. It issued an appeal *'to all Christian people'*, drafted by George Bell and Cosmo Lang, and based on the Lambeth Quadrilateral of 1888, but this time carefully stressing the spiritual validity of non-episcopal ministries. A recent study of the plethora of post-war ecumenical committees meeting in the wake of Edinburgh and in the early planning days of Life and Work and Faith and Order has shown that this was as much a response to Free Church and wider discussions as an Anglican initiative. The appeal ran aground, as so often before and since, on the rocks of episcopal ordination, but not before six years of significant discussions had taken place at Lambeth. They brought together some of the ablest people of the day - from amongst the Congregationalists, Garvie and J D Jones (1865-1942), and from English Presbyterianism, Patrick Carnegie Simpson, professor of church history at Westminster College, and Moderator of the General Assembly in 1928. Carnegie Simpson placed the discussions in historical perspective when he noted that the statements on nonconformist ministries were *'the most notable thing which Lambeth had said to any non-episcopal church since the time of, say, Bancroft or Laud.'* However, the long process of uniting episcopal and non-episcopal ministries in India eclipsed the English discussions in the 1930 Lambeth Conference. Conversations re-started in 1935, and an *Outline of a Reunion Scheme* was published in 1938. The Congregational Assembly of May 1939 welcomed it, but the discussions came to an end because of the war.

The Free Church discussions with the Church of England were

complemented by negotiations between the Presbyterians and the Congregationalists. Talks began in 1932, focused on both doctrinal matters and methods of practical co-operation. By 1935 it was decided that full union was impossible, but that fuller co-operation was desirable, and discussions took place about the ways in which this might happen both centrally and locally. Those conversations were also ended by the war.

## The inter-war years

From 1919 to 1939 the churches struggled to find new voices and new ways of relating to a changed world. The Presbyterian Church of England had nearly 6,000 fewer communicants in 1939 than it had in 1919 (6.97% of the total membership). The English Congregationalists lost 10% of its members - just under 29,000 people between 1916-39 (no figures are available between 1917-26). Churches of Christ membership peaked in the early 1930s, but was in decline by 1939. By the late 1930s it was clear that what had been perceived as a temporary set-back in the fortunes of the denominations in the early 1920s was now sadly accepted as the inevitable norm.

Prior to the first world war the number of church attenders was two or three times greater than the actual membership of the churches. During the inter-war years the penumbra of attenders reduced, and attendance was lower than membership. The figures that we have are not precise enough to allow speculation to turn into fact, but it is likely that the age profile of congregations changed and became older, and that churches relied more and more on growth from within the families of existing members. That cannot be ascribed to a failure in evangelistic effort. One of the striking features of church life at this period is the number of imaginative and creative ways in which churches attempted to respond to their situation.

The unifying of Congregationalism continued apace. The introduction of a system of Moderators in 1919 was an essential step in the process of helping independent churches realise their common identity as part of one denomination. Under the influence first of J D Jones, and then Sidney Berry (1881-1961), its first full-time Secretary, the Congregational Union became an inescapable reality in local church life. Jones, minister of Richmond Hill, Bournemouth from 1898-1932 was a commanding figure in national and international Congregationalism. Author, preacher, ecclesiastical diplomat, always ready with a felicitous phrase, no gathering was complete without him. Berry, who served from 1922-48, became almost synonymous with the

Union during his long period of office. During the 1930s the denomination went through a long period of introspective self-analysis, and embarked on an 'Inner Mission' to revive its spiritual life in 1936, followed by an evangelistic 'Outer Mission' the following year. Plans for church extension were interrupted by the war.

Ironically the interwar years marked a theological and spiritual renaissance in the churches of our traditions as well as the first signs of serious decline. The Churches of Christ founded Overdale College in 1920, and William Robinson (1888-1963) became its first Principal. He was to have a formative influence on the Churches, re-interpreting their restorationist heritage in the light of the ecumenism of the 1920s and the best of current Biblical scholarship. Restoring the primitive church was not simply a matter of reading a blueprint in the New Testament and putting it into action. The New Testament was not that kind of literature. As he put it in his first book, *Essays on Christian unity* (1923):

*The historical method of interpretation has come to stay. The New Testament, like the Church, is freed from the dogma of indefectibility; but this does not mean that it loses its supreme place as the norm by which to test all future Christianity. This it will never lose. But it does mean that the New Testament is seen in its proper relation - historically - to the Church; and that in effecting Christian Unity we must make our appeal to Scripture, history and reason.*

Robinson was quietly convinced that the Churches of Christ had an important contribution to make to the quest for unity, and his own theological work was centred on ecclesiology. In his address to the Second World Convention of Churches of Christ (Disciples) which was held in Leicester in 1935, Robinson showed how the Churches combined Protestant and Catholic emphases within their own life and yet transcended them as '..*a Church which was neither Protestant nor Catholic but Christian.*' The essentials of Protestantism - freedom, an emphasis on the priesthood of all believers, personal faith in Christ and the centrality of Scripture - were united with a fundamental Catholicism - a hatred of schism, the centrality of the eucharist, respect for reason and tradition. As a teacher in Selly Oak (of which Overdale was a part) and in his work as a representative of the Churches in both national and international ecumenical councils, Robinson did all he could to share that vision as a contribution to the coming Great Church.

Congregationalism was also exercised by questions of ecclesiology, and with the interpretation of its own identity. Forsyth's work had renewed interest in the nature of Reformed churchmanship, and indeed raised the question of whether Congregationalism was part of the Reformed family, or whether its roots were to be found in the radical reformation. There was a spectrum of views. Forsyth, firmly rooted in the theology of the magisterial reformation of the sixteenth century, had his followers, but so too did the more radical tradition. During the 1920s appreciation of the significance of freedom and equality as valuable gifts of the denomination's history was heard anew in the writings of Selbie, Garvie, Peel and others. The doctrine of the ministry was the touchstone of the difference between them, Forsyth firmly convinced of its distinctiveness, the others carefully circumscribing the ministerial role. At a far, although winsomely attractive, extreme was W E Orchard, a wandering ecclesiastical gypsy of a man, trained as a Presbyterian at Westminster, serving as a Congregationalist at King's Weigh House, before ending up a Roman Catholic in 1932. The Weigh House was a distinctive and unusual church, the heir of a long tradition of concern about the beauty of worship which dated back to Thomas Binney's ministry in the previous century. Orchard's liturgical practice brought catholicism into congregationalism. The communion table became an altar, the minister wore Anglican style vestments, and *Divine Service*, an angular yet entrancing 400 page Prayer Book devised by Orchard became the liturgy of the church in its weekly eucharistic celebration. Many looked askance, but Orchard built up a congregation of over 400, and never introduced any changes without the permission of Church Meeting. Congregationalism was by no means monochrome.

Ecclesiology was also a concern within the Presbyterian Church of England. Carnegie Simpson's prominence in national union discussions was undergirded by his *Church Principles* and *The Evangelical Church Catholic*, and his New Testament colleague at Westminster, C A Anderson Scott wrote on *The Church, its worship and sacraments*. Simpson's work is notable for his belief that freedom and order are, as it were, opposite sides of the same coin of Christian living. He defends the Free Churches' unwillingness to make all members conform to procedures, but at the same time is sharply critical of those who distinguish between external authority and the witness of their own experience and conscience. Order, he argued, was one of the church's most precious possessions. Whilst there were clearly nuanced differences between Congregationalists, Presbyterians and the Churches of Christ, the common concern with ecumenism and ecclesiology pointed to growing convergence.

The interwar years saw a flowering of nonconformist scholarship. It was as if our traditions were coming of age. The ancient universities had been open to them for several generations, and the expansion of higher education created a ready audience for their work. Adrian Hastings, a Catholic church historian, has suggested that the best theological teaching available in England in the 1920s was to be found at Mansfield and Westminster. They were indeed heady days at both institutions. The combination of Oman, Carnegie Simpson and Anderson Scott at Westminster, and the rising genius of C H Dodd at Mansfield in a staff that already included W B Selbie, Nathaniel Micklem and Vernon Bartlet makes the point. Excellence was not confined to those institutions though. Theologically Modernism was in the ascendant in England, and its leading exponent was C J Cadoux, on the staff of the United College, Bradford from 1919-33 before moving to Mansfield.

T W Manson (1893-1958), the great Presbyterian New Testament scholar, described Cadoux's *The case for Evangelical Modernism* (1938) as '*the swan song of Modernism*'. He was right. The theological world was undergoing a seismic shift in continental Europe. In 1919 Karl Barth published his commentary on Romans. It was a strange, extraordinary book. Barth was appalled by the intellectual bankruptcy of liberalism, epitomised for him by the unanimous support of the German theological establishment for the first world war. Here was a book which stressed the otherness and strangeness of God, of his judging and saving Word which stands over and against the world in Jesus Christ. It heralded the theology of neo-orthodoxy, which had been uncannily anticipated by P T Forsyth. When a student quoted Forsyth to Barth, Barth is reputed to have replied '*If Forsyth had not said what he said when he said it, I would have said that he was quoting me.*' The mood eventually changed in England, although the English theological establishment was never wholly convinced by Barth.

The finest contribution of our traditions to scholarship in the 1930s and in the immediate post-war period lay in Biblical studies. After a spell in Manchester Dodd became the first nonconformist to occupy a chair in theology at Cambridge for three hundred years. He was the Norris-Hulse Professor between 1935-49, and his books on Paul and John's gospel were landmarks in the history of biblical studies. He chaired the editorial panel of the New English Bible, which was eventually published in its entirety in 1970 (the New Testament was first published in 1961). Manson occupied the Rylands chair at Manchester and his work on the teaching of Jesus broke new ground in the application of critical methodology. The year after Manson left Mansfield to follow Dodd to Manchester, a brilliant young scholar arrived at Mansfield from Cambridge to train for the Congregational ministry. His name was George Caird (1917-1984), later to become

Mansfield's Principal in succession to John Marsh, both men maintaining the college's (and Congregationalism's) outstanding contribution to New Testament studies.

## The Second World War and its aftermath

The Second World War had a devastating effect on the churches. The Blitz destroyed countless buildings, including 99 Congregational churches in London alone, and the Presbyterian Church of England suffered grievously when their new offices in Tavistock Place were hit by a V2 rocket in February 1945, killing the General Secretary, W T Elmslie and eight other staff members. The pattern of local church life was dislocated by evacuation. Pastoral demands multiplied as in the first war. The second world war produced a very different effect on British society to the first. 1914 marked the end of innocence. Its ideological impact was profound. Between 1939-45 the war accelerated the pace of change in society which was already well under way. The destruction of city centres and the consequent need for rebuilding hastened the break-up of old patterns of community life and left many city centre churches as isolated islands.

Church membership had increased slightly after the first war; the second hastened the rate of decline, which roughly trebled between 1937-47. The decline has continued since then. Between 1947 and 1972 the Presbyterian Church of England lost 29% of its membership, the Congregationalists 32% and the Churches of Christ 56%. The formation of the United Reformed Church has not altered that overall pattern. That broad picture masks some significant variations. The Presbyterian Church of England increased its membership between 1947-9 and again between 1955 and 1961, which probably reflects the sharp rise in Scottish emigration to England between 1945 and 1960. The number of English residents born in Scotland increased from 366,000 in 1931 to 654,000 in 1960.

Active conversations between the churches, both multilateral and between the Congregationalists and Presbyterians, were curtailed by the war. However, the war did not stop everything. Some church work continued as usual. In 1940 the National Free Church Council and the Federal Council of Free Churches amalgamated, forming the Free Church Federal Council, and in 1942 the British Council of Churches was formed. All three of our traditions joined both bodies, but it was of particular significance for the Churches of Christ who had felt unable to join either of two Free Church bodies earlier in the century because of policy on intercommunion (ie.

admitting those not baptised as believers to communion). They had though been fully involved, particularly through William Robinson, in the world ecumenical movement. Their new membership was to re-align their relationship with the other churches.

The Presbyterian Layman's Conference continued to meet during the war and in 1943 it petitioned the General Assembly to recommence conversations with the Congregationalists. Their appeal was accepted and the Congregationalists expressed themselves willing to begin again, so in 1945 a Joint Conference was called. The Congregationalists were represented by, amongst others, Nathaniel Micklem, the Principal of Mansfield, Sidney Berry, the General Secretary and the church historian Geoffrey Nuttall; the Presbyterian delegation included the historian S W Carruthers, Roy Whitehorn of Westminster College, and Arthur Macarthur, later to be the General Secretary of the Presbyterian Church of England. The work was quickly done and a Scheme of Union was laid before the churches in 1947. Three options were presented - outright rejection, acceptance, or the possibility of closer co-operation. The churches chose the path of co-operation. A Joint Advisory Council was established, and an act of covenant between the two churches was celebrated in Westminster Chapel in May 1951. The Joint Advisory Council worked away in the 1950s, but produced little real impact on the lives of the churches.

Those conversations were part of a wider concern with ecumenism. In 1946 archbishop Geoffrey Fisher, delivering a university sermon at Great St Mary's, Cambridge, invited the Free Churches to take episcopacy into their systems. It was an attempt to break the ecumenical impasse. The experience of war, the formation of the British Council of Churches in 1942 and the first Assembly of the World Council of Churches in 1948 spelt out the need for British initiatives. The problem seemed intractable - Anglicans could not accept non-episcopally transmitted orders, and the Free Churches and the Church of Scotland would not accept that their ministries were deficient. Fisher was not seeking any organic union:

*It is, I think, not possible yet nor desirable that any Church should merge its identity in a newly-constituted union. What I desire is that I should freely be able to enter their churches, and they mine, in the sacraments of the Lord and in full fellowship of worship.*

Fisher's invitation had a profound effect. It set in train a series of negotiations between Anglicans and Methodists which eventually resulted in a report published in 1963, and an amended Scheme of Union in 1966, which was rejected by an alliance of Anglo-Catholics and Evangelicals within the Church of England although it gained the necessary majorities within Methodism. It thus rendered wider conversations between the Free Churches impossible, and it weakened the role of the Free Church Federal Council. It also affected the Congregational-Presbyterian conversations because the Church of Scotland responded positively to Fisher, and the English Presbyterians became partners to discussions about the possibility of introducing a modified form of episcopacy into both the Church of Scotland and the Presbyterian Church of England. During the 1950s the energies of English Presbyterians were directed there rather than to the work of the Joint Advisory Committee which was working with the Congregationalists. Agreement was reached in 1957 to take bishops-in-presbytery into the Scottish system. They would be ordained by Anglican bishops and act as permanent Moderators of presbyteries. The scheme floundered on the rocks of nationalism rather than theology as the *Scottish Daily Express* orchestrated a fierce campaign against what it saw as Anglican, English imperialism. The Church of Scotland turned the scheme down, and it was never tested in the Church of England. The path of British ecumenism was clearly not going to be an easy one.

The English Presbyterians were left in some confusion about future direction. Should they try what their predecessors had attempted in the 1860s, the creation of a united British Presbyterian Church ? Should they become a Synod of the Church of Scotland ? Should they look to a union of all English Free Churches ? Should they talk further to the Church of England, or should they renew their conversations with the Congregationalists ?

Matters were further complicated by the formation of the Church of South India from a union of Anglicans, Methodists, Presbyterians and Congregationalists in 1947. There was rejoicing amongst Indian Christians and consternation in the Church of England about whether they could be in communion with a church which included non-episcopally ordained clergy in its number. They agreed that they could in 1955, provided the non-episcopally ordained did not celebrate at Anglican altars.

In 1959 the English Presbyterians held a conference of Presbytery Conveners in Rugby to discuss their dilemma. In the car park after the meeting the Presbyterian General Secretary, F G Healey told Arthur Macarthur that he had been approached by his Congregationalist opposite number, Howard

Stanley, to ask if the time had not come to begin formal conversations. An informal private conversation was arranged at Memorial Hall between six church leaders which resulted in a proposition being taken to both Assemblies in 1963. A Joint Committee was established under the chairmanship of John Huxtable and Alec Neil.

For English ecumenists the 1950s had been a decade of frustration. That may be why so many of its committed and able people offered their services to the world scene. Bishop George Bell, that most honourable and far-sighted of Anglican bishops, was elected chair of the Central Committee of the WCC in 1948, Oliver Tompkins, later bishop of Bristol, Ernest Payne the Baptist leader, and Norman Goodall, the Congregationalist secretary of the International Missionary Council, all played crucial shaping roles in the early development of the World Council.

At home, the Free Churches were enjoying an Indian summer. It was the last decade of the great preachers - Donald Soper at Kingsway Hall and on Tower Hill, enjoying his role as prophetic irritant and unofficial chaplain to the Labour Party; Leslie Weatherhead at the City Temple, exploring the relationship between religion and psychological wholeness. Stephen Winward and Ernest Payne were pushing the Baptists towards new sacramental order. In the universities the Congregationalist C H Dodd and the Presbyterian T W Manson dominated New Testament scholarship. In Cambridge Newton Flew and Gordon Rupp were amongst those who established Wesley House as an institution of excellence. Rupp came to Wesley House in 1967, combining the principalship with the Dixie chair of Ecclesiastical History from 1968, and re-writing the history of the continental reformation. Herbert Butterfield, Regius Professor of History and Fellow of Peterhouse combined a robust Methodism with a high Tory view of history. In Oxford, another Methodist, Charles Coulson, the Professor of Applied Mathematics, brought together the world of the natural sciences and the calling of a Methodist local preacher.

Indian summers soon give way to winter. Below the surface the old antagonisms of church and chapel were crumbling in the face of secularism. Ecumenism, for all its disappointments and follies, was providing a sub-text which suggested that being Christian was more significant that being Anglican or Methodist, and the Methodist minister who in 1957 ran through a list of ex-Presidents of Conference whose sons and daughters had joined the Church of England would have found Congregationalists, Baptists and Presbyterians who could have provided him with similar stories.

If denominationalism was the determinative feature of English

Christianity in 1945, by 1960 the agenda was ecumenical, and the Week of Prayer for Christian Unity and Christian Aid Week were part of the liturgical calendar in the widest sense.

Billy Graham came to Britain for the first time in 1954. His visit was symbolic and prophetic. It was a symbol of a change of religious mood. If the inter-war years were marked by the primacy of liberalism and the Student Christian Movement in theological life, the 1950s and 1960s saw the resurgence of evangelicalism in British church life. It was prophetic because evangelicalism has always been less observant of 'vertical' denominational structures than other spiritualities, and one of the notable aspects of church life over the last thirty years has been the loosening of denominational allegiances. At the same time evangelicalism has brought a sense of renewal to all churches. The charismatic movement became part of British church life in the late 1960s. It too has had a profound effect on all the mainline churches. In an odd way it was a typical manifestation of the 1960s in its celebration of feeling and rejection of inhibitions.

For the churches the 1960s were an era of profound, and for some shocking, change. They were brittle, exciting years, fragile and superficial maybe, but full of verve and life and a creative inventiveness which had not been seen in British society for generations - perhaps not since the mid nineteenth century. In was seen in the plays of Pinter, the films of Lindsay Anderson and the Boulting Brothers, the novels of Kingsley Amis and John Fowles, the designs of Terence Conran (Habitat started in 1964), the architecture of Basil Spence (Coventry Cathedral was consecrated in 1962), the sculpture of Elizabeth Frink, the paintings of David Hockney, and (of course) the pop revolution.

That creativity was the cultural correlative of deeper changes. Britain was becoming distinctively multi-cultural. 260,000 Caribbean immigrants arrived in Britain between 1955 and 1962. The first riots rocked Notting Hill in 1958, harbinger of the grim reality of a racial discord which would get a lot worse before it got better. Britain acquired her own hydrogen bomb in 1957. The late 1950s and early 1960s were the years of protest, the years of the Campaign for Nuclear Disarmament. The mushroom cloud was the backcloth of cultural revolution.

The 1960s may have been brittle years, but they were also humane years, years in which sexual segregation was steadily outlawed in the institutions of British public life. Compulsory military service had ended in 1960, and Britain became steadily de-militarised (in contrast to America).

The whole structure of class, which is the most determining factor of British life, seemed to be irrelevant. The last hanging took place in Britain in 1964. The Race Relations Act was passed in 1968, the same year in which abortion and homosexual acts between consenting adults were legalised, and the Divorce Reform Act was passed in the following year.

As society changed, so too did the churches. In 1962 the bishop of Woolwich, John Robinson, suffered a slipped disc. He decided to make good use of his enforced leisure, and wrote a short book which became the surprise best-seller of 1963, *Honest to God*. It was a rare moment in church history, theology as front page news! Suddenly, thanks largely to an article in *The Observer*, the gap between the pulpit and the pew was bridged. The book's impact lay in its honesty. It brought together insights from three German theologians, Dietrich Bonhoeffer, martyred by the Hitler régime, the New Testament scholar Rudolf Bultmann and Paul Tillich who was teaching systematic theology in America. The works of all three were commonplace to theologians, and they were very different and indeed contradictory thinkers. Robinson's synthesis of their works was arresting to a non-theological readership. The 'God out there' was replaced by Tillich's 'ground of our being', traditional incarnational theology by Bonhoeffer's 'Jesus the man for others', and orthodox Christian morality by situation ethics. It might have passed unnoticed but for Robinson's *Observer* article which some bright sub-editor entitled in a huge banner headline, *'Our image of God must go.'* By 1966 it had sold 1 million copies.

South bank theology, as it was called, was a brave attempt to speak the gospel to an increasingly secular world. Many seriously disagreed with Robinson, not least his fellow members of the guild of professional theologians. However, no-one could doubt that here was a church leader wrestling with real questions. In the Battersea deanery of the Southwark diocese of which Robinson was a suffragan bishop, only 1% of the population attended an Anglican church in 1960. In Woolwich itself the rector, Nick Stacey, was busy trying to revive the life of its parish church with discos in the crypt and a coffee bar in the gallery. In 1963 the Southwark Ordination Course was founded to train worker priests. The church of the sixties was not moribund. That in itself was a cause for optimism.

Another source of hope was the deepening of ecumenical relations. It is hard to underestimate the impact of John XXIII's portificate. The decade began with archbishop Geoffrey Fisher paying a private visit to him as part of an ecumenical pilgrimage which also took in Jerusalem and

Constantinople. A story is told of these two elderly clerics exchanging formal greetings in the pope's study. The Pope read a statement which referred to *'the time when our separated brethren should return to the Mother Church.'* To which Fisher replied, *'Not return, Your Holiness.'* *'Why not ?'* asked a puzzled John. *'None of us can go backwards'*, continued Fisher. *'We are each now running on parallel courses; we are looking forward, until, in God's good time, our two courses approximate and meet.'* The Pope paused, and thought. *'You are right'*, he said. A very long tide began to turn. Six years later Fisher's successor, Michael Ramsey journeyed again to Rome, to meet John's successor, Paul VI. Those two meetings took place either side of the most significant and far reaching event in the church history of the twentieth century, the Second Vatican Council. The contrast was remarkable. This was a public meeting, marked by an ecumenical service in the basilica of St Paul's-without-the-walls and the signing of a Common Declaration announcing the birth of serious dialogue aimed at union. The result was ARCIC (The Anglican-Roman Catholic International Commission) and the growing involvement of the English Catholic church in the ecumenical scene.

The early 1960s were full of ecumenical promise. The Joint Committee of Congregationalists and Presbyterians met for the first time at New College, London on New Year's Day 1964. A few months later the British Council of Churches Faith and Order Commission meeting at Nottingham challenged the British churches to covenant for unity by Easter Day 1980, and to set up local ecumenical initiatives, thus changing the context of the Congregational-Presbyterian conversations almost before they had begun. The challenge seemed both feasible and attainable.

## The creation of the United Reformed Church

The Committee proceeded in the way that all such committees work, reading papers, building up trust and discussing papers. Arthur Macarthur tells how, at the first meeting, he and Howard Stanley, the two General Secretaries, described their churches. Congregationalism had 2,990 churches, 212,017 members and 197,544 children, the Presbyterians 346 churches, 71,329 members and 28,885 children. They were very different animals, Presbyterianism strong in the north yet represented by single congregations in many larger towns, but almost entirely absent from large tracts of the South and West; Congregationalism more evenly spread, but with a great number of small villages churches and a presence in the English speaking part of Wales. *'I recall'*, he remembered, *'some anxiety on our side as Howard Stanley described some of those village churches and indeed the number of churches of all sorts with less than fifty members, closing at the rate of fifty a year. Presbyterians, used to a central stipend system, trembled for the economic future.'* That initial meeting agreed that they must accept that the past had made both churches what they now were, but that their work was to explore what the church might be in the future. The most ardent exponent of that view was Hubert Cunliffe-Jones, the Congregationalist Professor of Theology at the University of Manchester. The committee asked him to prepare a paper for their next meeting. He returned home on the train, writing. That was the genesis of a Statement of Convictions about the possible shape of a united church which was both Catholic and Reformed. Ill-health forced Cunliffe-Jones's resignation from the committee soon after this, but his was the creative act which was to determine its direction.

More papers were commissioned - from Martin Cressey on ministry and the sacraments; Kenneth Slack on union and mission; Stanley Ross on the nature of the local church; David Geddes on membership and initiation, and Noel Salter on why bother with Presbyterian-Congregational Union. These six papers formed the agenda for the rest of 1964, and a six section document, a Statement of Convictions (keeping to Cunliffe-Jones's original title) was presented to the Assemblies of both churches in 1965. Both Assemblies gave approval for it to be circulated, and the debate passed into the wider sphere of individual churches.

In the meantime the British Council of Churches-initiated discussions about wider union were getting underway. Every encouragement was given to the Congregationalists and Presbyterians to continue their work as part of that wider process. The committee re-organised themselves from the six groups which had been responsible for work on the initial papers into four. The first was to be responsible for Statements of Faith, ordination formulae and the confessions made at baptism and confirmation. The second and third considered how the councils of the new church should work in theoretical and practical detail, and the fourth faced up to the financial and legal work which would be necessary to bring about union.

When the replies to the Statement of Convictions were received, it was clear that the churches were not yet fully persuaded. Of the 90 Presbyterian replies, two-thirds were in favour, but only half the 229 Congregational replies showed similar enthusiasm. The committee identified the areas which they felt needed further study, but felt it right to seek the permission of both 1966 Assemblies to prepare a draft Constitution. This was agreed. It was presented in 1967, and sent down for discussion. The further work which the committee had undertaken was rewarded.

Many more responses were received - 941 from the Congregationalists, 641 in favour, 130 from the Presbyterians, 87 in favour - 68% and 66% respectively. This was both a mandate to continue, and a signal that caution was required. The committee began to smooth sharp edges, with all the concomitant risks of ambiguity. An interim report in 1968 was followed by a Scheme of Union in 1969 which set out a full picture of what the new church would look like for the first time.

During this period the wider ecumenical scene was changing. In 1968 the carefully prepared Anglican-Methodism scheme floundered on the rocks of a minority combination of Anglo-Catholics led by bishop Graham Leonard, some Evangelicals and a few die-hards of no particular allegiance. One Anglican observer commented glumly that it *'reduce[d] the Church of England from comprehension to incoherence.'* It was sadly symbolic, a puncturing of the balloon of optimism. In 1960 Kenneth Slack, the Presbyterian General Secretary of the BCC had published a book called *The British Churches to-day*. A revised version appeared in 1969. In the new preface Slack regretted that *'Passage after passage of the book has seemed strangely optimistic and has had to be excised.'* The Congregational-Presbyterian proposals were the one point of hope on an increasingly bleak horizon.

The crucial votes were eventually taken in the Assemblies of 1971. The debate took place simultaneously on the same day, the Congregationalists meeting in London, the Presbyterians in Newcastle-upon-Tyne. The Congregationalist vote was taken much earlier in the day than the Presbyterian, but the outcome was naturally kept from the Presbyterian Assembly until they had finished their deliberations. The Assembly vote was to be decisive for the Presbyterians, and the debate was therefore a long one. It lasted four hours. Late in the evening it was learnt that both Assemblies had consented with the required majorities - 89% from the Congregationalists (1888 to 233), 79% from the Presbyterians (434-115). The nature of Congregational church government meant that the Scheme now had to be approved by more than 75% of the membership of each of the local churches. The Joint Committee met at St Andrew's Hall, Birmingham to receive the votes. All 31 of the County Unions were in favour, as were 1,668 local congregations representing 136,856 members, 82.2% of the total membership of the church. 597 Congregational churches, 26%, voted not to join. That was a matter of great sadness, and not a little pain, to all concerned. Two Presbyterian churches, in Jersey and Guernsey, opted out and petitioned to join the Church of Scotland. There was a measure of sense about this because the Jersey church in particular owed its growth to immigrant Scots, but there was also a sense of irony. Thomas Cartwright, the originator of English Presbyterian theory, had been chaplain to Castle Cornet in Guernsey from 1595-1601, and the church order of the islands had been presbyterian between 1576 and 1623 in Jersey and 1662 in Guernsey.

Once the votes had been taken, the new church had to be given legislative shape. Both churches shared the belief that the government of the state was distinct from the government of the church. They were equally aware of the legal judgement of the House of Lords in 1904 which granted the rights of church property to the dissenting minority of 'Wee Frees' following the union of the Free Church of Scotland and the United Presbyterian Church in 1900. They therefore heeded the sage advice of their legal advisors, and the formation of the new church was made the subject of an Act of Parliament.

The United Reformed Church Bill was introduced into the Lords in November 1971, sponsored by Lord Wade. Support was lent by the bishop of Hereford, Lord Balerno of the Church of Scotland and the Roman Catholic Lord Longford. Difficulties arose when the bill reached the Commons. It was introduced by the Methodist MP for York, Alex Lyon who was then a member of the British Council of Churches. Because opposition was voiced it was sent to an opposed committee which met for two days. The case was argued principally by John Huxtable, the Minister Secretary of the Congregational Church before five MPs. The case against was put by Austen Spearing, Ivor Morris and David Watson, arguing that the act so altered the legal status of independent churches as to be a betrayal of trust. The committee agreed to forward the bill provided a statement was made that an assurance be given that a local church wishing to secede from the URC could seek the consent of Assembly to leave with its property. The rapid drafting of that clause meant that it was less than comprehensive, and in the end it was withdrawn during the third reading on 17th June. The debate on the third reading began at 11.12 pm and lasted three hours. There had been a possibility that those opposed to the bill might talk it out, and as one of the leading opponents was Ian Paisley, that was perceived to be a real threat. That could be avoided if more than 100 members were present when the vote was taken. With the help of church leaders of other denominations, the necessary numbers were present.

The debate was opened by Alex Lyon who, in a speech of judicious clarity, stated that this was one of the most significant pieces of ecclesiastical legislation to come before the House, for it was the first union of separate denominations since the Reformation. He resisted the new clause by first outlining the procedure which the churches had undergone to reach their decision, and then by arguing that a church which wished to secede from the URC should do so under the forms of governance of the new denomination which had been agreed by the vast majority of the memberships of the Congregational and Presbyterian Churches. By doing so the Congregationalists had agreed to give up their rights of independency for the sake of the new church. The amendment, if passed, would completely undermine the governmental structure of the new church and wreck the Scheme. As the majority of the churches had given their assent to the Scheme of Union, it was likely that they would do so again, so all the House would be doing, were it to amend the bill, would be to delay the union. He then proceeded to a wider issue. Did the House have any right to tell the churches how to conduct its affairs ? He pointed to the disastrous intervention of the House in the 1928 Prayer Book revision as evidence that they should not, and expressed the hope that that ghost might be laid by the present debate.

Nigel Spearing agreed, but stated that his reasons for opposing the bill were legal rather than theological. He had no desire to stop the bill going forward, indeed the church of which he was a member had voted in its favour. He did, however, believe it was Parliament's duty to consider such a wholesale reversion of the terms of charitable trusts, particularly as he had been approached by members of his own denomination who were deeply anxious about it. Properly based church union was dependent on a solid legal foundation, and that was the responsibility of Parliament. The proposed power of the new councils of the URC, which were foreign to the Congregationalist tradition, seemed dangerously authoritarian. The amendment sought to limit those powers.

As the debate continued, support came from Michael Clark Hutchinson and David Steel, both members of the Church of Scotland. Hutchinson noted that the Church of Scotland favoured the union, Steel that as the son of a Presbyterian minister and a Congregationalist mother, he was automatically prejudiced in favour! Marcus Worsley, the Anglican MP for Chelsea added his support. Opposition was voiced by Tony Benn, himself the product of a distinguished Congregationalist family, and Ian Paisley. Benn supported Spearing's attempt to protect the rights of any minority that might wish to secede. Paisley, in a sharply perceptive if occasionally irate speech, noted that the House had no right to interfere in the decisions of the churches, adding impishly that it was about time the Church of England was disestablished. The House did not have the authority to stop the proposed union. The parallel with the 1928 Prayer Book debate was a red herring in his judgement, for it was about doctrine. The true parallel was the Free Church case of 1904, which was about property rights. His concern was about the property rights of those who might dissent, and in their defence he proposed that the words from the preamble of the bill which stated that both Assemblies were convinced that the union was the will of God be deleted, for those words suggested that those of dissented had not discerned God's will.

At this point the debate was getting heated, and Norman St John Stevas, the Catholic MP for Chelmsford, made a characteristically witty and far-sighted intervention. Members of the Congregational churches in his constituency had sought his support in the debate. The debate, was not about property. It was actually about ecumenism. The bill before the House was, he hoped, a stage on the journey to wider unity. He looked forward to the day when his own communion and the national church might become one, indeed to the day when all Christians might be one, and noted that:

*There cannot be, in ecumenism, any cast-iron guarantees. It is not possible to move forward with a whole series of insurance policies guaranteeing one against what might happen. We simply do not know. No Congregationalist, no Presbyterian, knows where this path to which they have set their feet will end. All they can do is to make an act of faith, which is what this Measure is, to move together, to grow together.*

He disagreed with Tony Benn's comment that ecumenism meant the end of Congregationalism, for *'In the ecumenical movement there is no loss but only gain. No one loses his own traditions; people add new perspectives to those traditions. They are enriched by others, not impoverished.'*

The debate continued a little longer. It was wound up by the seconder, John Roper, son, grandson and great-grandson of Congregational ministers, whose father had been minister of a united Presbyterian-Congregational church. In a thoughtful speech he reviewed the debate, noting how lessons could be learnt from other united churches in the world, particularly those of Canada, Jamaica and Ghana. He requested Ian Paisley to withdraw his amendment which he considered a *'gratuitous insult'* to the churches. Paisley refused, but his amendment was lost. Nigel Spearing withdrew his amendment lest it be thought that the House was doing anything other than demonstrating its support for Christian unity. So it was that in the early hours of the morning of 22 June 1972 the United Reformed Church Act was passed. It received royal assent two days later.

The attention of the churches turned to practical details - combining offices, bringing the new church into being, and planning the uniting Assembly. It was held in Westminster Central Hall, by kind permission of the Methodist Church, and the service of celebration took place across the road in Westminster Abbey. The Assembly passed resolutions declaring the end of the two churches, and the birth of the new church, which made the Act of Parliament effective. The uniting service, a stirring, moving occasion, was planned by Eric Fenn, a distinguished Presbyterian minister whose varied career had included an important role in the development of religious broadcasting. At the heart of the liturgy was an act of commitment when the leaders of other churches, Cardinal Heenan, Archbishop Michael Ramsey (himself the son of a deacon of Emmanuel Congregational Church, Cambridge), and the Moderator of the Free Church Federal Council, Dr Ironwy Morgan, brought greetings and pledged their communions to the quest for unity. That was what the new church was about. Two denominations had agreed to die that this resurrection might take place, and the United Reformed Church itself was created to die in the sense that those who brought it into being thought of it as a staging post on the pilgrimage to a greater union. Uniquely amongst the British churches, the URC has built the quest for unity into its very constitution in the Basis of Union.

At the first meeting of the United Reformed Church Assembly, on the 5 October 1972, the Churches of Christ responded to the new church's call to further unity by asking for negotiations to begin between the two bodies. A long history lay behind that decision. The Churches had been re-thinking their theology over the previous forty years. Two commissions - on Ordination (appointed in 1936, reporting in 1941) and on the Work and Status of the Ministry (appointed in 1947, reporting 1950-53 and finally approved in 1953) were central to that change. The first suggested that Evangelists be ordained nationally at Conference. The latter whose report was largely drafted by William Robinson, modified the independence of local churches, and argued that the ministry should *'in some way express this unity and continuity of the one Church.'* It also challenged the restorationist view that the Churches of Christ contained within itself the only true pattern of New Testament ministry. Episcopal and presbyterian systems, it admitted, might equally well express the essentials of New Testament ministry. It also accepted that there was no theoretical barrier to the ministry of women. The task of the Churches was to *'..aim to set forth the unity which was a mark of the New Testament Church, and which must be a mark of the re-*

*united Church.'* Evangelists should be known as ministers. Although the report was gradually accepted, its thinking was ahead of its time. Not until 1973 was approval finally given to the ordination of women. If internal considerations had given rise to these two commissions, it was involvement in the wider ecumenical scene through membership of the British Council of Churches and the Free Church Federal Council that led the Churches to re-think their understandings of baptism, communion and church unity.

The established practices of believer's baptism and closed communion meant that the Churches were particularly interested in the doctrine of the church, for both those positions are an expression of a specific understanding of ecclesiology. As ever, William Robinson was at the forefront of the debate. How, he asked in one essay, *'can we restore the true church without continuity in history, and with the major part of the church left outside?'* Restoration of the true church was impossible without union. It was that belief that led the Churches to re-evaluate their attitude to ecumenism in the 1950s. Put bluntly, could a united church include those who practised infant baptism, and could the Churches, particularly when working on the mission field, exclude members of other denominations from communion ?

Given their stance on believer's baptism, it was only natural that the Churches should find common cause with the Baptist Union. The Baptists, however, kept an open communion table. Between 1948-1956 they discussed the possibility of closer co-operation, but in 1957 the Baptist Union Council rejected the project without giving reasons. In an important Conference paper, *Intercommunion*, given in 1954, Norman Walters set out the dilemma on the issue of closed communion. The growth of ecumenism in the twentieth century meant that the Churches faced a very different world to that of 1861 when the resolution about closed communion had been passed. The question now was *'..whether we are finally going to decline into a narrow sectarian body, or whether we are going to venture in faith, grasping the countless opportunities of the moment towards furthering the cause of Christian Unity.'* Conference responded by permitting 'guest communion' some two years later. In 1962 James Gray, who had been the Churches' representative at the New Delhi Assembly of the World Council of Churches, made a speech at Conference which challenged the Churches once again to face the implications of the ecumenical movement, and which was to prove a turning point in their relations with other denominations. They should, he suggested, be active proponents of union, and as evidence of that willingness, extend the practice of guest communion to 'guest membership' particularly in mission contexts, thus allowing those who had been baptised as infants in other churches to play a full part in the life of the Churches of Christ. He later explained that he had become convinced at New Delhi that the churches of the world would never abandon paedobaptism, despite the fact that theologians from many different communions agreed that the New Testament evidence clearly favoured believer's baptism. Guest, or ecumenical membership, as it became known, was an idea whose time had come, and over 80% of the Churches practised it by 1972.

When in 1964 the British Council of Churches challenged British Christians to covenant together for unity by 1980, the Churches of Christ were able to take an active part. They were involved from the beginning in the multi-lateral conversations in Scotland which were part of the response to 1964. The Union Committee of the Churches also decided to approach the Congregational-Presbyterian Joint Committee and the Baptist Union. The Union thought there would be no difficulty in the Churches joining the Union, but were chary of organic union. The Joint Committee, on the other hand, were already expressing the hope that their union might be open-ended as well as organic, and warmly welcomed observers from the Churches of Christ in 1966. In 1968 the Churches devised a plan to move themselves towards union if possible. This involved a careful consultative process with each church, prayer, and the formulation of a covenant to work and pray for unity. In 1969 71 out of 103 churches on the List (representing 85% of the membership) approved the covenant, and in 1971 they agreed to seek union with the URC on its formation in 1972.

A Joint Committee was set up, chaired by Dr Norman Goodall from the URC, with Dr David Thompson from the Churches of Christ as Secretary. It reported initially to the 1974 Conference when approval was also given to the Scottish Churches congregations wish to negotiate with the Scottish Congregationalists.

That year also saw the formation of the Churches Unity Commission for England. That was in part a response to the formation of the URC. The Commission, which included eight denominations, ranging from Roman Catholic to Baptist, was given the remit of spending two years to see whether the kind of union which had been achieved in the Churches of North India and South India might not be possible in England. John Huxtable, Joint General Secretary of the URC with Arthur Macarthur, was asked to act as its Secretary. The task before it was daunting - the reconciliation of episcopally and non-episcopally ordained ministries, women in ministry, the relationship between believer's and paedobaptism, establishment and disestablishment. The broad history of ecumenism in England since 1910 did not augur well for the process. The Commission produced Ten

Propositions about unity, and recommended the formation of the Churches Council for Covenanting to continue the work. It was formed in 1978 of those denominations who had expressed a willingness to move forward to a covenant. It was chaired by bishop Kenneth Woolcombe. The Churches of Christ, the Church of England, the Methodist Church, the Moravians and the URC were full members. The Baptist Union, the Free Church Federal Council and the Roman Catholic Church sent observers. It was, as John Huxtable later wrote, doomed to failure, not least one suspects because it tried to accomplish too much too quickly. However, the tight timetable was part of the conditions that the Church of England laid down in negotiations about funding. The General Synod of the Church of England failed to accept the covenanting scheme in 1981, and organic union seemed to have reached an impasse.

In the meantime the Joint Committee for Negotiations between the United Reformed Church and the Churches of Christ quietly got on with its work, publishing Proposals for Union in 1976. The proposals involved the Churches accepting the URC's conciliar structure, and both denominations acceding to a dual baptismal policy with due recognition of conscientious objection provided that both modes of baptism were available in each congregation. A new form of ministry, auxiliary ministry, for those in secular employment, was envisaged, and it was hoped that Churches of Christ elders would become some of the first auxiliary ministers. The URC Assembly accepted the proposals overwhelmingly in 1977, but they failed to command the necessary majority amongst the Churches of Christ. As with the earlier union between the Congregationalists and Presbyterians, three quarters of the membership of two thirds of the Churches had to vote in favour. Forty-five churches, representing 69.9% of the membership had attained the required majority, five more were not far short of it. Twenty-seven churches, representing 25.6%, voted against. The Central Council of the Churches called a meeting of the Consultative Council of all members of Standing Committees. It was clear that they wished to co-operate fully with the URC until a way forward could be found. The 1978 Conference asked those churches which had voted against to reconsider their position. If they had not changed their position, the Council was authorised to dissolve the Association to allow each local church to do as it felt fit. When it became clear that a sufficient change of mind was not forthcoming, the Association was dissolved - fifty-four churches were in favour, twenty against and one did not return its vote. Those in favour formed the Re-formed Association of the Churches of Christ, which united with the URC in 1981 to create the United Reformed Church in the United Kingdom. The impetus for the Re-formed Association came from the Scottish churches which had become frustrated by the breakdown of conversations with the Scottish Congregationalists who refused to make baptism a condition of membership, and the slow progress of the Multi-lateral conversations. It was once again a source of frustration that union could not be complete.

## The United Reformed Church in the United Kingdom

It is hard to write the history of the past sixteen years. The events and people that have created that history are too close, and little serious research has been undertaken on the contemporary history of the United Reformed Church. However, there are some features of our life which a future historian might see as contours on the map of our history. They may also be seen in a century's time as molehills in contrast to the surrounding mountains!

The United Reformed Church was created in 1972 when Edward Heath had been in power for two years. The politics of confrontation dogged his four year premiership. When he called the 1974 election the country was working a three day week, the miners were on strike, the Trades Union Movement was at the zenith of its power, and the country was gripped by a sense of industrial bitterness unparalleled since the General Strike. The Labour administrations of Wilson (1974-6) and Callaghan (1976-9) produced little change. The country's troubles simply seemed to intensify - Northern Ireland descended deeper and deeper into hellish violence, unemployment rose from 550,000 in 1968 to three million in 1981, and the true figure for 1985 was probably over four million, but by then the government had grown adept at massaging the figures. Neither liberal Conservatism nor moderate Labour seemed to have an answer. In 1979 Margaret Thatcher came to power. For the next eleven years Britain experienced something unique in its modern political history.

The Thatcher revolution was part of one of those odd shifts of international political gear - Ronald Reagan became President of America the following year, John Paul II had ascended the papal throne the year before. As she stood on the steps of 10 Downing Street following her election victory, Mrs Thatcher quoted St Francis's prayer, *'Where there is discord, let me sow harmony...'* By 1982 she was declaring, *'The time for counter-attack is long overdue. We are reaping what was sown in the sixties.'*

Mrs Thatcher set herself the programme of reversing Britain's decline.

What she wanted was a clean break with the past. The consensus politics which had prevailed since 1945 were at an end. If the creation of post-war Britain, and in particular the welfare state, had roots which reached into Christian soil in a tradition of Christian social thought which can be traced back to such different nineteenth century thinkers as F D Maurice and R W Dale, so too did its deconstruction under Margaret Thatcher. Her roots are nonconformist roots. She grew up in Lincolnshire Methodism, and unlike all her twentieth century predecessors, she cared about theology. That is a clue to the nature of her political revolution. As the American economist Milton Friedman once shrewdly observed, Margaret Thatcher was not a Tory by belief but a nineteenth century Liberal. She embodied some of the ideals that had once made nonconformity a power in the land - thrift, self-reliance, duty, family responsibility, self-improvement. In the nineteenth century the economic equivalent of freedom of religious practice was Manchester school economics, freedom from state interference, laissez-faire. Margaret Thatcher was the heiress of that tradition. She was formed by the culture of the chapel and the grocer's shop, and she believed in it. She was, she said, a conviction politician, not a consensus politician. That was why the monetarism of Friedman and Hayek was so appealing to her. Such unreconstructed Victorian liberalism was anathema to traditional, patrician conservatives like Sir Ian Gilmour who had been raised in the compassionate, paternalistic tradition of Disraeli's 'one nation' conservatism. In his book *Inside Right* he sharply attacked this new ideology, suggesting that its failure to create a sense of community might repel people from the rest of its programme. Such dissenting voices were rapidly dismissed as 'wets'. Mrs Thatcher did not believe in community.

The Churches of Christ and the United Reformed Church united in 1981. The bulk of the URC's short history has taken place against the backdrop of Thatcherism. Looking back on the Thatcher decade, it is now clear that she was unable to stem the tide of economic and industrial decline. That is scarcely surprising, for reversing Britain's industrial decline is the holy grail of modern British politics. When Mrs Thatcher was asked what her greatest achievement was, she replied immediately, 'Changing attitudes.' She was the creator of the enterprise culture, and the ideology that produced that culture partly determined the history of the churches during the Thatcher years.

Parliamentary opposition was ineffective, and the churches found themselves speaking for the nation, particularly for those least able to defend themselves and least likely to darken the doors of the church. The list of skirmishes between church and state is long - 1981 Nationality Act, the

1982 Falklands Memorial Service, nuclear weapons, the conduct of the police and security forces in Northern Ireland, and particularly the miscarriages of justice which produced the cases of the Birmingham six, the Guildford four and the Maguires, rules about refugee status and political asylum, community and race relations policy, inner city poverty, unemployment, the poll tax, benefit reforms and the restructuring of the National Health Service. It was focused on particular individuals - the bishop of Durham and archbishop Robert Runcie, and on particular publications like *Faith in the city* in 1985, because the popular media concentrate on Anglican bishops and Anglican reports. However, a reading of the reports given to denominational and ecumenical Assemblies and Conferences show that there was a depth and solidarity about the critique. It was not a matter of pink bishops versus the Iron Lady, but a sustained and serious reaction against the trend of policy.

The heart of the conflict was ethical. It was about the theoretical way in which enterprise culture works. Wealth would 'trickle down'. State support for the poor disabled, rather than enabled, because it denied them the incentive for work, creativity and enterprise. Mrs Thatcher seriously questioned the existence of 'society'. That led Robert Runcie to warn of danger of regarding success as *'a sort of blessing or reward for righteousness'* which in turn would lead to dismissive judgments about the value of the unsuccessful.

In 1988 Mrs Thatcher addressed the General Assembly of the Church of Scotland, and made clear her view of the proper relationship between religion and socio-economic issues. The distinctive marks of Christianity were not social but spiritual. The Bible, she felt, provided a *'view of the universe, a proper attitude to work, and principles to shape economic and social life'* and she went on to quote the text '..if a man will not work, he shall not eat.' Talents were given that we might use them to create wealth. Spirituality enters the matter when you decide what to do with the wealth that has been created. What mattered was individual responsibility and the church must not interfere with that. The Church of Scotland listened but, nurtured in Calvinism as they were, the Assembly's members had a rather less optimistic understanding of human nature.

Although the institutional churches presented a solid front against Thatcherism, there were many Christians who found the government's position Christianly coherent and ethical - John Selwyn Gummer remained a convinced supporter, so too did Professor Brian Griffith, who was for some time head of Margaret Thatcher's policy unit. There is always a gap between the deliberations of national bodies and local churches. Until careful research has been done it remains a suspicion, but it is likely that local churches were more seriously divided on these matters than a reading of national reports would suggest.

Future historians will see the churches attitude to social affairs as a major contour of church life during the late 1970s and the 1980s, and although the URC's part in that is hidden away in the minutes of denominational and ecumenical committees, they will note its contribution.

The second contour is the changing pattern of religious allegiance. The formation of the URC has not halted the decline of membership. It would have been remarkable if it had, for membership of all the mainstream churches has been declining throughout most of this century, and the ratio of church members to the total population has been falling since the 1840s. Between 1970-85 the total active membership of the British churches fell by 1.5 m to just under 7m. By the mid 80s only 15% of the population claimed actual membership of a Christian church. Within that total pattern of decline there were interesting variations. Church going remained six times more popular in Ireland than in England; the Roman Catholic Church became the largest single denomination; the independent and pentecostal churches experienced growth. One recent sociological study of religion in Britain in the post-war period has suggested that the crisis facing the churches is not one of believing, but of belonging. That is reflected in the ratio of members to adherents in the URC which is now roughly 2:1. The deep suspicion of all authority structures which is prevalent in Western society has led to the growth of a pick n' mix culture. Religion is back in the marketplace, often in esoteric and strange forms, and the rate of church decline is gradually slowing. Whether that trend will have an effect on the older Free Churches remains to be seen.

Lesslie Newbigin once said that contemporary Britain was the hardest mission field he had ever encountered. What matters in a post-Christian society is faithfulness to the gospel. We are called to be faithful, to preach the gospel and administer the sacraments. The result of our work is always in the good hands of God. *'For twenty-three years, from the thirteenth year of King Josiah son of Amon of Judah to this day, the word of the Lord has come to me, and I have spoken persistently to you, but you have not listened.'* (Jer 25:3 NRSV) wrote Jeremiah. We are not the first of God's people to find his gracious providence perplexing.

A sensitive future historian may discover a third contour, that the

URC has remained faithful to its calling. It has continued to proclaim the gospel in innovative and creative ways, often in the hardest of places. The membership of the churches has declined, the number of churches has not:

| | Members | Buildings | Ministers |
|---|---|---|---|
| 1972 | 200 000 | 2 080 | 1 841 |
| 1995 | 102 000 | 1 784 | 813 |
| Reduction | 49% | 15% | 56% |

Those figures may be interpreted in two ways. It may be seen as the heritage of a Congregationalism whose demographic pattern throughout the century has included a large number of small churches. It can also be understood as a refusal to forsake the 'front line' of missionary engagement. There has been a determination, for example, to do all that is possible to maintain a presence in our inner cities, and the development of the ministry of Church Related Community Workers has been a significant, if small, witness to creative thinking about the relationship of church and community.

Maintaining the front-line of mission with a falling ratio of members to churches has caused difficulties in providing ministry for all churches, and the denomination still struggles to find an appropriate pattern of ministry which is both responsive to its own needs yet also ecumenically responsible.

Another contour is internal and administrative. The real internal challenge for the URC has been to make sense of provinces, which were introduced largely to provide a conciliar setting for the work of Moderators. District and Provincial boundaries were prepared on the basis of the 1970 Local Government review, which became effective in 1974. However, the shrinking of the church and the further changes in local government structure in the 1990s raises questions about our ability to sustain them. The work of bringing the financial structures of the three churches into one system, and the creation of Provincial Trusts required much work and considerable energy. It has led to an increase in the power of Provincial Synods and that is unsurprising for politics and commerce have also drifted towards increased regionalisation. One unforeseen result of that trend has been an unequal distribution of resources within the Provinces, and that is an issue with which the church struggles. However, the tension between provincial and national structures is in other senses healthy, allowing a serious engagement with regional variation and needs. Wales is, of course, a special case because it is both a Province and a nation. However, the URC's provincial structure has enabled its Welsh churches to play a significant part in the creation of the Welsh covenant and in ecumenical developments since then.

Another contour which may be discernible on a future map is the church's attempt to honour the gifts of all God's people. The rôle of women in the church is slowly and painstakingly being recovered by historians. When that work is complete, histories such as this will need re-writing. The changing status of women in society has been one of the salient features of twentieth century history, and that has been reflected in church life too. The Congregationalists were the first trinitarian church to ordain a woman to the ministry of Word and Sacraments. Constance Coltman, who had been brought up a Presbyterian, was ordained in 1917 to that delightfully angular church, the Kings Weigh House during Orchard's ministry. The Presbyterians and the Churches of Christ had a longer journey to women's ordination, although both made it clear in the 1920s that there was no theoretical bar. The URC has tried to honour the calling of women to ministries of all kinds. Two lay women, Mrs Rosalind Goodfellow and Mrs Ruth Clarke, have served as Moderators of General Assembly, in 1982 and 1993 respectively, and currently three Provincial Moderators are women. Much remains to be done, and there is no room for complacency.

Like the other British churches, we are determined that people of all ethnic groups should play a part in the leadership of our councils. That is proving a more complex problem, but at least our Assembly has declared its conviction, and endeavours to provide a balance on its committees between men and women, young and old, black and white.

At the 1996 Assembly at the University of York, the Archbishop of York, Dr David Hope, was deeply moved by the fact that one of the lessons was read by a girl of primary school age. That, he assured Assembly could never happen at the General Synod of the Church of England. One of the most impressive aspects of our life is the seriousness with which the leadership of young people is taken. It is more obvious at Assembly than at other levels of church life, but it is a distinctive mark of our church life, reminding us that all have a contribution to make to the life of the people of God, regardless of age.

If the church has been faithful in its proclamation of the gospel in its mission and in its honouring of the ministry of all the baptised, it has also been faithful to its Basis of Union and to its promotion of the unity of all God's people. That is a predictable contour, and it is still a formative one. The URC is involved in countless Local Ecumenical Partnerships, and has contributed through its personnel to ecumenism at every level - in the last seventeen years the work of Martin Cressey on the Faith and Order Commission of the World Council of Churches, Philip Morgan's General Secretaryship of the British Council of Churches and his guidance of its dissolution to form the Council of Churches for Britain and Ireland, thus enabling a wider ecumenism including both Roman Catholics and the black led churches, and John Reardon's Secretaryship of the new body are the visible tip of an iceberg which reaches down to county and local bodies. Ecumenism has moved rapidly in a very different direction to that envisaged by the those who created the URC, but our commitment has been unwavering. Our experience as a united church will surely be of value in the ecumenical future.

That commitment has itself created tensions for us. The final contour we might point to is the formation of a specific identity. We are a church that was created as a stepping stone to something greater. We never intended to be here seventeen years on. The URC is therefore struggling with its identity, with what it means to be both United *and* Reformed, to be true to the heritages which are ours, and yet open to the promptings of God's Spirit to become what God would have us be. Only a church with an identity can produce a hymnbook. *Rejoice and Sing* (1991) with its blend of metrical psalms, Watts and Kendrick, Taizé chants and Iona songs, is clear evidence of traditions living together. We are Reformed, and we are re-discovering our traditions, and yet we are more than the sum of all our parts. We know something of the cost of living together whilst respecting divergent consciences - the questions of lay presidency at holy communion, two forms of baptism, human sexuality and Biblical authority exercise us. That is part of the spirituality of being 'united', and there is a gift of God there.

As Norman St John Stevas said in the parliamentary debate in June 1972, we did not know where the path on which we set our feet would lead. We were sure that in doing so we were being obedient to the call of God. There is good precedent for those kinds of journeys, as Abraham and Sarai, Amos, Peter and Paul and countless saints of God bear witness. Faith is about travelling into the unknown. When Edward Winslow wrote down his recollections of John Robinson's farewell to those members of his Leyden congregation who set sail in the *Mayflower* in 1620, he remembered Robinson charging them to follow his ministry *'no further than he followed Christ'*, and to be open to receive what God would reveal to them as they journeyed on, *'For he was very confident that the Lord had more light and truth to break forth from his Word.'* Those words echo in the hymns of our traditions. George Rawson, a Congregationalist solicitor who worked in Leeds in the mid nineteenth century made them the refrain of his 'We limit not the truth of God'. George Caird, hymnwriter and poet as well as Biblical scholar, found in them the inspiration for 'Not far beyond the sea, nor high':

Rooted and grounded in your love,

with saints on earth and saints above
we join in one accord
to grasp the breadth, length, depth and height,
the crucified and risen might
of Christ, the incarnate Word.

Help us to press toward that mark,
and, though our vision now is dark
to live by what we see;
so, when we see you face to face,
your light and truth our dwelling-place
for evermore shall be. (*Rejoice and Sing* 318)

That takes us to the heart of the Reformed tradition, to a church attentive to the Word of God, from whence comes both grace sufficient for all our journeys and the surprises of God's love, new every morning. Under the good hand of God, the pilgrimage continues.

This section is divided into two. The first part, suggestions for further

# Postscript

History forms societies and churches, giving them particular shapes and styles. The particular shape of the URC sometimes baffles those from other parts of the Christian family. Occasionally it perplexes and frustrates those who have grown up within it! But there are reasons for the way we are, and at this moment in our story it is worth stopping a while to take stock.

Ours is a heritage that reaches back over nearly half a millenium. In our beginnings we were formed from the work of both the magisterial and the radical reformers of the sixteenth century, for whom questions of church order and the place of Scripture in Christian life and worship were very important. We call ourselves, rather cumbersomely, yet none the less accurately, the United Reformed Church. Each of those words is important.

We are **Reformed.** We belong to that family of world-wide churches who understand their formation to have been determined by the reformations of the sixteenth century. Those roots explain several things about the way we are.

(a) why we place such a high value on Scripture in our worship and discipleship.

In some of our churches the Bible is carried into church at the start of worship, followed by the minister who is thus seen to be 'the servant of the Word'. We listen attentively to readings from Scripture, and the climax of our worship is often the exposition of those readings in sermons and other imaginative exercises. Our concern with the Bible is focused on Sunday, but it flows out into the rest of the week. Most churches will have regular Bible study groups, and many individuals find their spiritual nourishment in daily study and reading.

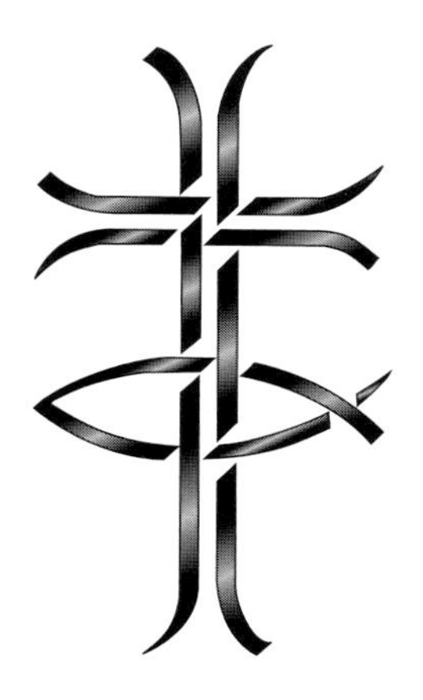

That deep commitment to, and love of the Word of God is, of course, not exclusive to the URC, but we could not be the church without it. The churches of the

Reformation differed from their Catholic (and later Anglican) neighbours by stressing the significance of Scripture as the starting point of theology. Catholic and Anglican theology gives equal weight to Scripture, reason and tradition. Reformed theology has always chosen to stand under the judgement of Scripture, for, as the Westminster Confession put it:

*..the whole counsel of God, concerning all things necessary for his own glory, man's salvation, faith and life, is either expressly set down in Scripture, or by good and necessary consequence may be deduced from Scripture.*

An echo of that can still be heard in our own Basis of Union which states that the church '*..acknowledges the Word of God in the Old and New Testaments, discerned under the guidance of the Holy Spirit, as the supreme authority for the faith and conduct of all God's people.*'

The Reformed tradition has treated the Bible with that kind of deep respect for good reason. It is primarily through Scripture that the Reformed have encountered God. The Reformed have always been wary of the human intellect. One of the firm convictions of the Reformed tradition is that we cannot reach God through our own unaided efforts and perceptions. However wonderful and creative our theologies may be, they could not even begin to comprehend the otherness and mystery of God. God must therefore reach out to us. Revelation is of supreme importance. God revealed himself in Christ. It is though the pages of Scripture that we encounter Jesus. Hence the centrality of Scripture.

(b) why we celebrate communion

For the reformers God's grace and love were mediated particularly through the Scriptures. That did not mean that they devalued the sacraments of baptism and holy communion. Those from the Churches of Christ tradition have recalled the United Reformed Church to an understanding of the centrality of holy communion in worship, for communion was the normal act of Sunday worship for them. Churches from a Congregationalist background often celebrate communion monthly, those from the Presbyterian tradition either monthly or quarterly. It needs to be stated clearly that the frequency with which communion is taken is no guide to the seriousness with which it is taken. What is interesting is that each of these patterns is historically conditioned. The medieval pattern of eucharistic celebration was quarterly, co-inciding with the great feasts of the year. That pattern passed unaltered into Zwinglian practice in Zürich, and eventually elsewhere in the Reformed world, including Scotland. In post 1662 England, one of the distinctive features of Congregationalism was its regular monthly celebration of communion. Anglican practice varied, but with few exceptions they too celebrated monthly or quarterly. The frequency of celebration in the Church of England increased following the Oxford movement's recovery of the centrality of the sacraments in the 1830s. Congregationalism continued with its established monthly pattern.

Whatever Reformed practice may be, Reformed theory has never doubted that Word and Sacraments are of equal importance, that the sacraments are the Word enacted, and that the Word is a 'sacramental' conveyance of the presence of God. Calvin wanted to celebrate communion weekly in Geneva. It was the city council which said no. The reformers thought they were restoring a balance between Word and Sacrament which had long been lost in the medieval church by emphasising the importance of Scripture and preaching.

(c) why we have conciliar government

Throughout history the church has struggled with the relationship between personal and corporate authority under Christ. Our traditions believed conciliar government to be Scriptural, and that the will of Christ was best discerned through the prayerful meeting of minds in church councils.

(d) why we believe in the ministry of all God's people

In the Reformed understanding of church order, there is one ministry of Word and Sacraments, and all ministers are therefore equal although they may exercise different functions. Ministers have a particular role in the life and work of God's people, but only as part of the people of God. In a profound sense baptism makes us all ministers because all the baptised share in the ministry of Christ. It is to our Reformed roots that we owe our understanding of the priesthood of all believers. One of the great achievements of the reformers was the breaking down of the medieval distinctions between 'sacred' and 'secular', for all the world belonged to God. The counting house was just as much God's space as St Peter's cathedral in Geneva for Calvin - '*..there shall be no work so filthy and vile (if it be such as thou obey thy calling in it) but it shineth and is most precious in the sight of God.*' God called people to serve him in countless ways. The old medieval world in which vocation was restricted to the work of priests, monks and nuns was thus swept away. Ministry became one vocation amongst many in the Reformed churches. All Christians were called, all were priests, serving God in their own particular place, raising that place to God in prayer, and mediating his love to it by their lives. For Luther and Calvin the priesthood of all believers did not mean that anyone could do anything in church for they both believed deeply in church order and were scandalised by some of the 'undisciplined' behaviour of the radicals. For them the doctrine was of much greater significance. Being part of the priesthood of all believers means taking the world seriously as the theatre of God's activity and therefore the focus of our discipleship as the baptised people of God.

The Reformation has had a determining influence on the United Reformed Church. A Reformed church though, is never static. It is always striving to be more faithful to Christ. That is why so many Reformed churches worldwide have been committed to the quest for unity and the healing of divisions. We are not simply a 'Reformed Church', we are also a United church. We are **United**, a product of modern ecumenism, which by the grace of God has brought together three very different ways of being the church into one body. We remain committed to the quest for further healing of the broken body of Christ.

Above all though, we are **Church** - not 'a' church, but part of 'the' church, the body of Christ which gathers within itself all the saints of God of all places and times. Our history doesn't actually begin in 1517, the 1640s, 1662, 1972 or 1981. It begins at the foot of the cross. However, the way our history has shaped us means that we come to experience 'the' church through belonging to 'a' church. Put more theologically, the catholic is found in the local. The catholicity of the United Reformed Church is expressed through a series of interlocking councils, local, regional and national and (in a consultative sense, international), but the centre of gravity is local. The first reality is belonging to that community, playing a part in its life and mission and taking responsibility for its government and life. That means, in turn, that the fellowship of believers is important. The more radical, independent strand in the Reformed tradition laid great stress on the importance of a covenant which bound a local community of believers to each other under God. There are clear similarities between the concept of the gathered independent church and the Benedictine monastic ideal. Commitment to God and to each other is a characteristic of both. In 1660 about a dozen like-minded Christians covenanted together to form a fellowship at Axminster in Devon. The form of their covenant is typical of many from this period and later:

*The Lord having called us into fellowship with his Sonne, and convinced us of the necessity of Church-fellowship: we do solemnly professe, in the strength of Christ, The accepting of the Lord for our God, And the giving up our selves to him, to walk, through the strength of Christ, together in all his holy Commandements and Ordinances according to the Rule of his Word: And we do likewise give up our selves to one another in the Lord, To walk together in the exercise of all those graces, and discharging all those duties which are required of us as a Church of Christ.*

It was through the covenanted fellowship of local believers that they experienced the church catholic. From the very beginning English independents realised that ordination meant little if done in isolation, so ordinations became (and still are) 'clan gatherings'. English presbyterians never doubted the value of a series of interlocking councils, although they did not have the chance to translate theory into practice until the nineteeth century. The history of the Reformed tradition, then, shows that the value and significance of the local has always been balanced by the importance of the church catholic. It is seen in the genuine openness of Baxter and Doddridge, in the informal and formal associations of churches prior to the growth of central denominational structures, and in the quest for the unity. Reformed spirituality is local and rooted.

All of the traditions which formed the United Reformed Church were conscious that they were part of God's great story of salvation. It is precisely because we are part of 'the' church, the great communion of saints on earth and in heaven, that we are able to live with the tensions between being 'united' and 'reformed'. The blessings of union are great, but unity sometimes means renouncing things that are precious to us for the sake of a greater blessing. The true benefits of unity come when the great gifts of Christ to each tradition are fully and honestly shared. All three of the denominations which make up the URC could legitimately claim to be churches of Reformation in that they could trace their origins or inspiration to that movement.

What did the three traditions which formed us contribute to the URC?

**Presbyterianism** was a system of church government which depended on ministers and elders taking counsel together under the Spirit's guidance for the welfare and mission of the church locally, regionally and nationally. Presbyterians placed a high premium on order, believing, for example, that normally only Ministers of Word and Sacraments should preside at communion. It is to presbyterianism that we owe our system of interlocking, mutually dependent councils - from the local church to the General Assembly. The 1972 Union created an extra 'level' of councils, the Provincial Synod, principally to provide a conciliar setting for the work of Provincial Moderators who were part of Congregationalism's gift to union. Modern

English presbyterianism grew out of Scottish ( and to a lesser extent, Irish) presbyterianism. That heritage is enshrined in metrical psalms and the distinctive accents of some of our congregations, and it is an inheritance which makes us a truly British church. We also owe the ministry of elders, which has become such an important feature of our corporate life, to presbyterianism.

**Congregationalism** knew that each local body of believers contained all the giftings and graces necessary to be the church of Christ in that locality. It is to Congregationalism that we owe the significance of the Church Meeting in which each congregation seeks to discern the mind of Christ for its life together. Congregationalism placed a high value on the ministry of all God's people, and one of the ways this was expressed was through the work of lay preachers. Congregationalists were used to lay preachers presiding at communion, if invited to do so by Church Meeting.

One of the tensions of our present life is the different ways in which Synods and District Councils interpret guidelines on lay presidency. What is important though, is that we understand that those guidelines were the product of a process which attempted to honour divergent consciences. Sometimes, as Paul realised, we need to refrain from doing things we feel to be natural and right for the sake of the consciences of others.

**The Churches of Christ** brought to the union a commitment to the healing of Christian brokenness which reaches back to their earliest days. They also brought a belief in believer's baptism, and an understanding that holy communion should be the normative act of Christian worship. That is why we offer both forms of baptism in the life of our churches. It was also their experience of eldership which helped the united church formulate its ideas about what was originally called 'auxiliary' ministry which became non-stipendiary ministry.

Historians should resist the temptation to gaze into crystal balls, because if history teaches us anything it is that the future is unpredictable. As the second millenium draws to a close, we have been privileged to know a little of the healing grace of God as the Holy Spirit has drawn three denominations into one. Nothing is wasted in God's economy. What we have become is part of what God wishes us to be.

# Suggestions for further reading and acknowledgement of sources

reading, is a small selection of books which is intended to guide interested students as they begin their own exploration of the subject. It is arranged according to the chapters in the book. The books vary in complexity, and I have tried to indicate those that are more advanced. The exclusion of articles is deliberate - they can be found in the sources section.

Some denominational histories and books about our traditions are listed separately. Most, if not all, are unfortunately long out of print. The United Reformed Church History Society provides a forum for those who are concerned about the history of our traditions to share their interests. The Society's *Journal* is by far the best source of specialised studies of our histories. Those who wish to subscribe should contact the Membership Secretary, c/o The United Reformed Church, 86 Tavistock Place, London WC1H 9RT.

The second section sets out the sources I have used. I hope this will enable those who are interested to follow up more detailed reading.

# reading

## 1. The European reformation

R Tudor Jones *The Great Reformation* (Leicester 1985) - accessible and easy to follow
Owen Chadwick *The Reformation* (London 1964).
Euan Cameron *The European reformation* (Oxford 1991) - a more advanced survey
Heiko Oberman *Luther, man between God and the devil* (ET London 1989) - the best biography of Luther
G R Potter *Zwingli* (Cambridge 1967)
W P Stephens *The theology of Huldrych Zwingli* (Oxford 1986)
T H L Parker *Calvin* (London 1975)
Michael Mullett *Calvin* (London 1989) - clear and concise
William Bouwsma *John Calvin: a sixteenth century portrait* (Oxford 1988) - a 'must' for the more advanced student

## 2. The English reformation

A G Dickens *The English reformation* (London 2nd ed. 1989) - an epoch making study and a great work of scholarship which should still be read, preferably in the second edition of 1989
Christopher Haigh (ed) *The English reformation revised* (Cambridge 1987)
Christopher Haigh *English reformations* (Oxford 1993) - both these works present serious critiques of Dickens
Eamon Duffy *The stripping of the altars* (New Haven and London 1992) - presents a radically new interpretation of the vitality of late medieval popular religion
Dairmaid MacCulloch *Thomas Cranmer* (New Haven and London 1996)
Claire Cross *The Elizabethan religious settlement* (Bangor 1992)
Patrick Collinson *The Elizabethan Puritan movement* (London 1967) - an outstanding analysis of Purian opinion
B R White *The Elizabethan Separatist Tradition* (Oxford 1971)
Kenneth Hylson-Smith's *The churches in England from Elizabeth I to Elizabeth II, vol 1 1558-1688* (London 1995) - provides a clear narrative of events of the latter part of the English reformation and is an accessible guide to the state of historical research.

## 3. The seventeenth century

Kenneth Hylson-Smith *The churches in England from Elizabeth I to Elizabeth II, vol 1 1558-1688* (London 1996)

Kenneth Fincham (ed) *The early Stuart church 1603-1642* (London 1993) - for the more advanced students
Ivan Roots *The Great Rebellion 1642-1660* (London 1966)
John Morrill *The nature of the English revolution* (London 1993) - outstanding collection of essays - for the more advanced student
Barry Coward *Cromwell* (Harlow 1991)
Christopher Hill *God's Englishman* (London 1970)
G F Nuttall *Visible Saints 1640-1660* (Oxford 1957) - incomparable on the Independents
Ronald Hutton *The Restoration* (Oxford 1987)
Ian Green *The re-establishment of the Church of England 1660-1663* (Oxford 1978)
G F Nuttall 'The first nonconformists' in GF Nuttall and Owen Chadwick (eds) *From uniformity to unity 1662-1962* (London 1962) pp 149-189.

## 4. The Eighteenth century

There are no good modern studies specifically about our traditions in the eighteenth century. Students should consult the detailed sources list below for specific concerns. The following books will provide a more general history of the church in this period.

John Walsh, Colin Haydon and Stephen Taylor (eds) *The Church of England c.1689-c.1833: from toleration to Tractarianism* (Cambridge 1993)
Henry Rack *Reasonable enthusiast* (London 1989) - the best biography of Wesley, which contains much more besides
Barrie Tabraham *The making of Methodism* (London 1995) - an easily accessible introduction

## 5. The Nineteenth century

David M Thompson *Nonconformity in the Nineteenth Century* (London 1972) - a series of documents with linking commentary
Clyde Binfield *So down to prayers: studies in English nonconformity 1781-1920* (London 1977) - a sparkling set of essays on Congregationalism
David M Thompson *Let sects and parties fall* (Birmingham 1980) - a wonderfully comprehensive history of the Churches of Christ
James Munson *The nonconformists* (London 1991)
Ian Sellers *Nineteenth century nonconformity* (London 1977)
B G Worrall *The making of the modern church* (London 1988) - an excellent introductory textbook
Hugh McLeod *Religion and society in England 1850-1914* (London 1996) - good summary of recent research - for the more advanced student

## 6. The twentieth century

Adrian Hastings *A history of English Christianity 1920-1985* (London 1986) - an admirable narrative history
Grace Davie *Religion in Britain since 1945* (Oxford 1994)

## 7. Denominational histories

**(a) Congregationalism**

R Tudor Jones *Congregationalism in England 1662-1962* (London 1962)
Alan Sell *Saints, visible, orderly and catholic: the Congregational idea of the church* (Geneva 1986)
Clyde Binfield *So down to prayers* (London 1977) - mainly on nineteenth century Congregationalism

**(b) Presbyterianism**

A H Drysdale *History of the Presbyterians in England: their rise, decline and revival* (London 1889)
C G Bolam, Jeremy Goring, H L Short & Roger Thomas *The English Presbyterians: from Elizabethan Puritanism to modern Unitarianism* (London 1968)

**(c) Churches of Christ**

David M Thompson *Let sects and parties fall: a short history of the Association of Churches of Christ in Great Britain and Ireland* (Birmingham 1980)

**(d) General studies of dissent and the Reformed tradition**

Michael Watts *The Dissenters volume 1* (Oxford 1978)
Michael Watts *The Dissenters volume 2* (Oxford 1995)
J H Leith *Introduction to the Reformed tradition* (Atlanta 1977)

# Sources and acknowledgements

## General

The following have been my constant companions. I have tried to indicate particular points of indebtedness below, but I hope the authors and their publishers will accept this general acknowledgement of my reliance on their works, and forgive me for any borrowings which I have failed to track with proper diligence.

R Tudor Jones *Congregationalism in England 1662-1962* (London 1962)
David M Thompson *Let sects and parties fall* (Birmingham 1980)
Michael Watts *The Dissenters volume 1* (Oxford 1978)

## Specific

### Chapter 1

**(a) The European reformation**

The idea of three 'phases' of the reformation is taken from Heiko Obermann *The Reformation; roots and ramifications* (Edinburgh 1994) pp 210-17; the quotation from Geoffrey Elton is from his review article 'Commemorating Luther' *Journal of Ecclesiastical History* 35 (4) October 1984 pp 614-19, from p 618; for popular religion, see particularly Eamon Duffy *The stripping of the altars* (New Haven and London 1992); the main source for Luther was Heiko Oberman *Luther, man between God and the Devil* (ET London 1989); the quotation from Gordon Rupp is taken from *Luther's progress to the Diet of Worms 1521* (London 1951) p25; the quotations from Luther's writings can be conveniently found in E G Rupp and Benjamin Drewery *Martin Luther* (London 1970) documents A1 and A5; for the implications of Luther's discovery for the medieval penitential system, see Euan Cameron *The European reformation* (Oxford 1991) pp 132-136; for Karlstadt see Gordon Rupp *Patterns of Reformation* (London 1969) and Felipe Fernandez-Armesto and Derek Wilson *Reformation, Christianity and the world 1500-2000* (London 1996) pp 146-8; for Calvin's Geneva the main sources used are Michael Mullett *Calvin* (London 1989) pp 30-38 and R S Wallace *Calvin, Geneva and the reformation* (Edinburgh 1988) pp 46-52; the quotations from Calvin are all from the Library of Christian Classics edition, edited by John McNeill and translated by F L Battles (Philadelphia and London 1960); for Calvin on the eucharist see Brian Gerrish *Grace and gratitude: the eucharistic theology of John Calvin* (Edinburgh 1993); on Laski see Basil Hall *Humanists and Protestants 1500-1900* (Edinburgh 1990) pp 171-208 and on the continuing life of the emigré community in London, Andrew Pettegree *Marian Protestantism: six studies* (Aldershot 1996).

**(b) The English reformation**

For Anne Boleyn and Tyndale see Eric Ives *Anne Boleyn* (Oxford 1986) pp 161ff; for the Elizabethan settlement Claire Cross *The Elizabethan religious settlement* (Bangor 1992); for the growth of presbyterian opinion and the development of the vestments controversy, Patrick Collinson *The Elizabethan Puritan movement* (London 1967) pp 71-101; the account of the separatists relies on Watts *op cit* pp 14-71, B R White *The Elizabethan Separatist Tradition* (Oxford 1971), *passim* and Kenneth Hylson-Smith's *The churches in England from Elizabeth I to Elizabeth II, vol 1 1558-1688* (London 1995) provides a clear narrative of events of the latter part of the English reformation pp 48-76.

## Chapter two

For Wales see Glanmor Williams 'Medieval Wales and the Reformation' in Sheridan Gilley and W J Sheils (eds) *A History of Religion in Britain* (Oxford 1994) pp 77-94; for the Scottish reformation, James Cameron 'The church in Scotland from the Reformation to the Disruption' *ibid* pp 129-151, and Gordon Donaldson *The Scottish reformation* (Cambridge 1960); the quotation, 'I am so far from being contentious...' is taken from the 1603 preface to *Basilikon Doron*, quoted in Kenneth Fincham and Peter Lake 'The ecclesiastical policy of James I and Charles I' in Kenneth Fincham (ed) *The early Stuart Church 1603-1642* (London 1993) pp 23-49, at p 25; the account of James's reign relies on that essay, Hylson-Smith *op cit* pp 92-141, and John Morrill 'The Scottish national covenant of 1638 in its British context' in John Morrill *The nature of the English revolution* (London 1993) pp 91-118; the estimate that 10% of the clergy were Puritans is taken from Nicholas Tyacke *The fortunes of English Puritanism* (Dr Williams's Lecture 1990, London 1990); the quotation 'Then Jack and Tom...' is to be found in David Edwards *Christian England volume 2* (London 1983) p 170; for the Jacobean separatists see Watts *op cit* pp 41-76 and Hylson-Smith *op cit* pp 108-117; for the growth of Arminianism and anti-Calvinism, Nicholas Tyacke *Anti-Calvinists - the rise of English Arminianism 1590-1640* (Oxford 1987) and Alan Sell *The great debate* (Worthing 1982) which sets out the theological issues clearly; the quotation from bishop Davenant 'Why that should now be esteemed Puritan doctrine...' is taken from Tyacke *op cit* p 138; for the account of Prynne, Bastwicke and Burton see C V Wedgewood *The King's Peace 1637-1641* (London 1955) pp 160-1 and Hylson-Smith *op cit* pp 170-73; for the religious motivation of the civil wars see John Morrill 'The religious context of the Civil War' in John Morrill *The nature of the English revolution* (London 1993) pp 45-68, particularly p 61-65; the account of the fumbled dismantling of the English church relies heavily on John Morrill 'The church in England 1642-1649' in Morrill *ibid* pp 148-175; the quotation '..such things among us' may be found in Hylson-Smith *op cit* p 193; the judgement of Cromwell '..one that is worth more...' in John Morrill 'Introduction' in John Morrill (ed) *Oliver Cromwell and the English revolution* (London 1990) pp 1-18 at p8, footnote 19; for the sectarians see Christopher Hill *The world turned upside down* (London 1972), Watts *op cit* pp 117-208, Hylson-Smith *op cit* pp 199-223; the commentator who counted 199 heresies was Thomas Edwards *Gangraena* (1646).

## Chapter 3

The quotation from the Declaration of Breda is taken from Anon *Documents relating to the settlement of the Church of England by the Act of Uniformity of 1662* (London 1862) pp1-3; for the celebrations following Charles II's return to the throne, see Ian Green *The re-establishment of the Church of England 1660-1663* (Oxford 1978); my account relies heavily on Ronald Hutton *The Restoration: a political and religious history of England and Wales 1658-1667* (Oxford 1987); for John Owen, see Peter Toon *God's statesman: the life and work of John Owen, pastor, educator, theologian* (Grand Rapids 1973) ; for Sheldon's role see Hutton *op cit* p 176; for the ejected see G F Nuttall 'The first nonconformists' in G F Nuttall and Owen Chadwick (eds) *From uniformity to unity 1662-1962* (London 1962) pp 149-189; the quotations from the sermons of the ejected are from the following sources, Bates, Hylson-Smith *op cit* p 241, Joseph Caryl, Tudor Jones *op cit* p 60; for Richard Baxter see G F Nuttall *Richard Baxter* (London 1965), N H Keeble *Richard Baxter, Puritan Man of Letters* (Oxford 1982); D G Cornick 'Starting with oneself: Spiritual Confessions 7 Richard Baxter's *Autobiography*', *Expository Times* June 1990 vol 101 no 9 pp 259-63; for his attitude to Hereford and Savoy, see Nuttall *art cit* p 184-5; the accounts of persecution are taken from Watts *op cit* pp 230-238; for the Glorious Revolution and the Toleration Act, see Roger Thomas 'Comprehension and indulgence' in G F Nuttall and Owen Chadwick *op cit* pp 189-255, Hylson-Smith *op cit* pp 275-296; the quotation from John Locke is to be found in Johannes van den Berg *The idea of toleration and the Act of Toleration* (Dr Williams's lecture 1989) p 17.

## Chapter 4

For a re-evaluation of the eighteenth century church, see John Walsh, Colin Haydon and Stephen Taylor (eds) *The Church of England c.1689-c.1833: from toleration to Tractarianism* (Cambridge 1993); the quotation from Pope is from 'Essay on Man' (11) 266/7; 289-94; for eighteenth century dissent see Duncan Coomer *English dissent under the early Hanoverians* (London 1949) - the 'Bold Whigs' quotation is from p 5; for the 'Happy Union' Watts *op cit* pp 289-297, Jones *op cit* p 109-119; for occasional conformity, Jones *op cit* p 20, Coomber pp 93-99; for the account of Queen Anne's death, Watts *op cit* p 266; for the Protestant Dissenting Deputies see Bernard Manning *The Protestant Dissenting Deputies* (Cambridge 1952) ed. Ormerod Greenwood, the quotation from Walpole is taken from pp 29-30, and for the Deputies vs. the City of London pp 119-129; the Evans' list statistics are taken from Watts *op cit* pp 269-70, my account relies on his analysis; for worship see Watts *op cit* pp 303-15 and Horton Davies *Worship and Theology in England volume 3, From Watts to Wesley* (London 1961) pp 94-114; for Mark Lane and Isaac Watts see A P Davies *Isaac Watts, his life and work* (London 1948), B L Manning *The hymns of Wesley and Watts* (London 1942), and Watts *op cit* pp 311-13; I am indebted to John Taylor for the comment about Watts's involvement in denominational affairs; the account of the subscription crisis relies heavily on Watts *op cit* pp 371-382 and Jones *op cit* pp 133-143;

for the theological issues see Alan Sell 'Presbyterianism in eighteenth-century England, the doctrinal dimension' originally in *The Journal of the United Reformed Church History Society* (JURCHS) vol 4 no 6 (1990), but reprinted in APF Sell *Dissenting thought and the life of the churches* (San Francisco) pp 118-169; for Doddridge see Malcolm Deacon *Philip Doddridge of Northampton 1702-51* (Northampton 1980), G F Nuttall (ed) *Philip Doddridge 1702-51, his contribution to English religion* (London 1951) and R L Greenall (ed) *Philip Doddridge, nonconformity and Northampton* (Leicester 1981) - the analysis of his readers is taken from Alan Everitt's essay in that volume 'Philip Doddridge and the Evangelical tradition' pp 31-54; the thesis about the Evangelical Revival is from W R Ward *The Protestant Evangelical Awakening* (Cambridge 1992); for the Countess of Huntingdon see Edwin Welch *Spiritual Pilgrim* (Cardiff 1995); for the relationship between the Evangelical Revival and old dissent, see G F Nuttall 'Methodism and the older dissent: some perspectives' *JURCHS* vol 2 no 8 (1981) pp 248-259; the quotation from Harris 'I travelled about 600 miles...' is from Watts *op cit* p 397; for the Evangelical Revival and Methodism, see Henry Rack *Reasonable enthusiast* (London 1989); on William Roby, see Gordon Robinson *William Roby (1766-1830) and the revival of Independency in the North* (London 1954), particularly pp 93ff; the quotation from Thomas Morgan 'Religion at low ebb...' is to be found in Jones *op cit* p 159; for the development of itinerancy in older dissent see Deryck Lovegrove *Established church, sectarian people: itinerancy and the transformation of English dissent 1780-1830* (Cambridge 1988); the quotation from David Bogue about the LMS is from Richard Lovett *The history of the London Missionary Society 1795-1895* (London1899) vol 1 pp 6-10, at p 7; for the formation of the Congregational Union see Jones *op cit* pp 239-244.

## Chapter 5

For the 1851 religious census, Michael Watts *The Dissenters, volume 2, The expansion of Evangelical Nonconformity 1791-1859*, appendix 1 'Interpreting the religious census of 1851' pp 671-6 and pp 24-27, and David M Thompson 'The 1851 religious census: problems and possibilities' *Victorian Studies* 11 (1967) pp 82-97; the comparative figures for 1715 and 1851 are derived from Watts's work; for the relationship between nonconformity and industrialisation, see Alan Gilbert *Religion and society in industrial England, church, chapel and social change 1740-1914* (London 1976); for the study of 28 towns in the 1880s see Robin Gill *The myth of the empty church* (London 1993) and Hugh MacLeod *Religion and society in England 1850-1914* (London 1996) pp 27-37; the quotation from Augustine Birrell is to be found in D M Thompson *Nonconformity in the Nineteenth Century* (London 1972) p 169 (document 66); the Whitehouse quotation is taken from a letter in the Whitehouse envelope, URC archive, London; for Miall and political nonconformity, see Clyde Binfield *op cit* pp 101-25; for the affiliation of nonconformist MPs see MacLeod *op cit* pp 91-92; for nonconformity and Liberalism see David Bebbington *The nonconformist conscience* (London 1982) and Stephen Koss *Nonconformity and modern British politics* (London 1975); the quotation from Matthew Arnold is from *Culture and Anarchy* (1869) -

conveniently to be found in Thompson *op cit* pp 183-5 (document 71); for worship see Jones *op cit* pp 298-303; for suburban noncomformity, the Armitage family and Mansfield College, my account relies heavily on Binfield *op cit* pp 162-185 - Elkanah Armitage's diary entry is on p 165; for English Presbyterianism see D G Cornick ' "Catch a Scotchman becoming an Englishman!" Nationalism, theology and ecumenism in the Presbyterian Church in England 1845-76' *JURCHS* vol 3 no 6 'Essays in honour of R Buick Knox' pp 202-15; the section on the Churches of Christ relies entirely on D M Thompson *Let Sects and Parties Fall* (Birmingham 1980) *passim*; the text of Thomas Campbell's *Declaration and Address* may be found in D M Thompson (ed) *Stating the gospel: formulations and declarations of faith from the heritage of the URC* (Edinburgh 1990) pp 118-183; for Wales see Robert Pope and Geraint Tudor *The history of Christianity in Wales* (Bangor 1996) and John Davies *A history of Wales* (ET London 1993) pp 419-29 and 500-507.

## Chapter Six

For Mudie Smith and attendance statistics see Jones *op cit* p 319-20; for the 1902 Education Act see James Murphy *Church, state and schools in Britain 1800-1970* (London 1971) pp 76-94, James Munson *The Nonconformists* (London 1991); for R J Campbell and 'the New Theology' see Keith Clements *Lovers of discord* (London 1988) pp 19-49, which I follow closely, especially pp 29-32, and Peter Hinchliff *God and History* (Oxford 1992); the quotation from Campbell is from Clements *op cit* p 30; for Forsyth see Trevor Hart *Justice the true and only mercy: essays on the life and theology of Peter Taylor Forsyth* (Edinburgh 1995); the Forsyth quotation 'I could not contemplate conclusions...' is from D G Miller 'P T Forsyth the man' in D G Miller, Browne Barr and Robert Paul *PT Forsyth, the man, the preacher's theologian, prophet for the twentieth century: a contemporary assessment* (Pittsburgh 1981) p 15; 'The minister's study...' is from P T Forsyth *Positive preaching and the modern mind* (London 1907) p 117, '..that he and it together...' *op cit* p 69; for Oman see Stephen Bevans *John Oman and his doctrine of God* (Cambridge 1992), F G Healey *Religion and reality: the theology of John Oman* (Edinburgh and London 1965) and H H Farmer 'Theologians of our time III - John Wood Oman' *Expository Times* 74 no 5 (1962/3) pp 132-135; 'Laboratories...' is quoted by Bevans *op cit* p 39; '..a varied and secular procession' is from J W Oman *Grace and personality* (Cambridge 1925) pp 81/2; 'what all life does say...' *ibid* pp 14-15; for the first world war see Alan Wilkinson *Dissent or conform? War, peace and the English churches 1900-1945* (London 1986) ch 1-3 from whence come the quotations from Clifford, Guttery, Robertson Nicholl and Morgan; for the Churches of Christ see D M Thompson *Let sects and parties fall* (Birmingham 1980) pp 123-125; S W Carruthers quotation from *Fifty Years 1876-1926: a brief survey of work and progress since the Union* (London 1926) p 45; for ecumenism see Ruth Rouse and Stephen Neill *A history of the ecumenical movement 1517-1948* (London 1954), E K H Jordan *Free Church Unity* (London 1956), D M Thompson 'Theological and sociological approaches to the motivation of the ecumenical movement' *Studies in Church History* 15 (1978) pp 467-479 and 'The unity of the church in twentieth century England: pleasing dream or common calling ?' in *Studies in Church History* 32 (Oxford 1996) pp 507-531, and various articles in Nicholas Lossky et al (eds) *Dictionary of the Ecumenical Movement* (Geneva and London 1991); on Selbie and Mansfield see Elaine Kaye *Mansfield College, Oxford, its origin, history and significance* (Oxford 1996) pp 167-8; on the run-up to Lambeth 1920 see Thompson 'The unity of the church...'; Carnegie Simpson quotation is from P Carnegie Simpson *Recollections* (London 1943) p 78; on the interwar years see D M Thompson 'The Older Free Churches' in Rupert Davies (ed) *The testing of the churches 1932-1982: a symposium* (London 1982) pp 87-119 and 'The Free Churches in Modern Britain' in Paul Badham (ed) *Religion, state and society in modern Britain* (Lampeter 1989) pp 99-119; on the Churches of Christ see Thompson *Let sects passim* and James Gray (ed) *WR The Man and his work: a brief account of the life and work of William Robinson MA BSc DD 1888-1963* (Birmingham 1978); for Congregationalism see Jones *op cit passim*; on W E Orchard see Elaine Kaye and Ross MacKenzie *W E Orchard - a study in Christian exploration* (Oxford 1990); the material on the 1950s relies heavily on Hastings *op cit*, particularly pp 462-72; the material on the 1960s follows Hastings and Clements *op cit* pp 178-215; the story of John XXIII and Geoffrey Fisher is from Hastings *op cit* p 523; the formation of the URC follows Arthur Macarthur 'The background to the formation of the United Reformed Church (Presbyterian and Congregational) in England and Wales in 1972' *JURCHS* vol 4 no 1 (1987) pp 3-22 and John Huxtable *As it seemed to me* (London 1990) *passim*, and on the Churches of Christ, Thompson *op cit passim*; the details of the Parliamentary debate are from *Hansard* vol 839 no 140 Thursday 22nd June 1972, cols 629-72 - the quotation from St John-Stevas is from col 662; the political history of the 1970s and 1980s follows Chris Cook and Alec Sked *Post-war Britain 1945-1992* (London 1993); for the churches and Mrs Thatcher see Henry Clark *The church under Thatcher* (London 1993); on the state of religion and the crisis of belonging, see Grace Davie *Religion in Britain since 1945* (Oxford 1994).

[Scripture quotations are] from the New Revised Standard Version of the Bible, copyright 1989 by thr Division of Christian Education of the National Council of the Churches of Christ in the USA.
Used by permission. All rights reserved.

(page 169) *Nonconformity in the Nineteenth Century* by David Thompson published by Routledge & Kegan Paul 1972.
Used By permission.

Calvin quotations are from the Library of Christian Classics edition of Calvin's Institutes, edited by John McNeill and translated by F L Battles (Philidelphia and London 1960) - Westminster Press. Permission sought.

E G Rupp & Benjamin Drewery, *Martin Luther* published by Edward Arnold 1970.
Used by permission.

Euan Cameron, *The European Reformation* published by OUP 1991.
By permission of Oxford University Press.

Nicholas Tyacke, Anti-Calvinists - the Rise of English Arminianism 1590-1640 published by OUP 1987.
By permission of Oxford University Press.

Parliamentary copyright material from Hansard is reproduced with the permission of the Controller of her Majesty's Stationery Office on behalf of Parliament.

I am deeply grateful to the following people and institutions for their kind permission to use photographs and other illustrations:-

- the United Reformed Church for the picture of Edward VI granting the licence to John Laski; and for the Westminster Confession.
- the Director and Governors of the Cheshunt Foundation for the Tyndale New Testament and the portrait of the Countess of Huntingdon and her family
- to John Potter who photographed the portraits of Cartwright, Campbell and Barbour
- to David Thompson for David King and William Robinson
- to Carr's Lane URC Birmingham for R W Dale
- to the Revd Charles Brock for Mansfield College chapel
- to the Revd Ron Bocking and Mrs Joan Huxtable for the uniting service and Assembly

# Index

## People

**Places**